# THIS IS MY SEA

# THIS IS MY SEA

*An exploration of grief
and recovery*

**Miriam Mulcahy**

First published in the UK by Eriu
An imprint of Black & White Publishing Group
A Bonnier Books UK company

4th Floor, Victoria House,
Bloomsbury Square,
London, WC1B 4DA

Owned by Bonnier Books
Sveavägen 56, Stockholm, Sweden

— @eriu_books

— @eriubooks

Hardback – 978-1-80418-400-4
Ebook – 978-1-80418-444-8

A CIP catalogue of this book is available from the British Library.

Designed by Alex Kirby
Printed and bound by Clays Ltd, Elcograf S.p.A

1 3 5 7 9 10 8 6 4 2

Eriu is an imprint of Bonnier Books UK
www.bonnierbooks.co.uk

*To my family, swimmers, sea-discoverers, soldiers*

*A word then, (for I will conquer it,)*
*The word final, superior to all,*
*Subtle, sent up – what is it? I listen;*
*Are you whispering it, and have been all the time,*
*you sea-waves? – Walt Whitman*

# 1. WHAT COLOUR IS THE SEA

*Eleutheromania (n) – an intense and irresistible desire for freedom*

THE FIRST SWIM IS never easy. It's more an act of defiance than anything enjoyable. I walk out to my waist, shivering as the water rises. My hands hover; my shoulders are curled in. I hop over the waves and look out beyond the rocks, past the pier, to where I know she is.

It's a decision, I tell myself firmly as I force my shoulders in and gasp, exhale rapidly and do everything I can not to scream at the bitterness of it, the icy, icy cold. But I have done it; I am down. Now I just have to move, keep moving and ignore every impulse from my brain that is telling me: *leave the water now.*

I leave the sea floor, leave my depth and strike out, past the boats, the strokes coming more smoothly now as I settle into the temperature and adjust. I never swim parallel to the shore. For me the whole point of swimming is escape: leaving the beach, leaving land behind. I swim out past the pier, to the outer rocks until I can see the secret beach.

The Atlantic, at first forbidding and cold, is now warm and smooth, holding me. I feel so secure and safe, they are here.

My mother and my father are swimming with me, smiling at me. Ais sits on the corner of the pier, smoking, her face scrunched in the morning sun, her legs extended, always seeking a tan. Dad dives and surfaces like a whale, his black hair gleaming and wet. Mam is so happy to see me, so happy to be swimming with me again. She is beautiful, tanned, wearing her gold jewellery, and she gives little tosses with her head as she moves through the water.

Me, I tread the surface, my legs barely moving, my shoulders out of the water, my arms, my hands pulling the water through them and effortlessly keeping me afloat. I feel happy again, truly happy. I can feel them, sense them. I know they are here, in this tiny scrap of water, deep and green.

I know this is where they came when they died.

The sea conspires to wash my grief away momentarily. Just as I placed my clothes in a heap on the beach, so too I put down the weight of my grief for the half of my family I lost over a shocking and brutal seven years. The sea holds me, minds me, lets me rest. I cannot take my grief into the water; they do not sit or meld together. The water is too green, too clear, too clean for something as murky, difficult and complicated as grief.

So here I am, swimming with my dead parents, treading water and dreaming. I love being back in the sea again and want to stay here forever. Everything I know about the sea, all its secrets, were taught to me by watching them swim. I try to uncover its truth, unmask its secrets by immersing myself in it. I come at different times of the day, early, before breakfast, often to a tide that is far out. It seems nearly like a penance until I feel the freshly minted sand beneath my feet and know that this is not penance; it is privilege.

*   *   *

I remember swims the way I remember books I have loved. There are swims that will stay with me all my life. Once when I was ten years old, after an enormous storm, it had been raining for days, and the sea was boiling. Mam and Dad had gone for their morning swim – we were in our caravan in Wexford. As we turned over in our beds, Dad flung open the caravan door and told us to get our togs on and come down to the beach, now.

Sleepily, half-awake, we obeyed and ran the short distance to the beach. The caravan was beside dunes, which gave onto an enormous beach: a huge sweep of sand, bookended on one side by a pier full of trawlers, rocks on the other, with an endless arpeggio of beaches beyond. Normally crowded and busy, in this weather, at this time of the morning, it was deserted.

We ran down the dunes and dropped our towels and ran for the water, where Mam was being tossed around by the waves. They were enormous, frightening in their height, but we all got in. Dad took us out, beyond where the waves were breaking. The water was surging and roaring and strong, green. Above all else I will never forget the colour of the water and how I felt: safe. Out of my depth, tossed relentlessly about like a cork, but my mother and father swam round us, circled us, and they were laughing. It began to rain – hard, fast, fat raindrops, but we kept swimming.

Were they mad? Possibly. But my parents were alike in that they both loved it; they were swimmers, sea creatures, sea-discoverers. You had to swim in everything, in anything.

After the deaths of my father, my mother, my sister, swimming became a place for me to be, to rest, to put my endless burdens down and stop the running circles of thought and sadness that consumed me. I began swimming in winter whenever I could. I took overnight trips to Kerry in November, January, drove two hundred miles, went straight to the beach when I got there, often in darkening skies, threw myself in. That first gasp and initial shock was like coming back to life for me in the midst of numbing, crippling grief.

Coming home to where there was no sea, I went to the pool – always a poor substitute, but necessary. I cried as I swam punishing amounts of lengths, my goggles filling with salt water even if the rest of me was washed in chlorine. In spring and summer I carved out every bit of time possible in Kerry and swam every chance I could. I medicated with the sea.

When I wasn't swimming, I surrounded myself physically with everything I could to remind me of it. I divided my share of my mother's collection of seashells and placed them in every room of my house. She never left a beach without a shell or a stone, so I add to the bowls and vases, the glass jars full of the pale white curiosities she favoured, bringing bags home after every trip to Kerry. These collections are a constant reminder of all the swims she had: alone, with Dad, with us, with her beloved grandchildren. They mean the sea is never out of my eyeline.

I am never not thinking about the sea. It laps at the outer edges of my consciousness, my thoughts, all the time. It's a longing that only quiets or subsides when I am there. I'm cursed to live in a landlocked county that is so far from where I love.

Where I want to be is a tiny corner of south-west Kerry, on the Iveragh peninsula, a series of stunning beaches and coves on the Kenmare river and around one of the headlands, on the Atlantic. Caherdaniel is the village, Derrynane is the harbour, which hosts a sweep of famous beaches but my soul-palace, my haven, is on the other side of Lamb's Head, the peninsula that bookends the long beach in Derrynane.

This is the place they loved the best, Rath, a tiny beach near Caherdaniel, Kerry. This is the pier, the sea they came to every morning before breakfast. First brought here by their friends, the Hurleys, after a trip to the Middle East with the UN in the 1970s, August weekend trips turned into weeks, turned into renting places, turned into spending as much time as they could here in a mobile home facing the sea. They walked down a fuchsia-filled boreen to this small grey beach, to this toy pier with its handful of boats. They negotiated the steps, covered with slimy green seaweed, and unfailingly launched themselves into the water every day.

There was no choice involved: the sea called them, called something in their souls, and by immersing their bodies, they answered the call. It was ingrained in them. More than habit, it was a need, a deeply defined necessity of purpose with which they started the day. It brought them great happiness and great closeness as a couple.

Our parents adored the sea. They grew up by the sea around Dublin, and all our summers were centred around beaches. They loved swimming, and this love was passed onto us as completely as the dark hair, the sallow skin, the hazel eyes that run through our genes. This love created an avid wanting, a craving, that swims in the Irish Sea; in Dublin and Wexford where the water is often impenetrable and murky can never satisfy.

And then there is the Atlantic, wild, clear, unpredictable and magnificent. It holds secrets you have to go deep and far to hear. It's a startling, vivid green that other seas dream of being. Yet it holds qualities of night that are visible during the day, it's a green of sleep and dreams and rest, it's the green of peace and perfection, it's the work of the moon, the shifting of the tide, it's mercurial and magical, and when I swim in this water, I know I am home. This green, this impossible green that intensifies and builds into a combination of white, turquoise, aqua, blue layers, this is my soul's colour, pure and the best part of who I am – it is my parents' great gift to me.

*     *     *

The mobile home near the beach in Rath has three bedrooms, a galley kitchen, and picture windows overlooking the sea. The view is stupendous, so much so that when we are there, books languish unread on laps, papers are cast aside, laptops remain unopened, and the TV is rarely switched on.

Because all we do, all we can do, is stare at the sea. Choppy, grey and rough on bad days with dancing white horses, thousands of them. When the winds abate and the sun shines, it turns topaz with shimmering glints and sparkles as the sun dances and invites. But we don't need the sun to entice us in. It is the sea that brought us to Kerry and keeps us here and makes us long for it when we are not.

The water is green, a pure and ethereal green, which combined with white sandy beaches, makes for nothing less than paradise. Imagine a green glass plate, not the dark green of wine bottles, but something lighter, brighter. Think of a green that is transparent, opaque, fresher and clearer and cleaner than anything you have ever seen, and you're not even close to how beautiful it is.

It is a green that is mesmerising, that haunts your heart, it's a green of many layers, hues and tints. It's the colour of the tropics in the south-west of Ireland; it's unquantifiable, as difficult to catch and describe as a star. It's more than what we see, what our eyes absorb and our brains register; it's what it does to our souls. And swimming in it is another level of experience, another way of being that is like nothing else possible.

The quality of the water kept us coming back here, year after year – it called something in my parents' souls, and their only way to respond was to answer and keep returning. This tiny, wild, magnificent corner of Kerry is the world they sought to understand, make maps of, something they did together and alone.

Their single greatest gift to me was the implicit understanding of the transformative power of swimming, how it taps into something profound. Yes, there is a sense of danger, especially when you swim like we do, out far and way beyond our depth, but we grew up knowing this is where we were meant to be. We learned early of the veils, the hovering between worlds, how easy it would be to stop and slip beneath the depths, how beautiful swimming is but oh, its darkness, its danger, its mysteries.

Every time they entered the water, they taught us how to follow them, how to swim, how to move, how to be held by the water. They taught us the most bizarre of skills: how to feel completely safe in the most dangerous of environments. Swimming has an edge to it that a lot of sports don't. You don't run the risk of never coming back with tennis or cricket. If you pause on a golf course and stop moving, you're not going to sink.

The duality of swimming is what captures us. There's intense pleasure and heightened risk in how we swim, going out of our depth on beaches that are small and not lifeguarded. Our ability to go in all year round, in any weather, our lack of fear when it comes to taut, threatening waves – we have swum in all conditions and returned. We have coasted through all kinds of jellyfish and butted heads with seals. I was once lucky enough to share the sea with a wild dolphin that came unexpectedly close to shore – yet we always come back. They taught us how.

The point of the swim is to connect your body with the ocean, to put your tiny physical self into the body of water that life came from and reconnect with that in a powerful way. It's to absorb the goodness of the sea: the iodine from the seaweed-infused waters, the minerals sloshing in abundance; to be joyous and grateful that you can do this, that you are fit and well enough to go in and stay. The secret to swimming in the Atlantic is time – it takes a good ten minutes to truly warm up and get used to it. Your body untenses, becoming as languid as the jellyfish you must remain attentive to. You aren't thinking, you're feeling.

Breath builds on breath, stroke upon stroke. You never panic in boats or in the water; staying calm is everything. If you allow it to, the sea will hold you. By surrendering to it, relaxing and unspooling, you let it keep you safe. There's a photo from my parents' time in Israel, Dad floating in the Dead Sea, his huge feet aloft, reading a paper with a grin on his face. This is saltwater, not fresh; it has power you cannot imagine.

They taught us all this without ever telling us. It was in their eyes when they looked at the sea and shed their clothes and went straight in. It was in their happiness and confidence in the water. To be with the best of who they were, all we had to do was follow them. The sea to us, whether in Wexford or Kerry, Carne or Rath, was play, fun, light. There would be darkness enough in the winters.

* * *

When I lost them, when Dad died suddenly, when Mam died quickly, when Aisling's death almost broke us all, the sea kept me alive. Breath on breath, stroke on stroke, go out as far as you can. It doesn't matter how wild and turbulent the waves are; you can navigate anything. If you stay calm and focused, the sea, the lightest, darkest force on our planet, this body of water that connects every continent, every person on the planet, will hold you. You have to trust you will be held, that the waves, if you allow them, will carry you back to shore. It's in you, the power to make it back – this is what they taught you, this is how they made you, this is who you are.

You're a sea-discoverer, and your tribe is on the beach, awaiting your return. You hear them when you swim, your beloved dead ones, but you take their words and return. You bring their wisdom back and infuse it into your kids like a drip. The sea is always there for you. Rath, Caherdaniel, Derrynane, Coomakiste – wrap those place names around you like an invisible cloak, like the armour and protection they are, and go back to your life. Leave the sea and stumble across the stones that coat the beach.

Life needs you. Grief will not win today, soldier.

# 2. ARMY BRATS AND LITTLE GHOSTS

*Man cannot possess anything as long as he fears death. But to him who does not fear it, everything belongs. – Leo Tolstoy*

AGED EIGHTEEN, I PITCHED up at the University of Limerick. My degree was European Studies; a broad degree, taking in history, politics, law and economics. I was doing French, and in first year we studied *The Outsider* by Camus. That one little book changed my life. Camus' pagan trinity of the sea, sun and sex sang to me and the central idea of existentialism, that there was just one life and it had to be lived, as fiercely and vividly as possible, rang like a clear bell in my head, renouncing the Catholicism in which I had been reared.

I wrote an essay on Meursault, got an A, and my professor read the essay out to the class, to my mortification. I was never allowed forget this faux pas. Frédéric Royall saw something in me, a hunger for books, and directed me on my own version of European Studies: I read through the literature stack of the library and he discussed the books with me. Of course I understood the absent / present nature of existentialism. Of course I devoured Camus' novels like the sacred texts they are. The absent / present so threaded through these novels rang and resonated within me. Their words spoke to my dark core; I had lived with that duality all my life.

As a young child I spent a lot of time teetering at the lip of my mother's crater. Its ramifications and hollow emptiness spill over frequently into my own life. I chase and seek the unavailable, especially with men – a fear of abandonment entirely different to hers but savagely informed by it. She was there with us, physically, but psychically, emotionally, sometimes she was not.

There's three of us in the 1970s, Rossa, me and Aisling. Two other pregnancies bloom and wither, after Aisling I think – I am uncertain about the timings. They are never spoken about, these babies who never made it – one quite late, the other early. Yet they are little ghosts throughout our lives, surrounding us as we play. How many times, I wonder – when I become a mother and finally understand my own – how many times did she, Mildred Thunder, look around her house, her table, watch sleeping children, wave us off to school, welcome us home again, and ask, *what would the other two have been like?*

Stillbirths, miscarriages, unborn children were not talked about in Catholic Ireland. Women were churched after births, a practice many consider barbaric. But to me the greatest crime against my mother's generation was the

Marriage Bar. A blunt legal instrument, it enshrined women's place in the home and created a generation of frustrated, unfulfilled women who had endless potential and their careers ripped away from them. And it made for a generation of daughters whose only purpose was to work as hard as possible to achieve the careers and positions denied to their mothers.

My father was happier, with his army friends around him. A few of them bought houses in the same estate as us, so we grew up with other army brats, a transient collective, as people came and went on long UN trips. Officers could be transferred at any time – maybe that's what stopped us settling. Fathers disappeared for six months to Lebanon, two years for Damascus and Jerusalem, even sometimes the best of jobs, to the UN in New York.

It meant them knowing on some level they had to marry up, marry well, pick the best – these women would be running houses, rearing children, minding the fort, and that requires a certain kind of stamina, of courage.

All communication in those days was letters-based; I remember one phone call with Dad in the six months he spent away in the Lebanon. For those months, the mothers are everything to their kids: mother, father, teacher, counsellor, sports coach – whatever is required, there is no other to pick up the slack. They had to pick everything up and drive it on.

Maybe that's where the seed was sown for me, my knowledge that I could cut it as a single mother. I had grown up around women doing it, albeit temporarily, all the time. No one showed me the way, the path, better than my godmother Máire, Dad's sister, a single mother who kept her career, her identity, who radiated strength.

Most army houses are identical – the same heavy mahogany furniture; carpets from all over the Middle East, often hung on the walls; intricate, embroidered Damascene tablecloths in red and gold that the women picked up for half nothing; bowls of coloured glass; watercolours of Palestinian and Israeli landscapes we would never know. Brass shells stood to attention at fireplaces and inside doors, housing pokers and umbrellas. There were brass tables bought in souks, tiny marble pyramids brought back from Cairo.

Ours had all those things, but paintings too, heavy oils and valuable prints from my mother's home in Bray, antiques my errant grandfather, Francis Xavier Thunder, collected and left behind him when he died in 1976, three years after his wife Delia Conway passed. My mother and I shared horrific, mirrored decades of parents dying and children being born, of death and new life, of funerals and preg-nancies, of the relentless, unstinting demands of grief and motherhood. Neither abates, nor ever stops asking.

Mostly, though, our houses and homes had love running through them and holding them up. I didn't realise as a child how dark things were for us. Grief went under the radar, unexpressed; life went on. Mam had four grievous losses over a short seven years, with three young children.

I clearly remember Aisling coming home and how it felt like nothing could separate them. Born in August, I see them, mother and sister in white, two black heads bent together as Mam feeds her and sings. How happy she was with Aisling's arrival, even though, at the time, her father must have already been unwell.

\* \* \*

For someone who wasn't around very much, my grandfather FXT cast a very long shadow. His abandonment of my grandmother and their four children when my mother was a young teen was absolute. Granny was supported by her first two children. She had been a young widow when FXT blazed into her life. An accountant, he managed to drink away her pub and shop in Mayo, bringing her and her children east to Bray, where they lived in the grand, rented wing of a big house. I remember a huge basement kitchen, towering rooms full of antiques, instruments, paintings.

His leaving caused terrible financial stress and a fear of poverty my mother carried with her always. There was a sad solidarity between her and her siblings, especially with her eldest sister, Kathleen. They had an uncanny physical language: a shoulder shrug, an eyebrow lift, a rolled eye – they were fluent in an unspoken language of hurt and pain that could be read in their eyes when they were together.

\* \* \*

16

During their courtship, a lengthy two years of letters, my parents wrote to each other every day, Dad in the Curragh, a young lieutenant, Mam in the Bank of Ireland on College Green. A young teller, she constantly told him to forget her and find someone else. She argued she wasn't good enough for him, that he was kind and sweet and she wasn't.

She was haunted by her family's poverty, her father's drinking, his abandonment of his family. She quickly realised Dad's comfortable, civil-servant, middle-class family in Clontarf was a world away from hers. They delayed their marriage again and again as their letters became consumed with accounting. She gave a good portion of her salary to her mother to help her survive, and how would she manage without it? Because immediately on marriage, Mam's job would be gone, and she was furious about this.

Dad got an overseas trip to the Congo, and he saved all his salary while based in Elizabethville and sent it home. His letters were full of the light, the sounds, the sights, the heat of Africa. He described patrols through the bush, parties with fellow UN officers, days spent swimming in pools, new friends made easily, trips in planes with herds of elephants, zebras and giraffes hustling across the plains. He also asked his father to write a letter to Mam, welcoming her to the family, and he did. Paddy Mulcahy was a kind, generous man who adored his wife, and his son, my father, was pretty much cut from the same cloth. Kind, empathetic, this man exuded emotional intelligence before anyone even knew what to call it. At last they fixed the date and got married, FXT coming back from London to give his daughter away.

They are the epitome of light and darkness walking down the aisle of the church in Bray. She is black-haired, in a white satin dress she made herself, radiant, abundantly happy. Finally at last, there is enough; she is marrying her prince, and dreams are coming true. FXT stands at her side, glowering at the camera, white-haired, with moons of darkness beneath his eyes, and black tails. She is light and promise, being handed over to her husband, the future – he is darkness, obscurity, the past.

Her father truly gave her away, passed her from one life to another, from one of lies and hardship and struggle to one of sun, certainty and love. Dad was the most loving, happy and kind person we know. But even he, with his bright, eternal optimism, his certainty and steadfastness, his diligent work ethic, could not wipe out the darkness in my mother, which her father had created. There was a hole within her, one that was never truly filled, not by music, not by work, not by us. There was a constant dissatisfaction, a 90 per cent of happiness. There were, quite simply, parts of her that I could never reach.

* * *

My mother may have been emotionally disconnected at times, but it was not her fault. It was the result of too much grief. There had been too much damn death in her life over a very short period of years, and she was scoured by it.

Grief imprinted and stamped itself on my mother at a very young age. Her father was gone, she hated him for it and she hated his absence. He chose not just another city, he chose another woman, another life. She loved all the good things he gave her and taught her: the piano, singing, the violin, art – but she hated her grief for him. It began two decades before he died, and she carried it with her until the end.

She was crippled by a double load of grief all her life: grieving for a father who was alive but choosing to live elsewhere and grieving children who were never born, a dark, silent grief she could never talk about. Years later I tried to ask her about it, but she always shut me down. She only spoke about her two little ones when she knew she was dying. She said they were with her in those final weeks.

The miracle of Milly, my mother, was that she loved so much, so beautifully and so well. Her miracle was barely transmitting the hurt and the darkness, so that what we received was barely an echo, a shadow of what she lived with. What was beautiful was that the four of us grew up in absolute love, in a house with parents who loved each other so deeply that we always knew we were secondary to what was going on between them. We were moons to their planet.

What was astonishing about her in those years was her love and care for us. The house was perfectly run, all meals cooked, laundry done. We always made it out the door to school without fail. Grief had wrung her out. And yet she loved, so beautifully. She adored us despite her intimate acquaintance with a land full of holes. Maybe we dragged her out from there momentarily. She could never rest, always aware of how close it was. But home was fine; home was good. Home was love: warm and secure.

* * *

FXT cruelly came home from London to die. I will never forget the howl of pain that drew us from our rooms one morning. It rose up the stairs as my mother, bent over the black phone in her white nightdress, her dark hair spilling over her shoulders, wept to hear he was gone. Here for the first time I knew was the unanswerable scream of grief, ripping a rent through my tranquil reality.

In 1979, with the settling of FXT's estate, his children sold a Nathaniel Grogan painting to the National Gallery. Lady Blanche and Udolpho Crossing the Ravine was one of my clearest memories of the house in Bray: a massive canvas (so three-year-old me thought), dark and black, but with a slash of light running through its centre.

This painting was sold for £9,000. Divided among his six children, it was the difference that let my parents buy the new house in College Park, Newbridge, the house they needed with a new baby coming, the house that held us all until we left it. FXT came good in the end.

Maeve came that July. Mam was so happy, and all I remember is a summer full of light, of white beds in white rooms, of once again seeing two dark heads bent together as Mam fed Maeve. We didn't stay in Newbridge for too long. The sea was calling her, and within weeks we were packed up and headed to Wexford.

# 3. UP THE MULS

*If I stay here, there is a going in my staying; and if*
*I go there is a staying in my going. Only love and*
*death change all things – Kahlil Gibran*

OUR LIVES CHANGED FOREVER and we entered another
world in 1976 with the acquisition of a battered brown and
cream Roadmaster caravan in Carne Beach, County
Wexford. It wasn't Kerry, it wasn't Rath or Derrynane, but
it was two hours' drive from home, an easy commute for
Dad and a spectacular beach with beautiful dunes: a world
unto itself.

The campsite had several fields, playgrounds, a shop,
even a disco and games room. At the end of the long
beach was a pier, crowded every night with trawlers
coming in with their catch, gangs of children crab-fishing.
We spent every week of the long summer holidays there,
two months of going to the beach every day and endless
swims, discarding our shoes and running barefoot, the
shock of returning to Kildare and school at the end of
every summer visceral. Where was the soft Wexford light,
clouded by sea fog, the black nights punctuated by the

swinging beam of Tuskar Rock lighthouse – where had the sea disapperared to?

When cousins came to visit on winter weekends, we tidied our rooms, Army style. Everything was put away, dusted, cleaned, beds made to within an inch of their life. Once we were done, Dad assembled us outside our rooms, calling *Cadet Mulcahy! Cadet Thunder! Inspection begins!* He wore his officer's peaked hat for this exercise, and for us, there were Defence Forces berets. Pat Mulcahy was a company Commander of the Third Infantry Battalion, and I have never seen anyone love their job so much as he did his.

Dad loved the army and brought everything about his job home. He had us debating around the kitchen table and talked to us seriously during elections about politics. The early 1980s were quite unstable, with multiple elections, fragile coalitions and the IRA campaign raging in the North. We were acutely aware of the army's importance in protecting and upholding the constitution. I think now, looking back, our fathers must've known more than they let on. There were threats to the state that maybe were foiled, and they would have been privy to intelligence in a way most people weren't. They took their responsibilities seriously and signed up for peacekeeping trips abroad, even if it meant leaving the family behind.

Still, we were tight, close and happy. We were as happy as any Irish family could be, incredibly lucky to grow up in love, with parents who adored each other. Dad had grown up in Clontarf, also with parents who adored each other. His father was a civil servant in the Department of Posts & Telegraph and worked on setting up the first Irish television station. Our paternal grandfather, Paddy, was kind, clever and brave and raised six children beautifully and well – they were also close and tight, and there were many happy nights spent together in Clontarf, at his sisters' homes in Ranelagh and Monkstown, in ours in Kildare.

Nights of conversation, debate, song, beautiful tables full of good food, lots of whiskey, beer and wine. Pretending to be asleep when we got home so Dad would have to lift me inside and carry me upstairs, with a tousle of my hair and a whispered *I love you, Mirs* before I fell properly asleep, safe in my castle, in my father's kingdom, his happy family, the Muls, unassailable. We thought those walls could never be breached.

But of course they were. Cannons of death: unborn babies, loss and grief hurled themselves at our walls. There was nothing singular about my family, we were a confection of light and dark, of wounds from older worlds warring with possibility and optimism. Because of my father's career as an army officer, we never felt at home in the inland town we lived in, close to the Curragh. My mother craved the embrace, the light, the air of the sea; she had lived all her life in a seaside town before moving after her marriage to a town she always hated. She had spent so much of her life grieving – and the 1970s, with the loss of her parents and the loss of two babies, were especially heavy for her.

Because she was so tired, so fragile, so hammered by multiple pregnancies – five in ten years – Dad took over at weekends and took us out. He instilled, early, in all of us a love of wild places: orienteering at weekends, sailing during the summer. He'd take us to the Glen of Imaal with his army friends and their kids, on hikes through the Wicklow Mountains with picnics served from the boots of cars after we had prised our wellies from our soaking feet before driving home. Winter Sundays were all about rugby, following the benighted campaign of the Curragh Rugby Club through the minor clubs of Leinster. Home games were the best, as we could spend the hours our dads stayed pitchside on the army obstacle course, then run riot around the clubhouse, fuelled by crisps and coke as our fathers sank pints of Guinness.

They were still heading off on rugby trips in their late 60s, right until his death – he got to see Munster win the Heineken Cup in Cardiff with his best friends beside him in 2008. They all married intelligent, strong women. My abiding memory of those women of my childhood, those other mothers, is how razor sharp they were. They could dissect you with a single glance.

All the hurt and pain my parents endured and shielded us from only became apparent decades later, when I became a parent myself. My father carried Mam through all her tragedies and kept us immune from the sadness that repeatedly swept through our home. When Dad was away in 1981 and '82 my most vivid memories are of Mam's exhaustion, her eyes bleached with tiredness. She was utterly haggard. I remember my secret delight that for those few months she was all ours and we did not have to share her; I'm sure that particular feeling was not reciprocated by her. She longed for her husband, and they wrote to each other every day.

He came home in early May, just before my birthday, handsome and tanned in his summer uniform, his hazel eyes shining as he picked us up and crushed us in his hugs. Six months of missed love crammed into one early summer evening, the cherry-blossom trees in the front garden flowering a pink snow. We sat around the kitchen table and listened to stories of the villages in South Lebanon: Tibnin, Beit Yahoun, Bra'shit.

These UN trips paid substantial dividends, and most of those funds were used for house renovations, new kitchens, new cars, college funds. That May Pat Mulcahy told our teachers we were finishing school early and took us to France for six weeks' camping. It was June, and every campsite, every night had a different vibe, a different memory.

Mam's frustration at the daily packing up and nightly pitching was evident. I remember these battles better than I do the endless monuments and châteaux we were dragged to, from Mont Saint-Michel through to the Loire and on to Carcassonne in the south.

Somewhere in the middle (it was lush, green and not too hot), Maeve, two years old and curious to see what this swimming lark was all about, tipped herself one evening into a deep lake. Rossa, without a second's hesitation, jumped in and saved her. We wandered through Montpellier's historic alleys, the first of many visits there for me. We stayed around Montpellier for a couple of weeks, found some huge, golden beaches and spent our days swimming in the Med.

Every time we passed under a bridge, under a motorway flyover, Dad beeped the horn and shouted out through the open window: *Up the Muls!* I never got to ask him what this was: a tradition from his father, an old tired joke he spun out over the years, something he had picked up from a UN colleague, something he sought to instill in us? Who knows what *Up the Muls* even meant?

Dad's sister Máire tells me long afterwards, as I'm finishing up this book. It came from their mother, Eileen Farrelly. I can see her, tiny, birdlike, dressed in blue and ensconced in her beloved Paddy's succession of Volkswagen Beetles as he toots the horn. On their travels she chirrups *Up the Muls!* for every bridge they pass beneath.

One night in a campsite below the giant dunes of Arcachon, I'm on my way back to the tent with Maeve when I hear a gang of young French people shouting and laughing, then I hear it: *beep, beep beep, UP ZE MULS!* I run back to the tent tell the others, and we all hush and listen. Then we hear it again and again – the French people think this is hilarious. So do we. We laugh about it, and it turns into something funny, not cringey, until we as adults start inflicting it on our own kids, some of whom aren't even called Mulcahy, but still we pass under bridges and flyovers, toot the horn and call out *Up the Muls!*

I think what Dad was trying to tell us was that we had something special, unique, a heritage to be proud of. The walls of our castle are inviolable and soaring, and we are a happy family, his mini platoon. The Muls are strong. We are gathered, knit close and tight. We prevail, we persevere, and quite simply, we never give up.

Dad wrapped us in such love that we felt we were untouchable, impregnable, unassailable, that the ground beneath our feet was rock solid, carved from the hardest granite, and nothing could upset us on our path through life.

He taught us well, our father, wrapped the watchwords of resilience, duty and service around us. The ability to keep going in the face of adversity was stitched and sewn into us as surely as his company's medals and insignia were stitched onto their greens. As a soldier, giving up is not an option. You pull on your boots, you keep your kit in order, and your rifle is always clean. You're alert and ready for the worst when it hits you.

When death and grief came at me, when they threatened to take down my walls, I often pictured myself clad in a bombproof vest, picking my way through a minefield. That's what the early days of death felt like to me, like if I put a foot wrong, everything would explode.

But being an army brat, I knew how to use a compass, how to read a map. I knew where to find Polaris in the night sky. Thanks to my father, I can stand anywhere and know instantly which direction I'm facing and where I need to go. He left us so many gifts, so many treasures, but this to me is one of the most precious – the certainty I can find my way through anything.

Dad's positivity, his relentless cheering of us all means that all I remember from my childhood is happy times. When we lost him, way too young, we discovered the opposite of all of that. The ground beneath our feet was ripped away as surely as we lowered his body into the earth. Our castle walls were crumbling, and we entered into other lands, new, strange worlds full of craters and holes. The maps that would show us the way were cruelly ripped from our hands the moment he died.

# 4. THE FIRST FUNERAL

*But O heart! Heart! Heart!*
*O the bleeding drops of red,*
*Where on the deck my Captain lies,*
*Fallen cold and dead – Walt Whitman*

MY FATHER GETS IN first. He always does, with everything. Up first in the morning, pulling us out of our comfortable beds for the cold walk to school. When we get up there is a warm kitchen and porridge, bowls of it at the red Formica table, his hand on our heads. With the sea, he never hesitates. With black togs on – togs that match his coal-black hair – he plunges in like an arrow, always first. He dives to the bottom and surfaces, takes a breath, checks on us, and dives again.

Losing Dad started in June of 2008 on Skellig Bay golf course, where he had a heart attack on the ninth hole and continued to play. That tells you a lot about him, that something had obviously gone very, very wrong, yet he carried on. Nothing came between him and his pursuits, whether they were golf, fishing, swimming, acting, rugby, gardening. When he retired he drew up a planned timetable of activities; everything he wanted to squeeze into one day. It amounted to twenty hours. I laughed when he showed it to me. *When are you supposed to sleep?* I asked him, o*r eat?* He looked at me as if to say, *Sleep? Who needs it?*

But he needed it. He had worked so hard all his life, putting in long days at the school where he worked as bursar to pay for our college fees when he left the army early. As soon as he arrived at home, he would kiss Mam, greet all of us, then go straight out to the line to take in the day's laundry. He'd help Mam as much as he could, organising us to do our chores so she could rest.

By eight, he was out the door again. He counselled married couples two nights a week – voluntarily. There was always a tottering pile of files he needed to get through, case notes that ate up hours more of his evenings. When he had all the counselling work done – he tutored counsellors for years as well, then taught and trained the tutors – he would pull his own files to him, his personal and family accounts. These needed a glass of whiskey to get him through as he tried to balance everything out, but four children denied him the neat and diligent accounting he achieved at work. He smoked, filling the kitchen with a miasma. He sighed – deep, troubling heavy sighs we could feel in our bedrooms upstairs. And this honestly, is where we lost Dad, to the historic heart disease and damage caused by forty years of heavy, relentless smoking.

But if not the smoking, it could have been lupus. In his fifties he was diagnosed with the condition, a fairly rare autoimmune disease that a cousin on his mother's side had died from in her forties. Lupus weakens the heart too, attacking the muscle, blocking up the valves. His was manageable with frequent doctor's appointments, strong drugs and steroids. He kept active and seemed to be doing okay. But he was on steroids for almost twenty years. What damage did they do to his already weakened heart, worn fine by four decades of heavy smoking?

So it probably should not have been the shock it was when Rossa rang me one June evening and told me Dad was in Cork University Hospital and needed a bypass. After the surgeon came out of theatre, he held up his hands as if to say they were powerless against what he had encountered – heart walls worn paper-thin by decades of abuse.

In the end, smoking killed him. And I find it's unbearable, to think it could have not happened at all.

* * *

Every illness seems to have a narrative, something that is parroted at you endlessly by family and friends. I now know, having been through it three times, that it's often more important to listen to what doctors are not telling you, rather than what they are. They can hold back and conceal a wealth of information to protect a family, and this to me is part of the problem we have with dealing with death in Ireland.

The story around Dad we kept hearing, all summer, was that he would recover. Everyone we met had a bypass story (this is Ireland, after all), and we kept being told, over and over, that he would be fine. His progress and recovery was slower than it should have been, but he worked hard, like he did at everything, and tried to meet all his targets. Towards the end of August he deteriorated, and he had another heart attack just as we were getting the kids back to school.

I regret we didn't push Aisling harder to come home from the States and see him – the last time we had all been together was the previous New Year's. Miraculously, we had all made it to Kerry for a magical few days, Dad's last New Year, surrounded by all of his children and grandchildren.

My last visit was the second of September. I brought him over the *Irish Times*, and we chatted about rugby, Munster, the kids. My last sight of him was him waving me out of the ward, his face beaming, his eyes shining love. He seemed fine.

So it was an absolute shock to get a call from Mam the next day, crying down the phone. *Come, Miriam, come quickly! There's something wrong – they say he's dying.*

It takes twenty minutes' drive from Milltown to Naas. I got stuck behind a truck, and when I finally got to the hospital, I ran to the coronary care unit where he had been. His bed was empty. *Where is he?* I yelled at a nurse. She looked at me, directing me to the ICU, but I could see it in her. She knew and wasn't telling me. I ran blindly through the corridors, seeking the ICU, having no clue where it was. I found it and burst through the doors, where Mam absolutely fell on me.

33

The doctor had just stopped working on him. Mam was bawling. I went to where he lay, his eyes staring at the ceiling, seeing nothing. There was an expression of absolute terror on his face.

\* \* \*

I screamed – repeatedly I think, I don't remember. I flung myself at his body and had to be prised from it. Mam and I held each other up; the doctor tried to break our circle, explain, but we could not face her.

We left the hospital, leaving my father behind us, splayed on the table. Rossa carried his belongings in a green plastic bag. Even as we walked through the corridors of the hospital, he was being wheeled to the morgue. We got in our cars and drove the few minutes to Rossa's house. He handed us all glasses of whiskey.

The ground beneath our feet, the ground that had existed there solidly since we were born, had been ripped away in one terrible swipe. Certainty was gone, surety, confidence. How would we know we were loved without being able to look into his eyes? All of our systems were reset. The world went back to zero; the maps we had drawn were torn from our shaking hands. Our compasses swung wildly – there was no such thing as true north anymore. His hazel eyes were ever, ever closed, their guiding light extinguished.

Consider the language we use: he passed away, slipped away in his sleep. We deny death's existence with euphemisms; we cloak its power in a tepid language of excuses when we need clarity and clean, hard words.

He died. He is dead. He's not coming back. He hasn't passed anywhere.

*We* are actually the ones who pass, from one existence to another. Grief uproots us. From some peaceful, calm, happy place, we are thrown into another world entirely. They are dead, and you have passed – into a world of grief. Once you enter this world, you are here for life. This world is full of people like you, people who have lost someone they love, and like parenthood, there's no undoing it. But no one talks about it.

*When does it stop?* is a question I'm often asked, having been thrown into this world of grief too often. *When am I going to feel like I'm not wading through a sucking swamp that deadens and slows my every step?*

It doesn't. Welcome to my world; you live here too now. Half the time we don't even know we are there. This murky, nebulous, shape-shifting world is transposed on our own, an invisible layer we can't even see. As far as any of us know, life continues.

But hang around a bit, stay a while. Maybe there is still a way to draw a map.

\* \* \*

There are so many things about his funeral that are still as vivid to me now, fifteen years later, as they were then.

Making phone calls from Rossa's house barely two hours after he died, all the people we had to tell. Aisling refusing to believe what she had heard. She literally could not absorb the information, that our father had gone. Collecting Oisín and Aoibh from school at three and telling them the untellable. Getting the house ready for the removal, the streams of people calling to the door, the endless phone calls still to get through, the multiple decisions that had to be made at lightning speed. How incredibly hard it was for Aisling and Maeve to come home to a house without their father in it.

His removal was the greatest session the house had ever seen; so many people arrived toting bottles of Jameson. In an awful reversal of the many parties our parents had hosted over the years, the freezer was once again laden with food, the smokers passing by it on their way out to the garden. Our Thunder cousins formed high knots, towering in the corners of the kitchen. I drank and drank and yet could not get drunk; I did not know it but I was already pregnant with Doireann.

His friends were deeply shocked, and the roars of laughter subsided into men weeping at the loss of Mul, the best of them. When Aisling got up to read John O'Donoghue's poem 'Beannacht', she took a deep breath, shook out her hair, arched her eyebrows, and didn't cry as her words became a painting in the crowded church, packed to the gills. How beautifully Mam kept her composure coming out of the service, only to be engulfed in a sea of people.

The yawning of the earth, the lowering of the coffin, the impossibility of it all. He was only 68. We had years, decades of needing him still. People telling us constantly, everywhere, all the time: *There are no words.*

Every time, my head lifts, whips around and stares at the person shaking my hand, hugging me, looking at me sorrowfully and telling me this most ridiculous of platitudes. There are no words? There are countless words, 300,000 in most dictionaries, almost a million when you consider slang, other languages we appropriate, and endless, countless combinations. I stare at the person and think, I'll answer that but not now. Now is not the time for etymological arguments, here at my father's open grave.

* * *

When we were kids, and later when our own were small, there was a game Dad would play to amuse and distract a fractious toddler, to get a laugh from them. He would place the child on his knees and, bumping them, tell the story:

*Oisín is walking down the road . . .*

*on his way to the shop . . . he FELL into a hole!*

His legs would open, and the child would fall through, only to be picked up and this joke to be repeated, over and over again. And that's what it feels like, with him gone. Our world is now a series of massive craters, waiting for us to tumble in. There are impossibly high mountains we will never be able to climb and treacherous marshes and swamps that will swallow us whole. Only this time there is no happy, laughing Dad to lift us up, to laugh at the joke. Now we have to find a way to lift ourselves.

His slipping away was, in the end, so quick. When he slipped into the deep, he swam in a new sea we could not follow him into. We were left behind, on land, in a world we could not navigate, broken, shattered and smashed. We were lost in all those words, tasked with organising rituals, going from hospital to undertaker to church and graveyard.

We stood at the lectern in front of a packed house and used what we had been taught to speak to the person at the back of the room. Rossa gave a stunning eulogy, and when I read Kahlil Gibran at Dad's funeral, I looked straight to the back of the church and imagined him standing there, listening to me, like he had listened to my debates, my essays, like he had read my articles and poetry – closely.

We found the right words to express who our beloved father was and how deeply and profoundly we loved him, we shook hands and had hundreds of hugs, we cried too much, drank too much, talked too much, looked through hundreds of photos and put pictures of him alive around his coffin, where he lay dead, dead, dead.

How could we walk a single step without him? And why were there holes everywhere, now – holes into which we kept falling?

# 5. DEGREE: THE WORDS FOR GRIEF

*Obnubilate (vb) – cloud over, darken, obscure*

THERE'S A MOMENT EVERY SWIMMER will have or has imagined: the moment something happens and they go under. Maybe it's something they are waiting and ready for, maybe life is so damn hard and perpetually awful that you're ready for the water to take you. *Today*, you think, *is the day I will walk into the waves and not walk out again.* You know how simple, how easy it would be to just stop moving and sink, slip down into the deep. That's half the attraction of swimming out so far; how deep and dangerous everything is.

Or it could be something the swimmer experiences despite themselves. When the waves are working against you, when you get caught in a riptide you can't swim through, when the sea is telling you:

*Not today. Go home. I am not to be taken on or imagined. I am unconquerable.*

And that sharp stab of panic rips through you, and you start to go under.

Many days it was like that, the waves of grief and sorrow absolute. Complete loss threatened to take us under. But we were given the gift of the sea by our parents, and we knew how to swim. In water that is way out of our depth, in water that is wild, we can swim through anything. They taught us that the sea will always hold us if we stay calm, don't struggle, let one breath build on another. One stroke, another kick – one more breath, and you will be home.

After the funeral, when the house emptied of people, the letters and cards began to flow. We read every one that came through. So few of them bridged the chasm of yawning emptiness that had opened up after the loss of him. So many said the same thing: *There are no words.*

Something hardened in me whenever I saw that phrase. No, I thought, that's the greatest lie of all. As a writer and a reader, I know there are words existing for everything – they might be hard to find, but they are there – hiding, waiting.

We went through our war with death alone. People saw us hurt and suffer and grieve, and maybe that's what they meant when they said, constantly, that there were no words:

*I don't speak your language and you are speaking the language of death. It's hard, tough, concrete and cruel, it's a language that requires truth, honesty and bitter, unassailable facts.*

People didn't know; they could not know. They ran from us. We were too much: too much darkness, too much reality, too much suffering, harshness and pain. Who wants to be near that anguish? We were speaking the language of death and dying. It was irrevocably stitched into our every thought, move, look, word.

It was never about people being unable to express their sorrow. It was about their terror of our grief, because such a tragedy happening to them quite simply did not bear thinking about. They said, over and over again, *There are no words.*

But words are what I do. Words are who I am, and I knew, as surely as he was dead, that the words were there, concrete and calm. They were waiting, a long stone wall, ancient and dependable, a collective compass I could fashion to help me through the madness I was facing. Every time I heard that phrase, I would look at the person giving it to me, their hands open and helpless. I would stare at them a little too long and think, *No, the words are there, and I will find them.*

I thought of the wall in Ursula K. Le Guin's *A Wizard of Earthsea*, a low drystone wall that separated the land of the living from the land of the dead. It was unpassable, inviolable, a wall like the thousands I had seen throughout my life in Galway, Clare and Kerry, walls painstakingly created by the harvesting of rocks from fields, sliced and split and stacked into boundaries between fields, which lasted for centuries. I would build a wall like that, where the stones were words, and I would choose them carefully, stack them neatly against each other, and they would be strong enough to last several lifetimes.

I turned to my shelves, my notebooks, to my laptop, and wrote words in their thousands. It took me years to find the right ones, but they had a funny way of finding me. Sometimes I would come across them in poetry from centuries before me; sometimes I wrote them unconsciously in a text, a letter, an email. Other times the words screamed at me from books, making me weep with astonishment.

Here are some of the words: you put one foot in front of the other and you carry on. You keep watch, soldier, and maintain your guard. You answer the alarm every single morning, get up, and get your children to school. You shop for food you don't want to eat, but eating it keeps you alive, so. You pay bills. You go to bed, even though sleep is a long-forgotten mirage. You get up and shower because you are here and this is what is required of you.

Here are the words: courage, constancy.

Here are the words: you're not allowed to give up.

Here is the word, the answer to death: *love*.

\* \* \*

Somehow the pattern of days weaves an impenetrable armour around you. Breath builds on breath, night follows day follows night, and the nights are terrible and terrifying. The nights are when you lose the words, and everything – your very self, your inner core – unwinds and unspools, and everything you have fought to sustain unravels. The nights are when you fall apart – when the children are asleep and can't hear you cry. The nights are when your bed feels big and empty and you have never felt so alone. The nights are when your brain takes you back, rewinds time and throws you once again into all the bad things and screams, *They are gone, gone, gone.* The dark has no distractions.

You spend years and years wading through what feels like the most toxic, sucking mud, like the earth is one endless, hauling swamp. Grief bleeds the absolute fuck out of reality; you're walking down a street, through a shopping centre, you're drinking pints in a bar, doing normal, lifey things, but no, actually you're not, you're in an alternate reality to everybody around you whose life is normal and okay and who has not lost half their family.

But just as nights blur and soften into dawn, grief softens too, the hard edges of it blunted by the days of struggle and hardship. Still, your reality is grey, the colours bleached out. The laughs are hollow and echo blindly. Everything you touch is paper-thin, unreliable, and at any second your legs could buckle and the holes mutate into chasms.

You learn to live with a biting anxiety that never truly leaves you. Anxiety whispering in your ear: *you could lose anyone.* Anxiety, malicious and controlling insists, *Don't trust this; nothing holds.* The boat is riven and leaking. Trust is gone, forever. How can you trust in anything when the man you most adored, the man you loved most in all the world, the man who was the ground beneath your feet, whose eyes you only had to look into to know how loved

43

you were, is one day in a hospital bed, wondering about Munster's chances that weekend – and less than twenty-four hours later, that man is being wheeled to the morgue?

\* \* \*

Of the many heartfelt and beautiful letters that came in, one changed my life. Orla Studdert wrote to us from a monastery in Southern France, Lerab Ling, where she was a Buddhist monk. The daughter of one of Dad's best and oldest army friends, like everyone else she was devastated by his death. Her letter touched the rawest strands of our pain. Orla wrote directly about death and explained, according to Tibetan teachings, how Dad had moved through different states, and how she had held him in practice and prayed for him for a total of forty-nine days:

> *I've felt Pat's presence every day for the past month. I believe that he does come, and that which was not possible in life is coming to fruition after his death.*
>
> *They say that the mind becomes extremely clairvoyant after death in the Bardo – the state between death and rebirth / heaven. They say that the dead person visits their relatives and home and can hear all our conversations to them.*
>
> *If this is so, I would really encourage you all to continue loving Pat and to use this time to say all you ever wanted to say to him, to say the goodbyes you*

*weren't able to do in person, to tell him what he means to you and to help him to let go.*

*Many people came up to me here telling me about how wonderful and kind Pat looked – just from his photograph! I regularly told them about him and all of you. Just know that we all sent you so much love through the medium of the practice. I will continue to do so, every day from November to April.*

*You are family to me and to all my family. You are not alone, and we grieve the loss of Pat along with you. I think he is going to be okay. I think he knew how much we all loved him and how enriched our lives have been through knowing him.*

\* \* \*

A few weeks after Dad died, I had a dream, or something stronger than a dream, where Dad, Rossa, Aisling, Maeve and I were on a ferryboat, going down a bay, high cliffs all around us. Lots of people were on the boat, families, and every so often the boat would come to shore, and someone would disembark. The sky was grey, the sea pale blue. The cliffs were dark. Then the boat pulled in and Dad said, *This is where you get off, here.*

I argued with him, saying there's no beach, I couldn't swim here. *What about you,* I asked, *aren't you coming?*

*No.* He smiled. *My boat's over there, this is for you, you have to get out here.*

He was all smiles, so happy and healthy, and in the dream I could see his eyes again, his hazel-green eyes that were always full of love. Dad just had to look at you to tell you he loved you. At the end of the peninsula, his adored white fishing boat was moored and waiting with his two favourite dogs in it. I hugged him and got out, standing at the base of sheer cliffs and watching as he hopped into his boat.

Waving, smiling, he rounded the corner and was gone.

I woke up, not knowing what it meant, but a sort of peace settled on me; I knew he was okay.

\* \* \*

As the weeks dragged on, and the friends who kept talking – really talking, about what really mattered – dwindled to a precious few, I turned to the book we had placed on his coffin: the *Tibetan Book of Living and Dying*. I heeded Orla's advice and headed for Dzogchen Beara, a Buddhist retreat in West Cork. Strings of Tibetan prayer flags, tattered and whipped by the sea, adorn a whitewashed cluster of buildings at what feels like the edge of the world. It's a place where people who are ill and dying can visit for respite, built on a site hewn from bog and rock. It was inspired not by financial motivation, but by one woman's death and the teachings of a book. The woman was Harriet Cornish, an Englishwoman who came to West Cork with her husband Peter in the early 1970s. Their dream was to establish a spiritual centre.

Peter and Harriet Cornish travelled all over Britain on their quest, and they were close to quitting when they came to Castletown Bere and made enquiries. They were brought in a horse and cart to look at a derelict farm a few miles outside the town. When they stood on the clifftop, and saw the ocean spread below them, they knew they had found the place they'd dreamt of.

Over twenty years they renovated and built a series of buildings, creating a retreat centre that now has a hostel, offices, cottages and a prayer centre with kitchens and tea rooms. Inspired by Tibetan Buddhism, the centre is the perfect location for reflection, peace and meditation. In 1986 the couple invited Sogyal Rinpoche, author of the *Tibetan Book of Living and Dying* (*TBLD*), to visit and gifted the centre to his organisation, Rigpa. He chose the name Dzogchen Beara. It means the highest teachings in the Buddhist tradition: *great perfection*.

In this country we can talk forever about the weather, money and politics, but when it comes to really important things, birth and death, we don't talk about them so well. Some people can do it, are good at it – like children. In Dzogchen Beara, I experienced something completely new and unexpected: here was a place where it was okay to be bereaved.

Maybe it's the location, in far-flung West Cork, clinging to the edge of the Beara peninsula like a limpet on a rock, tenaciously dug into the cliffs that guard Bantry Bay. Maybe it's the isolation from cities, how realities melt and dissolve over distance and the crises that clutch everyone in a vice-like grip disappear. It could be the orientation of the centre. All windows, all the terraces and gardens, all the paths and walkways display one thing: a vast expanse of shining sea, intercut by white ribbons of surf that dance around the cliffs. All you can hear is the eternal thump of the ocean as it encounters land over and over again.

The horizon is wider because of the height. Boats work the waters below, and colonies of seabirds criss-cross the silver vista of sea and sky that changes relentlessly yet somehow always stays the same. The people who live and work and study here are not disturbed by death; they embrace it as part of life. They understand what it's like. Many of them came here because of a death that led them to the *TBLD*, as they call it, and onto meditation, study and practice.

The shrine room where the group meditations take place has a beautiful altar with a large Buddha. Photos of Tibetan lamas and posters of Tibetan deities hang on the walls. Outside the shrine room is a butter-lamp house. There, you light a lamp for a soul who has passed on – or to pray for someone. The experience of meditating in that room, even for a novice, is not one that is forgotten quickly. It is a gift of pure peace.

When I arrived in Dzogchen Beara it was late and dark, and the next day the mist was down. Director Matt Padwick was worried it would not lift and I wouldn't see the views. The mist did lift – in the afternoon on the first day. Nothing could have prepared me for that view. I had seen it all before – in my dream. They were the same cliffs, the same sea, the peninsula, everything I had seen in my dream of Dad, it was all laid out before me. I told Matt what I had experienced.

Matt told Sogyal Rinpoche about my dream, and the Lama concluded that Dad must have come here after he died – while Orla was practising so hard for him – and then come to me in a dream to tell me about it. He placed Dad on his prayer list. Years later, when Mam was dying, Matt contacted him again, and he placed Mam on his prayer list as well.

I did not find this out until I visited Dzogchen Beara again, but what a comfort it is to know one of the foremost lamas had done practice for both of our parents. And how lovely to think that they both had a connection with this place – Dad after his death and Mam when she visited – that after reading the *TBLD* they were both held in practice.

I love that word, *practice*, and I love the way the Buddhists use it: *to hold* – to hold someone in practice. Because what they do here is what most of us run a mile from: they hold death squarely in their heads and hearts. This is where their unique calmness and equanimity comes from, because when anything is held as closely as death is held here, it dissolves the fear around it. And this is what they do here with death. They hold it, accept it, face it and say it is part of life. A death can be beautiful and meaningful and full of hope. It can be, as Matt says, a great gift.

What people experience when they come here is that deep, profound need we all have, especially after loss: to be held. You can see it here, in practice. People are being held – held by other people, held by meditation and practice and mindfulness, held by the great serenity and beauty of this wild, forlorn clifftop outpost, held by the constancy of the sea, by the eternity of the mountains. What is our grief after all, but a transient incursion, a fleeting raindrop, merged and absorbed by the sea below? And so too our tears. We just need to know we can be held in our grief.

# 6. SKELLIGS / SIX HUNDRED STEPS

*So comes to us at times, from the unknown*
*And inaccessible solitudes of being,*
*The rushing of the sea-tides of the soul; –*
Henry Wadsworth Longfellow

WE ARE SURROUNDED BY islands in South Kerry, and there are none as remarkable as the Skelligs. Seen as shadows behind Deenish and Scariff, not always visible, they appear and disappear through clouds and mist and rain, stark or nebulous on the horizon. Twelve miles out to sea, they are an outpost of lonely civilisation. Man's devotion to God was never more punishing than here.

Alongside the history of prayer, there is a corresponding history of protection: the Skelligs are also home to two lighthouses, one active and one abandoned. Their construction is as much a miracle as anything the monks ever did. Like the six hundred steps hewn from the rock that lead to the monastery, a road snakes around three sides of Skellig Michael, from the east landing to the first lighthouse, and continues on, a road that leads nowhere, to the second abandoned lighthouse, proof, if ever it were needed, how history can break our hearts.

It is the loneliest place I have ever been.

Loneliness has been something I've had to learn to live with the last ten years, and when it's bad I think of the others who knew it too. My grandmother, raising children in a cold, unheated house at the top of a long avenue, with none of the comforts and distractions I enjoy. She lived in her kitchen, cooking, baking and cleaning her way from one meal to the next. The loneliness my mother endured when Dad was overseas and she too, had a houseful of children to raise and cope with. Her acute, terrible loneliness after Dad died.

I constantly asked her out to mine, for dinner, for wine and a movie, for nothing, just to hang with us. She didn't come as often as I hoped or wanted, and she finally confessed to me why: *It's too hard going home after being out, walking into the dark house, turning all the lights on, then turning them all off again as you climb the stairs, alone.*

And I got it. I understood why she would stay in her house and keep the lights on, creating a lighthouse, making that transition from day to awful night easier. I know what it's like to leave a warm sitting room, with music, books and wine. It softens the loneliness, but it hits you again and again when you go to your dark room and contemplate another night in your huge bed with just you in it. Mam made College Park a lighthouse on winter nights, lit candles to keep the darkness, the grief, the loneliness at bay. But the wave is only receding; we can't stop it coming in again. Loneliness is something we have to live with, and maybe it's grief's greatest challenge.

Isolation does not come much greater than Skellig Michael, the largest of the Skellig Islands and the site of the monastery that dates from the sixth century. Thousands visit every year to witness for themselves the solitary isolation the monks lived in. The beehive huts at the top of the treacherous steps hewn from the rock are otherworldly. It elicits a chorus of hows: How did the monks get here? How did they make those steps? How did they construct those tiny, immaculate, still standing cones of stone that housed them through savage, howling winters and the endless fog that wrapped itself around this island, the rain that lashed them for days? How did they build that terraced garden and survive on gulls' eggs and paltry plants? There was another beehive hut above Christ's Saddle that a monk could retreat to and do penance and spend time apart from the community. How could they endure loneliness heaped on loneliness?

As fascinating as the story of the monks is, it is the other stories and presences on Skellig Michael that attracted and drew me. It is the tiny grave in the middle of the monks' graveyard, which houses the bones of the two Callaghan boys, sons of a keeper of the upper lighthouse. Their father served on the island, lost two sons and finally requested a transfer when another child fell ill.

Another keeper fell to his death while tending his cows on a strip of grass beside the upper lighthouse. When you stand beside the ruin and look at this few feet of turf, you wonder: how did anyone get – let alone keep – an animal up here, and you shiver, knowing this is where he fell.

These are the presences that haunt the island and make it feel so lonesome: the ghosts of those who never made it home. The upper lighthouse was closed and unmanned when Inishtearaght, off the Blasket Islands, was built in the 1870s. But previous to that it had served, shining its light out west, with a range of fifty-three miles. Its sister below had but a range of eighteen miles.

When you climb up the punishingly steep switchback road that zigzags up the escarpment leading from the lower lighthouse to the upper – a road so steep it hurts the lungs – and come across the ruin of the upper lighthouse, it is such a poignant, sad ruin, devastatingly beautiful in its derelict desolation. Hemmed in between a towering cliff face and tightly packed together are the lighthouse, the keepers' houses, and a series of outbuildings, with the sheer drop to the sea below. All the necessary requirements for life were here, but what a life it must have been. The rooms now lie in ruins, staircases long fallen in and roofs collapsed. Windows frame the sea and nothing but the endless sea; there is nothing else here. There is no land in sight, just the vast Atlantic, beating on this slate, marine mountain.

The lighthouse is half disappeared, and that is its pathos and wonder. The construction is astounding, covered in overlapping concentric rows of slate that still cling to the curves of the ruin a century and a half after it was abandoned. Still visible in the crevasses of rock are traces of the whitewash the keepers once painted on the walls. Around the corner runs a low series of huts, used to keep animals and store supplies. Up here is the end of the wall that begins at the east landing and snakes around three sides of the Skellig, capped with Yorkshire slate, built high to prevent children falling.

In the tower of the lighthouse the sound of wind and sea fall away, and all I hear is the clack of fallen mortar at my feet: a dry, sad sound. There is the air of something incredibly bereft about this place, but it is where, more than at the other lighthouse, you feel the spirits of the families and children who lived here. You are at the edge of the world. You have left land and civilisation behind. Maybe that edges the openings of other worlds closer.

It's hard to say why the lighthouses on the Skelligs drew me so much, why they fascinated me. I could not explain the power they exerted on my imagination. As soon as I was in the lower lighthouse, it was like I could catch hold of all the ghosts that flitted through it, all the lives that had lived there. Maybe it's resonant because apart from light-house keeper Richard Foran's brief visits, it has been empty for years. The monks' beehive huts have hundreds of tourists visiting them and tramping through them every day. There is no sense of peace or isolation there.

When the guides tell us where we cannot walk, I want to say, *I was here when all these others were not, I know every part of this place, I climbed and walked all over it, I*

*saw sunsets set the western cliffs on fire, I sat here in the*
*beehive huts as darkness gathered and ghosts pushed closer.*

\* \* \*

The lighthouses were operational from 1829, and the upper lighthouse closed in 1870 when Inistearaght, the most westerly Blasket Island, was established. Families lived here, well supplied with fuel and food. They even had schoolteachers to educate their children. They kept chickens, goats and pigs, and compared to the privations on the mainland, they were comfortable. By the turn of the twentieth century, homes had been built for the keepers on the mainland – in the case of the Skelligs, life was transferred to another island, Valentia – and families ceased to live here.

But this is what amazes me about the Skelligs: the women who raised children here. How they kept a routine in such a solitary place beggars belief. The children had no gardens to play in. They must have used the road down to the landing, the steps up to the monastery itself as their playground. Each lighthouse had two houses attached to it, one for the principal and one for the assistant keeper. In 1987 the lower lighthouse became automated, in line with lighthouses all around the coast.

On the Skelligs, when there was active lighthouse service, there had to be three keepers on the island at all times. One on shift, one on rest and one on watch. Nothing was left to chance or hazard. If there were just two, it would be too easy, with six weeks' service before they could get home, for something to go wrong. Two men could kill each other. Or one could kill the other and go insane. Three kept a balance. The third man was to stop the other two going mad, and also to raise the alarm if anything did happen. Three was the optimal number for survival in such an isolated place.

I learned all this when I got out to the Skelligs in 2009, on a story for the *Irish Times*. We flew out by helicopter with Irish Lights at the end of October for one night. Our one night turned into three days: keeper Richard Foran told us when we came down the first morning, *Better start rationing the water, we're not getting off the rock today.* As happens so much in this part of south Kerry, a sea-mist had descended.

But there was too much to do, too much to see and to experience to worry about anything so insignificant as food or water. The days drew in sharply once the sun set – and what magnificent sunsets they were. Our lighthouse windows gave onto the rocks and cliffs on the western side of the island, the sun a red globe plummeting into the distant horizon. The sea blazing, the mists surrounding the island momentarily parting and occluding, gathering again, like a vast cloud of rosy candyfloss suspended over the heaving sea.

The sea never stopped dashing itself against the sides of Skellig Michael. It was beautiful and awe-inspiring to watch as it curlicued around the rocks, and I leaned over the white wall, hung over it and happily watched the dizzying dance between water and rock unfolding beneath me. As the evening of the first day advanced, the wind picked up until Richard told us to come in, and I sat in my room and the sea threw itself against my window, so high were the waves. Richard told us stories; he said the waves would frequently cover the top of the lighthouses, come down the chimneys and douse all the fires.

When night fell, Richard took us up into the tower so we would see the operation. Keepers' duties included maintaining the light and maintaining a constant watch for fog. What weather did for the monks, technology did for the lighthouses. The lighthouse is fully automated now, and the keepers have left the building and the island forever. And just as electricity and remote monitoring signalled the end of the keepers' permanent presence on the island, maybe GPS will see these lights dimmed and forever closed down. What will be the fate of the lighthouses then?

The OPW is restoring the lighthouses, but to me their beauty is in their decay and ruin. When the upper lighthouse buildings are repaired, the sense of history attached to them will be undone. The tumbling mortar and falling stone, the rusting porch and empty windows evoke lives lived and struggles overcome all in the name of duty, a forgotten watchword. And this sorely neglected slice of marine heritage should be seen by more, so we could truly appreciate the heroism of those who kept the lights shining onto a dark sea, giving hope and promise of journey's end to the weary sailor.

*   *   *

One night I walked down to the landing to experience what it must have been like for the keepers. The rain lashed my jacket, the wind whipped and howled, threatening to lift me off my feet. I clung to the red rail hammered into the wall expressly for this purpose. This was dark – a dark like I had never experienced. Pitch black, but reassuringly punctuated by the swing of the lighthouse beam. I understood what it meant to be out at sea, in howling gales and stormy waves, and to see the reassuring beam pierce and disrobe the night of its menace and threat. When I reached the landing it was covered in water; waves pounded the steps and platform angrily.

I stood there and thought about wild nights and wilder water and the power of nature. I was lucky enough to explore the island on my own for those couple of days. I walked that road, that miracle of engineering, twenty times. I climbed the steps to the beehive huts every day and sat there in the still, stony silence. All the birds had left in October, with only the gulls and fulmars remaining. The only other creatures were the seals. I wondered what it would be like on a summer's day, full of puffins and tourists. I felt the loneliness of the Skelligs, the beauty of their isolation – I found them in the dark as I would never have understood them on a bright summer day.

I was lucky enough to get out to the Skelligs again, about six months later. This time a Tibetan lama, Dzigar Kongtrul Rinpoche, was visiting the island with an Irish philosopher, a monk from Glenstal Abbey, an Irish sean-nós singer and her sons, as well as four boatloads of Irish Buddhists from Dzogchen Beara. This was the island I had wondered about in the darkness, now bathed in sun, the sky an impossible blue. This was the Skellig I had not seen, awash with tourists inching up and down the steps, taking pictures, recording their experience of this extraordinary place.

I observed the Buddhists at the beehive cells, sitting on the terraces and softly taking up the chants of the Riwo Sangchö, melodious and calm, with an insistent yearning and searching. The collected voices resounded off the ancient walls of the beehive huts, one ancient culture and tradition, passed down through the centuries, enacted again in the heart of the ancient monastery. Between the chants a silence fell, as the Buddhists meditated and the cries of the seabirds were amplified. Then slowly, quietly, the chanting was taken up again, in perfect synchronicity.

It was incredibly strange to see a group of Westerners gathered around a Tibetan Lama, chanting in Tibetan at the top of the most inhospitable of rocks miles out to sea, but the weird thing is, it was completely right. There was an eerie sense of connections being made, the present colliding with the ancient past, the boundaries of time blurring, of doors to the past slipping silently open and Eastern culture bringing itself to the West in the most spectacular of locations. I stood near the oratory while the chanting continued and said a silent prayer for the spirits of the two tiny Callaghan boys.

Then it was the turn of the Irish. Noirín Ní Riain, Fr Gregory and Ní Riain's sons, Moley and Eoin Ó Suilleabháin, sang 'St Patrick's Breastplate' and a twelfth-century chant to Mary. To hear the voices rising to the skies together, carried by the wind and accompanied by the plaintive crying of the seabirds and the ever-present bass line of the surf thumping hundreds of feet below was an experience not of this world.

Noirín told me, *We sang differently. There are things crossing your mind that don't happen anywhere else – you could hear voices around you.* She had also felt what I had sensed, the other spirits lingering or maybe echoing what was being done here today. There was something definitely searching, reaching and stretching back through time, time shifted and centuries weaved and warped around and between each other. Doors, spaces, gaps between worlds softening and opening. The dead dancing, unseen, around the living, as constantly as the sea danced off the rocks below us.

* * *

Our mother came straight back to Kerry after Dad died. We rented a house at the end of October, and Maeve and

I came down, I brought the kids. It was a dark time. She had rented the same house we'd been in the previous New Year's Eve. We were just up from the caravan, and the ghost of Dad was everywhere.

She was so quiet, so lost without him. One night she confessed she was deeply afraid no one would want to be around her anymore as Dad was always the fun, talkative one and she would never manage alone.

Being around her was like being around an eviscerated shell – her light had been extinguished. I listened as she went over Dad's death again and again, every detail. I realised after a few days of this that being in Kerry in October, as the light disappeared early and the darkness closed in, was no good for her. I packed her and us into the car and drove her home.

After my visit to Dzogchen Beara, she went down herself with Maeve. It was the first time she found peace after Dad's death, and it was a turning point for her. She announced she was going away for a month on her own, to work in a villa in Spain.

I loved her so much for this – for having the courage to travel alone, to go somewhere she didn't know. Comares is a tiny village in the hills above Malaga, and there she would play the guitar, shell almonds, swim in the pool. I was heavily pregnant, due at the end of April, and I loved that she was heading off and wouldn't be around for the first couple of crazy weeks.

Her leaving us was a reassertion of herself, of her spirit, an announcement of the kind of widow she was going to be. This bereaved wife was going to seek the sun; she planned to revisit the places she had honeymooned with Dad around the south of Spain. She found her time in Granada particularly hard. There were lots of phone calls and postcards for the children as she documented her adventures.

I gave birth to Doireann at the end of April and had to wait another two weeks before Mam came home, around my birthday. She walked into the kitchen, locked eyes with Doireann, and one witch recognised another. *She is a pure fairy*, were Mam's first words about her new granddaughter. It is one of my greatest losses, the relationship they would have had. Doireann is different, she feels things deeply, and Mam understood her immediately. She could soothe Doireann instantly, and they had a connection I know both would have treasured.

Mam went back to Kerry, back to Rath as soon as she could, and spent most of the summer there. We visited and spent time with her when possible, and Rath worked its magic on her. I saw the sea keeping her afloat as she swam every day. It must have been torture, going to the beach without him, swimming without him, making the walk back to the caravan and entering it without him, or emphasis to be alone for the rest of the day. But how punishing those walks must have been back from Rath, up the twisting road, missing his presence beside her, needing it still. Hanging her solitary togs and towel on the clothes line, making one cup of coffee, taking down a single bowl for breakfast, a lone plate for lunch. Having a hundred things to talk about every day and he wasn't there to say them to. Her little 'now' after every accomplished task with no one to hear it. The pain of walking up and down the steps into and out of the caravan, knowing the only thing waiting for her was silence.

Driving together one day, she told me a story of a widow she had heard about who stopped leaving the house when her husband died. Then she stopped opening the curtains, stopped cleaning, let dirt pile up around her. Finally she stopped getting out of bed. *I can't imagine it*, Mam said to me, *not doing your best every day*. She did it because she knew he would do the same if the roles had been reversed, if she had gone first. He would be in Kerry, swimming every day, golfing, taking the boat out.

When the water called them, they answered. Just like the monks on the Skelligs heard a call to go and find a lonely outpost and create a life there and responded by making a monastery out of nothing, an eternal prayer out of stone. Mam answered death and grief with an iron determination not to let the walls of her lighthouse fall into ruin; she kept the walls high and the light always on, shining into the darkness.

# 7. THIS IS THE WAY TO THE SEA

*Exultation is the going*
*Of an inland soul to sea,*
*Past the houses – past the headlands –*
*Into deep Eternity – Emily Dickinson*

IN THIS PART OF Kerry we are spoiled; there is a choice of strand and shoreline so fantastically different it is like having a holiday in several different locations at once. We often choose where to go depending on how the wind is blowing. There are many beaches at Derrynane – starting with the impossibly beautiful but treacherously dangerous long beach, which is seductively perfect, situated at the end of Derrynane bay. The sand is crunchy and golden, backed by dunes, but the sea is wild, full of hidden riptides and eddies. That does not stop us spending time here or, I confess, swimming here. When the tide is fantastically out and the sun is beating down on the shining sand on a blue-skied, hot day, it is possible and nearly mandatory to actively pity all the people who are not here.

It is a truly hot day; the younger two potter about in the pools left generously by the receded tide while their older siblings revel in the power of the water. We never leave our depth here, and always swim parallel to the shore. It was one of Mam's favourite places to swim – you could see as soon as she arrived on the beach she was itching to get in. We had lots of days, lots of swims here together, and spending time here without her is still brutal.

The water here is green, warm and powerful. Stop moving for a minute and you are swept metres by the hungry tides and rip currents. Its danger is its intoxication, and it's what makes swims here so memorable. Only here do you get huge, proper waves, waves that will knock you over if you stand against them. Only here do the kids get use out of their body boards, and here is where the surfers come. Families come to this beach and spend hours on end in the water. There is nothing like that feeling of cresting waves or diving through them, the feeling of communing with the sea, of acknowledging its power and going with it. And that is why, even though we shouldn't, we love the long beach so much.

One of the greatest joys of Derrynane is sitting on the shelf of high sand carved out by the relentless tides. There is an incomparable vista in front of you. Lamb's Head stretches its isthmus on the left out into Derrynane bay, and Oileán Dhá Cheann or Two-headed Island sits on the horizon. Then Abbey Island joins in on the right, and the land sweeps in an arc of incredible beaches, a vast circle

THIS IS MY SEA

of sand and rock, to where I sit, on my sandy perch. The waves roll in inexorably, endlessly, and every seventh wave is greater and more ferocious than the others, as I have always been told. I sit here and understand the connection between the sea and the moon, the pull of gravity on the tides. I know Polaris is up there in the north, over my right shoulder, unseen but shining, and I think of Dad. The vast expanses, the huge spaces allow the connections to be forged in my mind, that the moon, high and invisible to us on this beautiful day, is pulling and controlling the tides of the oceans.

And it is pure joy to sit here for hours, to watch the sun arc through the sky and slip slowly behind Deenish to slide from the sky, but before it goes, it fires up the sea in incandescent glitter so fierce and bright that when the lengthening rays hit the water for the last time my children are reduced to shadows, black silhouettes against the sparkling, glittering sea. They are immersing themselves for the last swim of the day because it is seven and the beach has emptied, but I have stayed because I cannot tear myself away from this sun-drenched perfection. I cannot rip my eyes away from the awesome beauty laid out before me, from the sun dancing on the waves and picking out the crags on the rocks and the mountains.

I cannot leave, because I am meant for this, one more dip, one last swim, pull the hoodies on and let the kids tumble in the sand, race down the dunes, lie beside me on the sand-laden rug with their own books and sunglasses while I struggle to complete a paragraph of the book in my hands because of the sweet, agonising, continual criss-crossing of word and wave as my eye flits from one to the other, and I am caught between my dual passions – words and water – and there is nowhere else that could bring me this infinitely rewarding beauty and sweetness that makes my soul sing and irredeemably gladdens and strengthens my heart.

This is who I am – a simple confection of words and water, of elements that are constantly shifting and always in movement, fluid, and what a great and enduring joy to know this will always be here for me. My children will grow up and leave home, leave me, but this will always be here, this beach, this sand, this sea, this immeasurable, intoxicating sky, and I know my mother is here with me, on this last precious swim. I cut into the waves and dive through their immense power, I know she is here with me in the green water, the water that tosses and tumbles me, that dries on my skin and leaves its precious, sacred residue of mineral and salt I am loath to shower off. And it is a gift, to sleep a deep, bone-tired sleep with the sea still on my skin, running through my blood, the ocean whispering through my soul.

These are our perfect days, our happiest times together as a couple. My ex does not understand or appreciate Rath, but he adores Derrynane, loves the light and space and immensity of the place. These golden days where he spends hours digging holes and constructing marvels of castles with

Oisín, running up and down the beach with Aoibh after swims, drawing enormous patterns in the hard shining sand left by the receding tides, holding onto Doireann as she takes tottering first steps in the water, days so good and fine we can put aside our indifference and call a truce.

It's a privilege to round up the kids after a long day in the sea and herd them home, climbing the dunes and stopping to marvel at snails, descending into the gentle, cultivated beauty of Derrynane House and its glorious gardens. The simple pleasure of packing everything and everyone into the car and smiling at the accumulations of sand on the seats and the floor that tell of a gift of a week that has seen us on the beach every day, revelling in the unaccustomed heat, our bodies slowly turning brown, our muscles getting sleek from hours in the sea. I drive my children the three miles back, along roads of fuchsia-laden beauty, under the sheltering giants of Coomnahorna, Coad, Farraniargh and Cahernageeha, and the sea is drying on our skin and stiffening our hair. We are sated, we are hungry, we are happy.

# 8. DROWNING

*Sunset and evening star, And one clear call for me!*
*And may there be no moaning of the bar,*
*When I put out to sea – Alfred, Lord Tennyson*

I BRING HIM TO the beach, but he will not swim. Some days when it is really hot and the sand starts to burn, he will go in to his waist, even sometimes as far as his shoulders, but he never dips his head; he never dives, so he never understands the world I want to go to, my green cathedral with its white floors and soaring naves of glittering light – he will never see what I see. He cannot touch my core, because that is only to be found in the water, far out at sea.

There comes a point in every bad pairing when someone finally acknowledges the truth: this can't go on. I'm drowning here, and I'm going to wrap my arms around your neck and pull you down with me as I go. We were together seventeen years, and every time we talked about getting married, I got pregnant. My dream was to get married away from the Church, a civil ceremony and a reception in Caherdaniel, to stand on the pier at Rath, surrounded by the sea I loved – and possibly jumping in

after the ceremony to celebrate – but he could not understand why I wanted this. After four pregnancies we dropped
any talk about marriage.

To me, the pier at Rath seemed like the perfect place to
get married, wearing a simple dress and carrying a bouquet
of wildflowers. This pier left its mark on me. At 16 I
stumbled and fell on the rough concrete, got a bad cut
which left a tiny, fixed indentation on my right knee. Built
during the Famine as a way of creating work for people
who were starving, its grey stone slices into the green sea
and forms the bridge for me between two worlds: between
Kerry rock and bog and the enticing Atlantic. I love sitting
on its edge, watching the waves dash against it, foaming
and bubbling at my feet.

But he won't come with me, move from one world into
the next, he stands on the pier and watches while I swim,
talks to people. He will never join me here in this world
that means everything to me.

There had been so many times over those years I had
wanted to leave him. But fear stopped me. A lack of
courage stopped me. Thinking what it would do to the
kids, what it would do to him, stopped me. If I left, I was
on my own.

I remember an afternoon years before, when Aoibh was
tiny and she had fallen asleep on my chest on the couch. I
should have got ten up and put her to bed, but it was so
sweet, the way her tiny body curved and curled into half
of mine, her baby sweetness lingering in her scant, fairy-

blond hair, and I dozed too, or fell into some kind of trance. I dreamed up two more children. I saw other souls, heard them, felt them. Maybe again, like has happened so often in my life, the veils between the worlds thinned and dissipated, and these unborn children called to me, telling me *No, Mam, don't give up, wait for us.*

You can read this and think it is ridiculous, but there are things women feel that can't be explained. We create life, for Christ's sake – we make new people in our bodies, clusters of cells that divide and conquer us, taking over. This is true power and strength: the infinite, incredible capacity to make new life. Sometimes we know we are pregnant when it's only been a couple of weeks. Sometimes we know our unborn children are out there, waiting, calling to us. Sometimes, if we are listening hard and deeply enough, we can hear them.

All I knew, persistently through the years after Oisín and Aoibh, was that. I wasn't done. I looked at my pair playing in the garden, on the beach, and knew there were siblings waiting to come.

Maybe this knowledge came from how I grew up – with my two unborn siblings dancing round us as we played. Accompanying us on God-knows-what adventures as we drank and laughed our way through our twenties, before real life and responsibilities assailed us. Our shadow selves, watching on as we lived the lives they could have lived – did they gasp and wonder at our bad choices, opportunities missed, men passed over? I have found that when I am really quiet and still, I hear things. This was one of those times.

In 2008, when Oisín was eight and Aoibh six, I came into money and had the chance to get out. But then Dad had his heart attack, and we went into the summer of hell, and I forgot about my tentative plans to leave.

Good things happened that year as well, in 2008. I got published for the first time in the *Irish Times*, and then that summer in the *Irish Independent*. We grew up with the *Irish Times* in the house every day. Saturday mornings were spent doing jobs, chores outside and inside, and at lunchtime we gathered around the table, jugs of black coffee, sandwiches, Mam on her eternal diet of cheese and tomatoes and hunger, and the paper and all its sections were passed round the table, Dad claiming sport, me diving into news and waiting impatiently for Mam to finish with the magazine.

Here was the section I loved, long-length features and interviews. I read every column, opinion piece and interview forensically, and thus, in a way, in my teens I started my apprenticeship for the paper I would eventually write for. By the time I had to actually write the articles, I overcame the huge waves of fear that threatened to freeze me by telling myself: *You have been reading this paper your entire life. You know how to write for it. Calm down. Just tell the story, as beautifully and clearly as you can.*

My editor at the *Times*, Patsey Murphy, was like some kind of fairy professional godmother. She responded to all my pitches and ideas, guided me through the painful process of getting that article right. I knew a chance like this came once in a lifetime, and I made every line sing.

The article came out, was received well, my editor was happy, the racing world I had depicted were fulsome in their praise, my parents were ecstatic. The day it came out, the day of the Derby at the end of June, it made Dad so proud. He bought so many copies of the paper, like the proof of it would disappear if it wasn't in every room of the house, shown to every one of his friends, that his daughter was published in the paper of record. I'm so very lucky he got to see that before he died.

* * *

When Doireann was still one, I got pregnant again. A couple of years previously I'd had a major gynae op and lost a fallopian tube. The pill never suited me, my fertility is ridiculous, and with half of my uterus not working, I still managed to get pregnant.

The pregnancy was horrific. My darling aunt, Kathleen, Mam's older sister, was dying of lung cancer in Wales, and Mam spent so much time going over and back to her, minding her, doing everything for her, even as her own tumour magnified and developed, unknown to us all. Mam looked haggard, exhausted, tired, and we all put it down to the stress of constant travel between Wales and Kildare: the ferry, the driving. Kathleen's house was in a complete state, unkempt and uncared for. Her immaculate cottage on top of the hill overlooking the sea had become a mess.

Aisling was home from the States, and she went with Mam to Wales to help. They were three witches in one house, drinking whiskey together at night. One day Ais went on a walk up the fields behind the house and texted me: *I saw three ravens alight on a huge rock and they just stayed there. Mir, I walked right up to them and they didn't fly away. Just staring at me.*

Did she know? *When* did she know? Was there too much to know, and she just couldn't turn to look at it?

Three witches: two sisters and a daughter – all beautiful, dark-haired Conway women out of Mayo, with malevolent tumours creeping over their organs, bronchioles, twisting round their blood vessels, invading breast tissue and lymph nodes, sitting together in the gathering dusk of Kathleen's sitting room, drinking whiskey, watching the lights of the night-time ferry docking below them.

Aisling would refer to those ravens again and again, after we lost Kathleen, after we lost Mam. She was half turning to face death but never quite managed the 360 required. Could anyone so young and entirely full of life be so resolute, so brave?

Kathleen died at the start of June, and everyone else went to her funeral; I was two weeks away from giving birth and stayed at home. They sang, her brothers, her sister, her nephews and nieces, all the way home on the boat. She had met her husband on the ferry to Wales years before, had spent years coming and going to Ireland on the boat. She was always much more than an aunt to us. Like Aisling was to our children, Kathleen was to us; a magician who produced surprises and unimaginable treats, who had the time to listen to our wishes, complicit in our secrets as we were in her surreptitious smoking.

Death stalked us all that summer, visiting not once, but twice, tattooing loss and indelible fear, inscribing the worst fear into my children's hearts, minds and memories: the knowledge you could lose it all, you could lose everything, that the most important person in your world could die.

When death comes and threatens everything you have no choice but to be strong. You're strong because you have to be, you pull yourself up by your bootstraps because you have to, you clean and polish everything and keep your kit perfect because this is not normality, you're in the centre of the storm, you're at fucking war, your enemy is death and you, soldier, are holding the front line.

\* \* \*

When you swim, you must swim with the waves. When you go against them, they work against you. It's easier to surf over them than to slice through. Labour is the same. If you breathe with the contractions, know each one is a wave to get over, that the pain will last 40 to 60 seconds and then subside; if your breathing is good and correct and you keep on top of the wave, the pain of labour is bearable.

76

We lose completely when we lose our breath. We lose control, the pain takes over, and we are slicing through the waves, battling them instead of surfing over. Every time I gave birth, I imagined myself back in that boiling, tumultuous Wexford sea of my childhood, with my parents swimming around me, protecting me. All I had to do was stay on top of the waves for me and the baby. I had quick, uncomplicated births; I was not afraid of labour – I was ready for it. Mentally ready.

My partner's sister died a week before Rebecca was born. I went into labour the night of her funeral, and in tears, I paced the floor of the kitchen, as if walking could stop the contractions. The children were in bed and he was with his family. I was on the phone to a midwife in Holles Street, telling her that it was impossible. I could not have a baby right now; I had just spent the day burying her aunt.

All through the pregnancy I could sense this baby's strength. She spun and reeled and pushed against my belly, her arms and legs thrusting themselves out of her confined space and into the world. She would be an athlete, I thought, she was so insistent and strong.

I spent a lot of time thinking about names. I wanted Sadhbh; Dad had loved the playwright John B. Keane, and it would be another Kerry connection, after Cathair Saidhbhin, the fort of Sadhbh. There was also the connection with the name Oisín, as Sadhbh was his deer mother, lover of Fionn. I loved the idea of the names being connected, interwoven, as the lives of the children would be.

We came down to Sarah, for the Thin Lizzy song, or Rebecca for the Daphne du Maurier book – not particularly for the character of Rebecca, who obviously is not a great woman to emulate, but for the literary masterpiece it is. A Hebrew name, it means knotted cord. And it felt like we could do with some ropes at that time.

After that Friday night of hours spent pacing the kitchen floor, the contractions subsided, but I was in a huge amount of pain the next day. When the first contraction came, the whipcrack of pain doubled me over and floored me. My births were always hard and fast, and a nagging fear through this whole pregnancy was that I wouldn't make it to hospital.

He was out so I rang Mam. In the ten minutes it took her to come out, I had two more contractions. I opened the door, all colour bleached from me, and she put me in a chair, wrapped me in a blanket, minded me through every contraction and stayed by my side until he returned.

We jumped in the car but I knew this baby was on her own timetable. Garda traffic police met us at Naas, and they flew us to Holles Street. At 4.30, an hour and a half after the first obliterating contraction, I got him to stop the car at the door of Holles Street. I walked in, bypassed admissions and went straight to the delivery ward, pushing the doors open and yelling, *Help! Help me please – this baby is coming!* A midwife caught me, brought me to a delivery room. Three minutes later, Rebecca was born.

As soon as we were checked and cleaned up, the midwives put us in a private room. Everything was white and filled with the light of high summer. Rebecca, like Oisín, was born in June. She came two days before midsummer. I laid her, wrapped in her blanket, on the white sheet of my bed and marvelled at her beauty and perfection.

Already, only hours old, it was obvious she was pure Mulcahy. She had the indelible paint of sallow skin, the curling black hair. And her strength – I felt like I could fling her against the wall of the old hospital and she would bounce back to me like a rubber ball. I never wanted to leave that serene white room with my calm, happy baby who looked like she had been delivered from the Mediterranean, she was so dark.

Rebecca brought a huge amount of happiness right from the start. She is the sunniest, happiest, most content person I have ever met in my life. She reminds me so much of my father; she has his colouring. Her hair is brown but also goes blond once the sun glances it. Her hazel, mischievous, inquiring eyes are his exactly. She also looks like Aisling, with the gap-toothed smile, the long face. She is bursting with a tensile strength that would lend itself to surfing or skiing.

Everyone loves her. She has that quality Dad had, of making people feel good about themselves, the rarest of talents. But we did not and could not cope with the pressure of another child on top of everything else. We dragged ourselves through a horrific winter, and the truth increasingly confronted me and would not be silenced: I would have to leave to survive.

# 9. GODDESS OF CARNE
# AND TUSKAR

*Athanasia – (n) immortality; deathlessness*

As CHILDREN WE SWIM far, wide and deep. We don't get into the sea and swim hundreds of metres, even though we could. We don't do rigorous crawls; we play, diving through waves, jumping over them, standing up to the torrent of water crashing over our heads and testing our young tensile bodies against the physics of wave, distance, force, water. The sea always wins.

We duck and dip our heads and dive – a swim to us is not a swim until we have seen and been underneath, under-water, where the true beauty lies. This is what we have entered the water for, what we are here for, this play of light and colour and wave, this sensation of being truly enveloped and held, of leaving one world behind and being possessed by another is who we are. It is how our parents moulded and created us.

These were the high-definition, saturated summers of the 1970s, back when the skies were eternally blue, the grass the colour of straw, and we were a collective nut-brown from our endless days on the beach. One of us would be sent to the shop in the early morning to buy bread; we cycled through the sleeping campsite, our bikes throwing up dust trails. Once Mam had her fresh loaf from the shop and dispatched us all outside, she set to making sandwiches.

As she boiled eggs and washed lettuce, stepped in and out of the caravan to get her ingredients from the icebox, boiled the kettle for her flask of coffee and made drinks for us, she became steadily more irritated. The caravan faced south, so the Wexford morning sun hit it with full force and brought the inside to boiling point. She would chase us out if we dared enter, insisting that if she could barely stand the heat, we certainly wouldn't be able to.

Dad was at home in Kildare during the week, working, with the car, so we walked to the beach with the long yellow canoe slung between us. It held everything: lifejackets and paddles, the beach bag and towels, buckets and spades. While Mam made the sandwiches it was our job to cram everything into the canoe, two windbreakers angled through the hole, leaving room for the all-important food bag.

Once this was squeezed into the canoe, Mam locked the door of the van, picked up Maeve – who refused to walk and also refused to go in a buggy – and we began the long haul to the beach. We were on the way early most mornings, and many of the caravans we passed still had curtains drawn. Mam and Dad did not believe in hanging around the campsite. The sole purpose of our being there was to get to the sea.

We hauled the cursed canoe up the dunes, then slid it down and collapsed, hot, cross and tired, and rolled through the white, soft sand. We lolled about until the heat got too much and the temptation of the sea too great. But nothing was easily done by our family. Before we could lose ourselves for hours in the water, we had to unpack the canoe, search for a large, flat stone and put the windbreakers up.

Often, as an adult, spending my own long days on the beach with not a windbreaker in sight, I have wondered how she did this. Why spend all day on the beach and shut yourself off from the one thing you were there to see, the sea? The older I get, of course I realize she must be so like me, or I more like her than I realized. The busy, packed-to-the-gills caravan site with hundreds of caravans was a trade-off, a bargaining – she put up with the crowds because it gave her what she needed and wanted: the sea. Her beach fortress, the cotton windbreakers circled together, was her sandy hermitage.

The sun moved. Hour by hour the shadows changed. The beach filled and emptied as the day progressed, and no matter where we were, in the water, on the dunes, miles down the beach playing with our friends, we could find our canvas castle easily, its bright yellow, orange, blue and purple stripes resplendent, pulsating in the strong sun.

Starving as we were, we delayed looking for lunch because Mam was strict about the no swimming for an hour after rule. She liked us to wait until two, her reasonable logic being that the longer she held us off attacking lunch, the longer she would keep us on the beach. Two o' clock bisected the day perfectly – we had arrived around eleven, would not leave before six.

We gathered in the windbreakers and, ravenous, snapped the lid from the sandwich box, tearing into the food. We twisted the caps off soda bottles and gulped the semi-flat, sugared water. Ais waited for the crisps and then would go wandering again. She was constantly gone, her little pot belly sticking out over her bikini bottoms, her skin a polished mahogany, black hair falling thickly over her laughing eyes, her mouth a cheeky, bold taunt.

For the hour after lunch, Mam paid attention to us, then relaxed again, lying on her towel, black sunglasses shadowing her eyes, her headscarf protecting her hair from the beating sun. She needed heat and warmth and sun like others needed food and drink. Like people needed sleep, she needed light; she locked herself into the glare of the sun the way other women kneeled in a church.

As the afternoon wore on and our castles and sand towns got more elaborate – by this time, there were gangs of us communally building streets, estates, back streets, we had time for schools and hospitals – she rose, and without saying anything, we knew. She went to the water and immersed herself. It was as if she had spent the day bringing herself to boiling point and had roasted herself so completely she was ready for the water now, ready to transform again, from mother to sphinx to mermaid.

We followed her, as unable to resist her power and serenity and charm as we were unable to resist the cooling flood of the sea. The water loosened something in her, and she relaxed and played and laughed and splashed with us. We knew she was ours again. And as the evening ticked on and the sun pushed long shadows down past the dunes, we dismantled her castle and packed the wet things into the canoe. We washed the sandy buckets, gathered up the far-flung spades we'd used for wickets, and she pulled her sundress on. She scanned the sea for the last time, hoisted Maeve onto her hip, and led us over the dunes, our goddess of the sun.

*   *   *

I think of her ferocious intent as I spend days with my own four on the beach. I spend all morning preparing food and getting ready. I pack everything into a waterproof bag, the same cadmium yellow as the old canoe, tether the dog on her lead, lash it all to two kayaks and we paddle to the beach. I will spend all day lying on a rug and dispensing food and drink, and I too, am negligent. Buried in my book, I am vaguely aware they are hopping and clambering over the rocks at the end of the beach, scavenging through the rock pools. The older two are out in the kayaks on their own adventures. I too can spend hours motionless, hypnotised by incoming and departing tides, waiting for the sea to call me. These placid, everlasting hours of supine solar rest are who we are at our very cores.

85

My mother taught me how to be. She taught me how to love, how to cook, how to mind children, how to keep the balance of their needs offset with the things I needed to do. I grew up in a house of music, of paintings and prints covering every wall. I know now her fingers itched for ebony and ivory keys, for Mozart and Beethoven as she peeled potatoes and washed nappies and bottles. I know that ache because it's mine; my fingers long for the discipline and the joy of the keyboard, word building on word as hundreds become thousands. My hands only want the thin slices of pages between them as stories unfold themselves to me and I lose myself in books. She taught me to value my children as individuals. The rules need to be slightly bent between them – there's always one who will need more reassurance and one who flinches from too many hugs.

She knew everything about me, no matter what I tried to hide. I look exactly like her, so much so that now, years after her death, I frighten people when they see me. She told me without saying a word that I would make it through. Her steely, unflinching gaze would meet mine on the days when things with my ex were really bad and I escaped my house to hers, for coffee and a chat. I sat, broken, at her kitchen table, fingering the tablecloth, wishing I still smoked, and we would talk of other things. Distracted, I calmed down and was able to go back. She would look at me, telling me with no words, *You are strong enough for this. You are strong enough for anything.* How it must have broken her heart, to see me so fundamentally unhappy.

Everything I am, I owe to her. We shared almost identical decades in our thirties of pregnancy, birth, sickness, death and loss, rewound in a sickening loop that lasted ten years – my first decade, but she made it through. So I had to too. I had no choice. Starting in 2008 when Dad died, through the years of grief we have tried to remake ourselves and carry on. We fought our war alone, and no one understood, every Christmas a travesty of loss and anguish.

I made it through because of her.

She gave me music, art and light. She brought me to concerts, galleries and beaches. She gave me Kerry and the sea, taught me it is never too cold to swim and every swim is worth it. All her life, through singing to me, telling me stories, all our chats, she told me the things I needed to know, over and over again, her daily repetitions of love as pervasive as her scales on the piano, clean clothes piled in the hot press, daily dinners despite her exhaustion. As she was dying she kept telling me, *When I die, you will be free.* It took me years to understand the depth of love in that statement.

# 10. NO HERMITAGE

*Lightning was all our light, and it rained more*
*Than if the sun had drunk the sea before. –*
*John Donne*

IT IS THE END of August, the end of the summer, and
Maeve is with Mam. They love this time of year, when the
caravan site empties; the families are returned home getting
children ready for school; the road to Rath is quiet now,
with only the odd local car or walker. They walk down the
road, Mam gathering the last of the lilies, the fading montbretia to put on the cairn of stones she made for Dad after
his death. This place is in her bones, like the Duplyanka
estate was for Lara in Pasternak's *Doctor Zhivago*: 'It was
dearer to her than her kin, better than a lover, wiser than
a book. For a moment she rediscovered the meaning of her
life. She was here on earth to make sense of its wild enchant-
ment and to call things by its right name, or, if this were
not within her power, then out of love of life, to give birth
to heirs who would do it in her place.'

They enter the water, going down the pier steps with no
hesitation. Maeve, just like Dad, dives deep and far, her

brown hair, pulled back, slick and shining with the sea, her tanned skin tattooed with salt water, a mermaid. Mam swims around her, her usual breaststroke, then turns over and screams in agony. A weight is crushing her chest, a searing pain, it is a tumour in her lung, twisting with her as she flips in the water. Maeve helps her out of the water and gets her back to the caravan. Neither of them know it yet, but it is the last time she will swim here.

It was the summer after Rebecca turned one. I was again on the point of making a move from my ex, making a decision, when Mam got sick. For months she had been complaining about pain – in her back, in her arms, in her chest. Her doctor diagnosed osteoarthritis. She ate painkillers. Any time I spent with her that summer she roamed at night, unable to sleep, haggard with pain and exhaustion in the mornings.

Two weeks after the torturous swim in Rath, she received a diagnosis of lung cancer. She'd been hospitalised with a blood clot that could have killed her, but the oncologist treating her refused to tell us she was dying.

He said that the large tumour in her left lung had been there for about four years. Had Dad's death been such an insurmountable shock to her system that a tumour started then, that September four years ago? I turned to my doctor friend Mike, and when I listed her metastasises and where they were, told me it would only be a few short weeks – it turned out to be only eleven.

By the time I could get to the hospital those evenings, it would be pushing seven. She would be worn out, exhausted, hanging for her last morphine dose of the day. Most nights I only got to hold her hand as she fell asleep, and, in a reversal of our roles, I stroked her hair and sang gently to her. The insanity of living while the person you love most in the world was dying descended upon me.

It's extraordinarily difficult to execute the 360-degree turn required to accept that someone we love is leaving us. To change our perception of the person who has been front and centre all of our lives, who created us, to accept they will be gone very soon and there is nothing remotely permanent about their existence is all but impossible. I used what I had learned in Dzogchen Beara and turned to face the truth.

The most important person in my world was leaving it, and what could I do? The only thing that mattered: give her all of my love, open my heart flat, butterfly it, hold nothing back and give her everything.

It was an impossible time as the leaves coloured and turned. With every tree that revealed its skeleton, I would think, *She will not be here when it greens again*. Going to the house in College Park to keep it clean and get the things she asked for was eerie. Would this be it, when she was gone? These rooms forever empty?

She only wanted two things – to be at home and to go to Kerry. To go down the road to Rath one last time, to stand on the beach and look at the sea, even if she could no longer swim. I asked her oncologist if this would be possible, could we take her? He flatly told me no; the drive to Kerry was not possible, but going home was a faint possibility. At the end of November she was allowed to leave the hospital for an afternoon. We got the house ready and cooked a fabulous lunch – all her favourite food – and invited her brothers to come see her.

We spent a lovely afternoon together even though she was extremely tired. She sat in the big chair beside the fire and kept shivering. She walked around her house, touching her things, went upstairs to her room, rooted through her wardrobe, sat on her bed. She came down the stairs as her brother Patsy was leaving. He took her in his arms and hugged her, knowing it was the last time they could see each other.

That night, back in the hospital, she finally confessed to the pain she was in, was taken for a scan the next day and we were told what had happened – riven with cancer, the vertebrae in her neck had crumbled, and her spinal cord was free, floating, unprotected. It was liable to snap, causing instant death, any time. A huge restrictive collar was wrapped around her neck. It only could be moved or removed to clean her skin when two of us were there to hold and support her head.

We asked repeatedly how we could get her back home and when. We knew at this stage that getting her to Kerry was utterly wishful thinking – magical thinking. Our sister-in-law, Lorna, a senior A&E nurse in Crumlin Children's Hospital, was our channel this time. When we were foundering, she asked the correct questions. She fed the information back to us as gently as she could.

December arrived and Mam was in increasing pain. We asked about surgery and were told there would be none. Chemotherapy? No, the cancer had progressed too far. Radiotherapy, even? No, no and again no. For the first time we heard the words *palliative care*. We were told about time frames.

On the ninth of December the hospital let her go. I rode home with her in the ambulance. She moaned with pain all the way home. The Christmas lights strung over the bridge were blurred by a freezing rain in the late afternoon as the light bled from the day. The ambulance men carried her into her house and up her stairs and gently laid her in her upstairs bedroom, on the hospital bed we had rented.

Lorna, with her cool, calm assurance, her leading of us all, her stepping up to help manage us, had given us the greatest, most unimaginable gift: a December present so perfect, so huge it could not be boxed or wrapped.

Mam was at home to die, and we were there surrounding her, on guard.

\* \* \*

The thing about living so closely with death, suffering through it and coming out the other side is it makes you re-evaluate life. You become acutely aware of the flip side of everything. In life there is death, but also in death there can be life. In the darkest of times, when you are losing the most precious person in the world to you, incredible things can occur. Human kindness can touch your heart like a healing hand, urging you to go on, to take another step, to keep breathing. If you know and accept that the person you love is dying, incredible power is placed in your hands. Most of our fears are diminished when we turn to face them, but turning to face death is something beyond most people.

Looking death in the eye and being as close as you can to the person who is dying can confer incredible strength. You have faced your worst, most fundamental fear and accepted it, embraced it. I said everything I wanted to say to Mam, but mostly I told her how much I loved her, up until a few hours before she died.

We played her favourite music, read her poetry – she asked me for Tennyson's 'The Lady of Shallot'. We sang songs back to her like she had sung to us all her life. We gave each other space and made time for each other to be there; we lit candles and put photos of Dad all around her. But we did not need photos. He was with her, as much as anybody else was, while we were trying to keep her with us, desperately scrabbling and begging for more of the impossible: time. He was there in the room, waiting to take her.

There was an atmosphere of beauty and peace in the room that everyone commented on. It was quiet, calm and serene. There was no panic, no fear. We knew death was coming, and we made ready for it. Dad was there, and his love for all of us was there, and that was what made it different, special. It was his love, so strong he had come back to take her with him.

He was not the only presence in the room besides us. *We're all here, Mam*, I had said to her the day Aisling was home from America, the first time we were all with her in hospital. The doctor had been to tell her the cancer was terminal and she would not recover. *And Pat*, she replied, smiling bravely, despite the pain she was in. *He's peeping in at me from around the curtain. And my two little ones are here as well.*

Her two little ones. Lost, miscarried, thirty-five and thirty-seven years ago. To her they were there, always there around her, giving lie to the fact she had four children. She had six. And if they were there with her, were they not there all the time with us, throughout our childhood and adult life, the siblings we never knew we had until she reminded us, that fateful day when the doctors told her she was dying?

\* \* \*

We had ten precious days together at home in College Park. She was in constant discomfort and pain with her neck brace and pulled at it endlessly. We played music for her, sat chatting or in silence, cooked her favourite foods, turned away unnecessary visitors. When the morphine pump went on, she began to slip into unconsciousness, but the last thing she did was gesture with her hand. We could not understand what she wanted. *Pa, Pa* she said until Maeve grasped her meaning and brought her the photo of Dad she kept as a cover on her diary. It was a photo of him that Maeve had taken, coming out of the water, head bent, hair slick with the sea. Mam loved it. We placed it in her hand and she exhaled and visibly relaxed and slipped into the morphine.

Sometime in the afternoon we were all in the room, sitting around her bed, Rossa took her hand and said to her: *I want you to take a walk with me, Mam. We're going down the caravan steps and the garden is beautiful. Everything is blooming. We're turning up the road, and all the people you know from the campsite are there, smiling at you. We're walking up the road and turning left.* As we walked down the road to Rath, everyone she knew came out of their houses to wave to her, all the families she knew so well, all the people she'd met every day on her walks up and down to the beach.

Rossa described the road with such detail, brought it to life and transformed that dark December bedroom into a tiny road bursting with colour in high summer: a blue sky arced over our heads, the bees hummed as they flitted among the fuchsia, the montbretia dipped their heads as she walked by. When they reached the cross, Rossa told her, *Don't go on to Hurley's, not today Mam, we're going down to the beach.* He came to the wall, the one recently built to separate the road from the beach below. The crowd behind her was swelling and he said, *You're breaking through the wall, Mam, and we're all going to follow you.*

We walked over the hill and stopped to look at the beach. *All the kids are there, Mam, playing, waiting for you, Brenda is over by the rocks, dishing out sandwiches and coffee. Sean is gutting fish. Everyone is here, Mam, everyone. We're climbing the rocks now and we're going to the pier. Everyone is with you. We're on the pier, Mam, and the water is so blue and the sand is so white and the sunlight is glinting on the water. You have to go down the steps alone, Mam.*

Rossa's voice broke. *We can't go with you. You have to get in, the water is beautiful and Dad is there, he's waiting for you, he's doing his special backstroke. You give him the most beautiful hug, and you're swimming away together. Say hello to Dad for us, Mam and tell him we love him, tell him we miss him.*

By the time he was finished we were all crying, holding her hands and hugging each other. In that moment, Rossa did the single most beautiful and powerful thing I have ever seen a person do for another. He recreated Kerry for her, he brought her back there. There is no doubt in my mind she was mentally and spiritually in her most beloved place when he did that. We were all there with her, standing on the black stone steps of the pier on Rath, we saw her descend them, enter the water, and, without looking back at us, she went to Dad.

Rossa had pulled back the veils between our world and Dad's and escorted her into it. My hope that she would see Kerry before she died was fulfilled that day. He also did the equally important and impossibly difficult thing of letting her go. He sent her down those steps and kept us on the pier, and she left us and went to Dad. There was a lifetime's expression of love in that action, a genuine deep love between mother and son, come beautifully, powerfully to fruition. It was the most generous and selfless thing he could do, and he did it.

He passed our mother from our care back to our father's. He gave her back to the man who loved her most: infinitely, beyond life and past death. Dad came back for her, and Rossa handed her over. After four long years of separation, their son reunited them in the most achingly beautiful manner possible. We could see the water, deep, green and glittering, and we could see them in it, swimming away from us, past the rocks, out to sea, together again, together for ever, in their world, the world we will never know the map of.

I was left with an impression of green and gold as she died – her hair glinting in the lamplight, her shirt the colour of the sea. The gold of the candles' glow as we looked through her jewellery and chose pieces for her to wear. Was it the aura of her soul I sensed, a golden glow in the room, a final expression of her love for us? There was a sense of light in the darkness, of hope in the bleak midwinter, of life being there to be lived and, in the days that would follow, a celebration of a life that had been well lived.

# 11. THE SECOND FUNERAL

*Sciamachy (n) – an act of fighting with shadows*

FEW OF OUR SENSES work while swimming. Underwater, vision is reduced to a blurry impression of colour, deepening with the walls of water pressing in on you, the white sand below, the incandescence of the shimmering water-ceiling above. Swimming, especially underwater, is an act of transformation, of understanding. In discovering the water we uncover something about ourselves, something intense, private and fundamental.

We are traversing worlds, the boundaries between land and sea are criss-crossed and navigated and we lose something and find something at the same time. In holding the meaning of the sea in our hearts and souls, we hold something about ourselves: who we are, what we are capable of, how far we can go.

Less than twenty-four hours after her death, the house was once again full of people. Christmas was coming, and we had to move quickly. She died on the nineteenth, we waked her on the twentieth, buried her on the shortest day of the year, the twenty-first.

We felt bolstered by the presence of people. We were half mad with grief and shock, we could not believe it. There was a woman, a cousin from Mayo, I could not let go of because everything about her, from the flashing of her eyes to her sculpted cheekbones, to her slanting teeth were the living embodiment of my mother. I had never met her, and she was telling me there were six in her family and three have died from the same cursed disease that took my mother.

The doorbell rang constantly and we took turns to stand in the hall, welcoming people in, because this is what Dad had always done: he opened the door, beamed, and pulled his friends into his warmth and love, and we did this all night, over and over, pulling people to us, pulling them into our grief and devastation, pulling them into the huge, yawning chasm our mother's death had made in us and begging them to help us bridge it.

Some people only stayed for minutes, a fleeting hug in the packed kitchen.

All the words spoken at her funeral were carefully chosen, measured and weighed, and loaded with meaning. We used those words to tell her life, that she had beauty, grace and talent, and in the face of terrible tragedies and difficulty and losses, she never gave up.

She carried on living, with intent and meaning and purpose, right to the end. She found a place she loved, friends she loved, and even though the man she loved was taken from her way, way too soon, she carried her grief with grace.

\* \* \*

In the weeks before she died, Mam kept saying her death would liberate me. Over and over again she said, *When I die, you will be free.* It was the only time she spoke about dying, and I could not understand what she meant. How could such a huge, momentous loss make me free? But she was right and it did. The worst thing possible in the world had happened to me; I lost my beloved mother and my best friend. I never knew how strong I was until I picked myself up in the weeks after her death and carried on.

That was the bleakest January I will ever know. I boiled with anger, a dervish, furious with everyone, lashing out at the world. Anger was all I had, in the early grief of those awful first months; it became an anchor to moor myself in an unpredictable sea.

I constantly looked at the hundreds of people I saw every day, asking, *Why were they still here?* Why weren't they taken and she spared? She was worth one hundred of every single one of them, and while I drove or walked or worked or shopped I was confronted by these ineffectual excuses for humanity and got angrier and angrier, *Why her?* Why me, again, why us? Why should we have lost both our parents, both whom we *adored,* while all these people are walking and driving and working and shopping and do they know? Do they know what they have, do they appreciate it? Do they know how incredibly lucky they are, how amazing it is to still have your parents?

Anger, once I recognized it as an anchor, as an aid, helped. Once I admitted I was cast off, alone in a sea of absolute nothingness, once I realised how vulnerable and helpless I truly was because the person I loved so much – and still needed – was gone, I cleaved myself to anger, my only anchor in an oar-less, rudderless, sail-less boat.

Anger gave my days structure and definition. I did my best to restrict it to strangers in the car park and checkout queue and school gates. I passed countless trios where a mother pushed her grandchild in a buggy while her daughter walked beside her, and I stopped myself from running over, shaking them awake and shouting, *Lucky, lucky you, to still have each other.*

On the first of February, the first day of spring and St Brigid's day, I left my family behind and went again to Dzogchen Beara. I had been there many times before, but this time was different. This time there was a need to go there, not just a curiosity. There was a sense of pilgrimage, of putting normality aside and placing my needs before everybody else's for once. I will never forget driving along the motorway to Cork and finding myself in the mountains again. I drove through Béal na mBlath: that part of Cork is like a fairy land, all twisted, mossy trees, steeply rolling fields and rushing streams.

The words of the childhood poem Mam had often recited to me went round and round in my head: *Down the rushy mountain, up the airy glen, we dare not go a-hunting, for fear of little men.* The mountains in winter are totally different – brown, tan and weathered, their rocky seams and veins exposed, not blanketed in heather and gorse. I stopped in Castletown Bere to stock up and remembered the last time I had been in this supermarket, on my way out to the Skelligs.

The evening light was fading, and the sea was dark as I arrived at the centre. A huge sense of sadness overwhelmed me – Mam and I had often talked of coming back here together. I entered the tiny cottage and lit a fire. I sat and looked at the darkening sea and the darkening sky and thought about my beautiful mother and drank wine and read and cried.

Up the next morning for the meditation at nine, and as usual there were lots of people there, even at this time of year. There are always volunteers at Dzogchen Beara, people who are taking Buddhism seriously and studying it. There are others, like myself, the fly-by-nights, the Buddhist flirts, interested in the practice, in meditation, but not willing to commit. The facilitator starts the session and rings the bell. He calls us to empty skies and mindfulness and talks about the *Tibetan Book of Living and Dying*, but all I can think about is all the other people and why they are here: what kind of grief are they holding in their hearts? Are they getting succour here? And I think of all my dead, all the ones I have lost, my mother, my father, my uncle and aunt, all dead within the last four years, my ghosts, the ones I love, who sit on my shoulder and mind me.

Over the years there have been days when I really struggled, days I felt I was walking through a loaded minefield. And this is my army heritage, but I pictured my twin angels, my guardians, my parents, donning me in flak jacket, helmet – always a blue UN helmet – and flanking me, walking beside me, urging me on, step by tortuous step, through this land full of craters, guiding me, guarding me, minding me. And I think of them, and wonder what happened to their souls.

Were they, as the Tibetans think, reincarnated after seven weeks – the forty-nine days of Orla's practice? I think of how they were connected to this place, how I have become connected to this place. How my parents were on Rinpoche's prayer list – a bit like the Pope praying for a Catholic. Her name was here and on the walls of the monastery in Lerab Ling, and while she was dying, she was held in the practice of many Buddhist practitioners. And whether you believe in any of this or not, for me there is comfort in the notion that these people, who are intimately familiar with death and in preparing for it, held her in their minds and did the phow'a practice, a death practice for her.

We always imagined her being around forever. I'd pictured her at the kids' graduations, maybe even their weddings. We had no reason to think it would be otherwise; Mam had a fierce desire to live, even though the person she adored had been taken from her. And these are my meditations, these are my thoughts, these are the words that come to me as I sit in this beautiful room with others, in silence, on a clifftop above the sea. And I watch the seabirds wheel in the wind, and I think about the generations that have gone and the generations that are still to come and my place in all of it.

I drive back into Castletown. It's a glorious winter's sunny day, the kind of day that is full of promise and possibility. I wander aimlessly around the town. While standing at the sea wall, watching the ferry to Bere Island and wondering if I'll take it, I'm struck with a shattering realisation. For the first time in years, I am completely free to do whatever the hell I want.

What did I want to do? What *could* I do? I looked at the sea, the sky, the mountains that surrounded me, and I knew. I would walk. I would walk for miles. I would walk until my feet were blistered and I could barely move my aching legs.

So I returned to the centre and did just that, took the cliff walk and walked on top of mountains, beside the sea and beneath burning sun that blazed incandescent on the ocean and reminded me of Camus' Meursault and how he was blinded. I left the path and walked and walked and walked over mountainous bog until I reached a road and I followed it, turning my back to the sun. The telegraph wires were full of birds and their birdsong, and I felt something creeping up on me I had not felt in six months – an episode of happiness.

Later, I went to a beach nearby. I sat on a boulder and watched the green sea surge in and recede, eating up the stones and sand as the tide advanced. I sat there for hours, took off my boots and dipped my feet in the freezing water and seriously considered stripping off and getting in. The sea called me, and I didn't answer it. But I sat on the stones on Garinish Beach, my head emptying of everything except the rhythm of the water. And I had another realisation – my third that day: this was my meditation. Looking at the sea was my mind at rest, in a way it could never be at home, caught up in the daily treadmill of worry and obligation. Here the sea soothed my mind, settled it, becalmed it with its eternal repetitions.

The sea was calling me, and my soul was answering it. I collected stones, white, grey and black – something Mam always used to do. And as the sky darkened and the green of the sea morphed to deep grey, I returned to the centre and pulled out my laptop and wrote, for hours, about Mam and my grief and my loss. I lit a fire and watched the darkness stealing across the water and sky and closed the laptop and finished the book I had been reading as she died.

Every time I go to Dzogchen Beara it gives me something. The first time I visited I found a place where it was okay to be bereaved and people were not afraid of death. The next time I came with my children and explored meditation. I did not succeed, but I found peace in the midst of madness. This time I had come in the depths of winter, and like the opening of spring, the place – the mountains, the sea – had cracked open a space in my weary, battered heart for happiness. It reminded me of the power of decisions and how the ability to take them can influence our happiness. It was significant that I felt a glimmer, a moment of true and proper happiness less than six weeks after my mother had died. I had been keen to get here within the forty-nine days, and I had made it and I felt a connection with her, a connection through the sea. If she was still around, she was telling me things.

This time Dzogchen Beara had given me a most precious gift: the realisation that the worst can happen, we can lose the most precious people in the world to us, but the world does not stop spinning. And we should not stop living. They, our dead, our loved ones, would, more than anything, hate to see us sad. They want us to live, to be bright and happy and optimistic, because at the end of the day, happiness is a choice. We choose it or abandon it. It is something that must be actively embraced and acted on. Wishing for happiness will not bring it.

It is said that those who have experienced extreme sadness and who are genuinely bereft are those who will go on to experience the greatest happiness. I believe that. She told me her death would liberate me. And it did. I took action, made choices, made decisions and saw them through. And now, years after her death, she is with me every minute of every day. My soul calls her, daughter to mother, and even in death, even though she is completely gone, she will always answer. I know in my heart I'm not alone. Nobody can see her, but my beautiful, glamorous mother is walking beside me, every step of the way.

And that certainty of strength will see me through the rest of my life. It is a fear we live with all our lives. From the time of infancy and early childhood, all those early separations are intimations of this, the ultimate severing of you from the person you need and love and want most in the world.

And I am liberated, I am free, Mam, because I have your strength and grace and love. My sky is your sky, your stones are my stones, your sand is my sand, and your sea is my sea: these are the words you gave me.

# 12. MASTERS: GIVING INTO GRIEF

*You are no more, but sunken in a sea*
*Sheer into dream, ten thousand leagues you fell;*
*And now you lie green-golden, while a bell*
*Swings with the tide, my heart; – Genevieve Taggard*

IN FRONT OF RATH and the campsite, out past Oileáin na bhFaoláin, the Island of the Seagulls and what we call the Point is a huge, undersea rock named Buillig. It is vast, and the seas around it are treacherous: it serves both as a wayfinder and weather observation post. To know how the calm or not the sea is, you look at Buillig. It was always to be avoided when fishing, and this is what grief can feel like.

The water is roiling, stormy, tempestuous. You are being tossed about, at the mercy of the winds and waves. You are in a tiny boat, helpless and defenceless before the shadow of the rock. There is no sail, no rudder, no oars, no engine. Your world has lost its shape, its form, its parameters and boundaries have dissolved and disappeared. There is nothing here but sky and water, water everywhere, and the vast deeps and kelp forests below you that are alive.

You are floating on top of another universe. How easily that surface shatters.

The worst thing possible has happened. I have lost the person I needed the most. Despite brief moments of happiness, it feels I will not be able to live without them, survive without their love. Grief feels immovable and rigid, an invisible boulder beneath the water, causing turbulence on the surface, making whirlpools and eddies, turning the sea into giant waves as it seeks a way around. There isn't enough space to navigate past it, but to get through the day I must.

Tears fall at the most inopportune moments, beyond my control. My heart feels every minute like it is going to crack open and fail me the way it failed them. My shoulders are high, hunched. Anxiety courses through me. How do I find my way through this world, this existence without them? Where can I find the map?

The boulder in your path is not going anywhere. The currents around it are too rough to sail through. It's too dangerous to swim. So cast down your anchor and maybe rest your tired head a bit. Think about the person you have lost. They are never coming back. Maybe have a little cry, quietly, all to yourself.

These tears you are holding so incredibly tightly, the tears you can let nobody see – not your children, your spouse, your friends – these tears you think will break you open if you let them flow, they are the key to moving forward. If you can't cry, then sit with the weight of the stone, sit with the grief. The further you run from it, the bigger the boulder is going to get.

It's easier to numb the grief, to keep it at bay and at a distance. Too close and it will smother and overwhelm you, demanding you examine that closed and battered heart, slice it open to the pain. But the pain is not going anywhere. This is not a tide that goes out. It's a whirlpool, constantly churning and if you get trapped in it, can take you down. It's easier to ignore it with activity: phone scrolling, keeping busy. That winter after Dad died, I bought and steadily worked through a ton of box sets. I barely remember the shows and the episodes, but I vividly remember the nights I cried; the hot tears, the shaking sobs, my ruined eyes. I remember how I felt every time I cried – a little lighter, a small bit clearer.

After Dad, I kept the tears in all day and let them out at night. I'm not a pretty crier. The crying drained me physically. It hurt in every way, on deep levels. My obscenely bloated eyes the next day, scarlet and puffy, embarrassed me. But every time you cry, the boulder shrinks. Every time you acknowledge how completely shit this is, how truly awful – every time you get angry with someone else for still having their parents, for still being part of a couple, for still having all their friends around them – the boulder shrinks a little.

When Mam died, I stuffed the grief down and kept it at bay with alcohol. I hadn't been able to drink after Dad, being pregnant with Doireann and then breastfeeding her.

I separated from my ex four months after Mam died, and there was no one there to judge my drinking. I only drank when the kids were asleep, and I functioned fine the next day, but it halted my grief and stopped me dealing with it.

Alcohol was an absolute crutch in those years after my mother. I don't beat myself up over it. I was never drunk around the kids, and in a way it saved me. The glass of red at night was like a soothing hug. It softened the searing pain and gave me something to look forward to during the day. There would be ease, later on, while the children slept. Alcohol blunted the edges of the awfulness. It allowed me to slip temporarily into another place, where the constant knowledge of my mother's absence did not press, roaring, against my brain.

The loss of my mother, my best friend, skewed my world. My grief was so immense I could not face it. Things felt, at the time, volatile and unpredictable, like anything could happen. I held no compass in my hand and Polaris had been extinguished.

I started smoking again, outside, at night, in the garden, as the first apple blossoms opened on the trees. All my coping mechanisms were silent and furtive. When the kids were gone to their dad at the weekend, I spent all my time writing, a book no one would ever read. As summer arrived and the nights were warmer, I sat out under the birches, made an outside room under the trees and puffed my pain away. It was fifteen years since I had successfully quit smoking, and now here I was, the packets swiftly worked through. Taking up smoking again felt like the biggest *fuck you* to the world I could imagine.

What stopped me from flipping into insanity that first year after her death was reading, writing and swimming. I read voraciously, zipping through novels, I found the writing of Karen Blixen who wrote *Out of Africa*. Her loneliness, her misery, her stoicism spoke to me across continents and decades. She had loved Denys Finch-Hatton, but he spent a lot of time away from her and died tragically young.

Writing anchored me when everything else threatened to wash away. Writing about the family – writing an early, discarded iteration of this book – helped me, as I wrote my way through my childhood, her decades of mothering and grief, realising our lives cruelly mirrored each other in our sustained loss. Writing about her brought her back to me, brought back her beauty, her strength and grace. These qualities infused me at the time I needed it most. She was my mother, I was her daughter, and those same qualities in her I treasured so much were laid down in my DNA, in my bones, in my core.

I thought a lot about what she had said in those weeks and days coming up to her death – *when I die, you will be free*. I took birthday cards she wrote me before she died, one for my fortieth with instructions to write that bestseller. *It will happen*, she wrote. She always believed in me, and with her gone, it was cripplingly difficult to resurrect that belief from within myself and tell myself those words: *I believe in you.*

Yet those words sustained me on dark days and nights after the loss, a double loss, as it is for lots of people. This kind of grief is incredibly hard and difficult to get through, because it is twice the work. You lose your mother and your best friend. Or your sister and your soulmate. You lose your husband or your wife, your person, the one who gets and understands you, someone you could talk to purely with gestures, looks and nods.

How do you deal with this double grief? How do you cope with two walls of your castle coming down – the wall over there marked *mother* and the one behind you marked *best friend*? You are left open, exposed, bereft, defenceless as a newborn. But the world is clamouring for you, your children are calling you, your house is shouting at you, and after a few days, work simply doesn't care. You are showing up, but they can't see that in fact you are unravelling. The shock and the adrenaline that carried you through the first few days – the hospital, the undertaker, the church, the graveyard, the afters – it's over, and the world wants you back.

But you're not in this world anymore, the world of your children and work. As surely as they are in the ground, buried and covered up, you have passed too, into a murky, shadowy world you weren't even aware existed. You are frozen yet uprooted, transplanted into an altered world, an emigrant, new and wandering. And you're here without navigation, without maps. Yes, you have a compass some-where, but you pull it out, and its arrow swings wildly, incomprehensibly. It's no longer working.

Grief must be given into. Grief, though it stops absolutely everything in your life, cannot be stopped. It must be faced, acknowledged, accepted and dealt with. Blunt it, sure, in those first, terrible months. It is too much to face, and that frozen state is your brain protecting you from reality. The terrible truth is that life is forever changed. It will take months, sometimes years, to recognise you are living in another world entirely.

# 13. PRAYER BEADS

*And is my body ocean, ocean*
*whose power runs to the shores along my arms*
*and breaks in the foamy hands* – D.H. Lawrence

THE TIDE IS OUT, and the sand is grey. The sea looks silvery as it often does early in the morning. I shed my clothes and walk over the long stretch of shining sand, slip into the sea as quickly as I can. It's cold. It's always cold. I swim in the cold, and it warms up, or I get accustomed to it. I dive repeatedly, I swim far out, I tread water, and I feel once more a measure of happiness and intense gratitude that I know this place.

This is where the true riches are, in the green water, as I dive down to the white sand, repeatedly forcing myself down for the simple, profound reward of looking up at the surface from the clear green depths. For a few seconds I revel in the shimmering play of water, the white circle of light over my head and the increments of light that dissipate and darken in the surrounding green, and already my brief seconds are over.

I rise to the top, bursting through the circle of light and taking a deep breath. Collecting and hoarding as much oxygen in my lungs as I can, I turn and dive. I return to the water again, and swim through the depths. I resurface and am glad, with every atom of my being, to be alive, to be here, to experience this, this great gift from the sea, this baptism, this immersion, this drowning of the body and resurrection of my soul.

Having time to myself that first summer after the split felt like a balm, a relief. After years of being enmeshed in a relationship I wanted to leave, the shock of being out the other side took time to fade. Three months after I left him, this was my first chance to breathe again. The last time I had spent in Kerry, on my own, with no family, boyfriend or children, had been the tail end of a summer after college spent working in the village pub, the Blind Piper. So many of us spend no time alone at all, and it's challenging to do so, lonely and quiet without the company of others.

But this week was necessary; I had to stop and pause. But in the pausing would I sink, like I would if I were swimming? My relationship was as empty as the shells on the beach, but I hadn't had the guts to leave. The thought of it terrified me, brought me out in cold sweats.

Now, I knew I would not sink, but that I had been falling. I was like a stone tossed into water, as every part of me was diluted and erased over the last couple of years by staying with someone whom I no longer loved. And me, a swimmer, the very last thing I should have ever allowed myself to do was sink. It went against everything

I knew and cherished and loved: the thing I am here on earth for, my favourite thing to do, is to always rise, to swim towards the light. Many things pointed me towards the exit, over and over again. The compass in my head and heart pointed me in the direction of the door, but I couldn't go through it.

Four months after Mam died, in April, I went for a run on the Curragh. It was a blustery, cold, miserable day: a spring day that felt colder than winter, where nothing could warm you up. On the Curragh I tried to run under the lowering skies, through the sheep shit. I am a useless runner. I struggled against the wind blowing me back and the rain soaking me, and a mantra or lifeline came to my head and stuck there: *You are strong enough for this. You are strong enough for anything.*

Those words turned into my fuel in the weeks that followed. How I got through those weeks of anguish and fear and exhaustion is something I never want to think about again. Single parenting is incredibly hard, and if I had known just how hard, how crushing the weight of that responsibility is, how every decision had to be made solo, how terrible the loneliness, would I still have done it?

The children were horrified by our split, even though they came to me later and admitted they were waiting for it to happen, the arguments were so bad. Doireann thrived in the peace, and Rebecca – there was an overwhelming sense that the youngest of us was the strongest. Her ability to cast joy and happiness around her like a flower girl strewing petals roped us together, the five of us. She bound us, our knotted cord.

The words that people think do not exist. They find me, or I find them, maybe because I am listening for them, waiting for them, hunting them down with a laser-like hunger and intensity. *I am strong enough for this, I am strong enough for* everything.

I turn and pass these words onto my children. I tell them every day they are just as strong, even if they don't know it yet. I place the map in their hands; I show them the stars, tell them to always know where north is.

After the split I go to the water as often as possible. This, now, is my happiness. In Kerry every day begins and ends with a swim. And I walk the road to Rath, or drive to Derrynane, and let myself across the sand and into the water. I love the solitude, the ritualistic quality of walking down the road and appreciating every instance of life and wildlife around me – the blue skies, with scudding, wispy clouds racing across them; the comforting hulk of Eagle Jill at the end of the road; the birdsong; the incredible cornucopia of wildflowers that crowd the verges of this sacred road.

I adore the freedom of walking unencumbered by children, I love the freedom of being single again. A weight is lifted from me, I shed stones of weight. At the end of the walk, I will launch myself into the water. This is my pagan prayer, being here in the centre of nature at her most infinitely charming.

I have no faith and yet I am worshipping. Rocks, sand, stone steps on the pier, shells scattered like treasure on the wet, hard sand, mountains that stand sentinel behind my most beloved Rath, encircling us, protecting us, I pray to you. Let me always be fit and able enough to do this. Let me come here every year with my children.

I take my towel and wrap it around me and turn again to look and wonder at and worship the sea. This is enough for me: this sand, this sky, this pier, these rocks, this expanse of ocean that ripples out for miles until it meets West Cork. Hungry Hill looms over everything, another protector, another sentinel, another guardian. May this always be enough for me, and let me always take the same joy in this water that I take today.

Swimming brought me back to myself after my worst year – 2013, when I lost Mam, learned Ais had cancer, and when I separated from my ex. But the weeks of that summer in Kerry restored me. Days after I arrived with the kids, a heatwave struck, and we basked in glorious sun, felt the sensuous joy of the heat penetrating our skin, our muscles, deep into our bones.

And I swam every day, for my mother and for me. Every time I entered the water I talked to her, listened for her, thought about her, felt her. Slowly, like the clothes I left behind me on the beach, the hard carapace of years of unhappiness dissolved and washed away with the countless, endless swims I took, and every swim made me better. The salt water softened my misery and eased years of stress and tension. I felt a stranger returning to me, a girl I had known years before, before children, before hardship and stress had angled me into a poisoned, unhappy creature.

She was still there, and every swim returned her to me.

I laughed more with my kids that summer than I have done in years. In the midst of terrible grieving, I found incredible happiness. I had lost the dearest, most beloved person in my world, but here, in the green deep water, I felt close to her again. She was here. Her spirit swam with me in the clear harbour and the middle beach waters of Derrynane. In the tumultuous breakers on the long beach, in the serene waves at Bunavalla, in the Caribbean-like crystal waters of the secret beach, she walked with me on the hard grey sand that never got a chance to dry out. She swam with me as I made lazy circuits of the rocks in Rath, as I trod water off the pier and watched her grandchildren joyfully hurling themselves into the water. And every day I grew better, stronger. I slept again for the first time in almost a year.

Every time I leave the water and feel the simple grace of salt on my skin, it builds another kind of layer. An accumulation of protections, of blessings, of graces, that sustain me through the long, sea-less winter. Like an armlet of prayer beads, I can finger and count and remember them. In arid days when I am struggling through wind and rain and school runs and endless work, I can recall the peace that has been granted to me. Like the books that I have read and loved are stored in my mind, these swims are treasured jewels of memories, to be taken out and counted when I am hundreds of miles and hours and hours away from my beloved Kerry.

My swimming sustains me, and that is why I must do so much of it. That is why I will swim three or four times a day, and that is why I swim when the wind is howling across the beach, lifting the stinging sand to our eyes, when the clouds are lowering and scudding across the sky, why I swim in the rain. I swim because I have to. It is my investment in my soul that sustains me when I have no sea. It is simply the thing in the world I love doing the most. It is something I could not do without any more than I can choose whether or not to breathe. It is in me, it is who I am, it is how my parents made me.

# 14. FIERY GIRL

*Tenebrific (adj) – producing darkness*

THERE ARE PLACES WHERE power resonates more deeply than others, and my family are united in the power of Kerry, in how it makes us feel. The magic runs deep here. It pulses from the rocks and the mountains; it reverberates to us from the green, shining sea. To be at one with it, we only have to climb the mountains, walk for hours, get in the water and swim, dive to the depths and hear what we are being told.

This magic is a part of me that I fiercely deny, but which my sister Aisling thoroughly embraced. It's a Conway thing, from generations of Mayo women, connected to the earth, connected to nature, aware of other worlds – an ability to see things, an awareness of the other, a deep knowledge of how fragile the veils between the worlds are, that the dead are not gone, but walking among us, beside us. It's how Mam felt so strongly her two little ones. It's how I met my dead grandmother Delia on two occasions when I was seventeen.

Those encounters frightened and scared me so much I completely turned away from it. You can't stop dreams, though, and the dreams came, unwillingly. I dreamt of people I knew dying before they did. Saw how it happened. Said nothing, because I was so damn terrified of this thing within me. I thought I could shut the power down if I ignored it.

In many ways, I shut down a huge part of myself, that inheritance which runs through our family. Keeping these other worlds at bay, silencing the ghosts and spirits that dance around me, refusing to see what is directly in front of me, dismissing important dreams the second I wake is a fight I am constantly undertaking. It's exhausting, shutting down a world that is constantly calling you. It came through in other ways. And maybe Ais hated me for that, knowing I had what she had, that ability in the mind to travel, to visit unknown spaces, to go so deep you left this world and visited others.

When we visit Kerry is the only time I fully accept this part of me, and maybe that is why I am so happy there. I accept there is magic all around me, and I fall into it as easily as the kids fall into the sea from the pier – naturally, magnetically, like we are called and our answer is to fall, to pierce the depths.

As firmly as I rejected this part of me, this psychic ability or power, which is what Ais called it, she embraced it, cleaved herself to it, made it a central part of her life. The older she got, the more it mattered to her. And maybe she was correct and I was wrong.

Maybe it's time to let the other worlds in.

\*   \*   \*

There's something about being one of four kids. We are eternally four quarters that make up a whole. We are the four corners that create a square, a solid, unbreakable foundation. We are the four walls that surround a room. We are the four winds, the four directions on a compass. We are double the two who made us.

We are woven together, impenetrable, bound together by hot, eternal summers and darkening skin and nights under smelly canvas and caravan ceilings. We are tightened and wound by family dinners, games of cards, tennis, rugby, cricket, rounders, Trivial Pursuit, charades, Pictionary – the more ridiculous the better. We are cleaved to each other by nights where we can't sleep and we burrow into each other's beds, the older taking and comforting the younger and secretly drawing strength and relief from our own dark thoughts and fears from the baby breath tickling your face. And you hold them, your baby sisters and know, *We are tight, we are four, we are love.*

But then cancer comes and tears its way through. Our walls aren't thick enough; cancer snakes its way in. Cancer, pernicious and unstoppable as ivy, can take a wall down.

A week after Mam is buried, days after Christmas, days before Ais flies back to She lived in New York before, I call to the house. She's drinking wine from a box at eleven in the morning. She can feel the pulsating black tumour in her breast but can't tell me about it. She can't tell anyone about it. She's burying her head in the sand and hoping it will go away.

It doesn't.

It grows and twists its way around her lymph nodes, merrily subdivides and sends its treasonous cell soldiers all through her body. Then the hammer blow. It's Sunday, 10 March 2013, Mother's day, and Aisling calls from San Francisco. *Mir, I've got bad news,* she says. *Triple negative breast cancer, stage 3. But I've got it, don't worry – I'm going to fight it and I'm going to win.*

I listen to her as she outlines everything she's going to do. Ais is determined to not go the medical route. Her cancer plan involves herbs and diet, light and sound healing, uncovering the root of the family darkness that stalks us. She will investigate and annihilate this cancer. It's an old family evil hanging over us. She has travelled back and found Thunder crimes we are all accountable for. We must all seek resolution with the dark past for her cancer to heal.

It's the craziest thing I've ever heard, and when she hangs up, I cry.

Her cancer is called triple negative breast cancer because it doesn't have the three receptors in its cells that typical chemotherapy drugs can attach themselves to. Most breast cancers have these receptors in their cells, allowing the drugs to obliterate them – but not triple negative. If it goes beyond stage three (where the cancer starts to invade other organs), only ten percent of women who get it will be alive after five years.

The most alive person I know got the deadliest breast cancer. She walked into any room and ignited it. Her friends adored her, her family loved her, but the kids were besotted.

They worshipped her. Aisling was the cool aunt, the one who lived in Nantucket and San Francisco, but never, ever forgot a birthday. She had that brilliant knack of getting the kids presents they could never have conjured up themselves. Nor could we, the parents, but it was exactly what they wanted.

She dossed her way through school, nicknamed Scruff. She disrupted classes but made everyone laugh. I meet her first boyfriend regularly around Kildare, and he's still a little in love with her. But they all were. She brought gangs of kids to the house in College Park after school. They sat in the kitchen, smoked, sometimes drank the parents' spirits and laughed hysterically.

After school and a course in beauty therapy she ended up in Galway, working as a masseuse, and her interests in alternative therapies were sparked. Ais loved crystals, incense, stones in velvet bags. Her alternative remedies and beliefs were as deeply woven into her as my books were into me.

Her laugh was more infectious than any damn virus – she would get giddy fits that had us all laughing, tears streaming down our faces, laughing so much our sides hurt, laughing over nothing and everything. These could strike anytime, without warning. Her dreams were vivid and powerful. As a child she was a regular sleepwalker, roaming the house at all hours.

My writing about her is the most difficult thing I've undertaken. Describing her is like trying to catch the heat, the intensity and power of the sun. My relationship with her was probably the trickiest in my life. There was love there, deep love, but also a difficult history of sibling fights and rivalry and arguments the others didn't have. Thrown together a lot as kids, we were wildly different – I was serious, bookish, overly sensitive. Even as a child she was always waiting for the party to start.

Ais was like a painting in the gallery, full of light and darkness; she was complex, sublime, ethereal and earthy. She loved too much, cared too much, felt too much, was generous to everybody around her when she hadn't a bean.

Ais loved Christmas, holidays, and birthdays. She loved times when we would get together and celebrate, she loved being the centre of attention, and it irritated me endlessly. As a child her favourite thing was pretending. She'd wrap herself up in curtains, old army uniforms – on occasions, the dog would be draped around her neck. She loved that mutt. Bruno was a mongrel, a cross, and the best, most beautiful, loving dog we ever had.

Rossa and Maeve would give you entirely different versions of Ais than I would. I don't trust myself to write about her, to describe her, because I'm missing something huge. The ease the others had with her, I didn't have that – or I found it too late for it to matter. From the time we were tiny, we bitched, argued and hated each other. No one annoyed me, infuriated me, enraged me the way she did.

Her banter and slagging could turn to twisted knives, plunged into my sensitive spots after too much drink. Those sensitive spots, hidden to all save those we have grown up with, throbbed for days after. In time I began to dread her visits home from the States, knowing it would be weeks of hurt that we had to skate over like thin ice, millimetres from plunging into the truth.

We existed, as sisters, on a cliff of love. A moment's anger, the wrong words could tip us into hatred, a canyon of rancour ever below us, an ugly, yawning chasm whose darkness threatened to swallow us. We danced on a knife-edge of civility and brutality. It took nothing for the mask to slip, the truth to rear its head, and there was no beauty in this truth. We had failed to leave our childhood behind us. Whatever horror we created between us, that toxic hatred, the opposite of love, a festering sore of jealousy and spite followed us, attached like a shadow. We carried these fighting, bitching children around with us. It was impossible to put them down.

Going to the States was a good move for her. She ended up living on Nantucket, and she loved it there, surrounded by friends. She married a gorgeous man we all liked, Chad, moved to San Francisco. Her friends were her fellow waitresses and bar staff, her housemates.

Her marriage broke up. At a point in most people's lives when they take stock, reassess, possibly take a long hard look at what's going on to figure out who they actually are, she escaped further, into a world of shamanism, healing, mysticism, women's groups. To me, it was more bullshit, but to her, absolute truth. Our interactions were difficult and painful. She lectured me on all the different ways I was not living fully or correctly, how I was damaging my children, that her way was the only way, her truth the only truth.

That night in March, only three months after Mam's death, we picked ourselves up and begin fighting side by side. We had no time for tears, no space for fear; we are four, and we take up sentry duty again, manning the walls.

This time we have more at stake, more to protect – Rossa and I face the impossible task of keeping this latest tragedy from the children. They have lost both their beloved grandparents. They cannot know they are about to lose Aisling, too.

\* \* \*

We lost Ais gradually, in bits and pieces. Her cancer treatment was a carousel that morphed into a train wreck, and we had no control over any of it. She bent her ferocious, indomitable will to her illness and did it her way. After Mam's death she returned to San Francisco and eventually, weeks later, told a friend about the lump in her breast.

She got the diagnosis of triple negative breast cancer and decided to fight it with natural therapies, eschewing chemo and radiotherapy, the surgery. She was offered everything but, unfortunately, stage three breast cancer doesn't respond to light and sound and good thoughts. The tumour grew so big it threatened to break through the skin of her breast.

It was hard for her, going through this alone. There was no man, no partner, so in typical Aisling style, she rallied her friends around her. They wrapped her in their love. Her friends, her roommates, her women's group organised fundraisers so she could stop working and get the treatments she wanted – Chinese herbs, acupuncture, sound healing. Mam and Dad's friends also rallied, organising coffee mornings, sending her cheques. Sean Hurley, at the annual Cadet Class reunion in April, had the 31st do a whiparound for her. The results were substantial. A San Francisco night with DJs, bands and drag artists and another one in Nantucket raised $12,000. That's how much people loved her and wanted to help her.

If it were today, we'd be setting up a GoFundMe page. Back then, social media wasn't the beast it is today. Maeve and her boyfriend, Ian, set her up with a blog, Aisling's Ark, (aislingsark.blogspot.com) to help her express what she was going through and keep people up to date with her treatment. She got diagnosed at 38, and the severity of it flattened her. Chemotherapy, which she would eventually agree to undergo, would take away her fertility. Surgery would take away her breasts, and she would lose her eyebrows and hair.

When I think of Ais as a teenager, I see her in front of a mirror, meticulously tending to her perfect eyebrows. She could arc one superciliously and convey everything she wanted by a slight lift. They were wonderful, framing her astonishing hazel-green eyes, the same colour as Dad's. Her hair was black, a thick, glossy mane that was tossed around, another feature in her armoury of beauty and seduction.

Her cancer changed her. She excavated parts of herself most of us never touch. She opened herself up to love and light in ways none of us can imagine. She not only sought and accepted absolute, pure, complete love from those around her, she soaked it up from the earth, from the sun, the stars and the moon. She demanded love come to her from the universe and radiated it all back tenfold.

Just as the surgery opened her up, she opened up her heart and laid everything bare. She travelled emotionally, psychically, spiritually. She squeezed every drop of joy, fun, craic and laughter out of every single situation she found herself in and challenged all of us to do the same. The party wasn't going to stop just because cancer had joined in – no way. She was alive, laughing. Crying most nights, on her own, at the fear and terror that ruled her now. But to her eternal credit, she kept laughing. She hated people being worried or sad about her. In chemo treatments, in wards waiting for or recovering from surgery, she still acted the clown and made people laugh.

All Ais ever wanted to do was travel. She had a hunger to go far, go deep, to explore new territories. I am allergic to the endemic misuse of the word 'journey'. Its precise meaning is 'an act of travelling from one place to another'. It is geographic, rooted in airports and boats and tickets and maps and physical adjustments of landscapes and locations.

The way people misuse it makes me want to scream. If your life changes, that's not a journey, that's a transformation. Journeys are physical, not emotional. You haven't gone on a journey, you have changed.

But Ais did travel. She went places none of us could follow. She saw things none of us could imagine. She battled and overcame and lived with fear and terror and heartache on her own, with no other half to hold her at night. There was no partner to be with her for the countless doctor's visits and appointments. She heard every bit of bad news on her own, with no one to hug her or hold her hand. Nobody knows her dark nights and how much she craved the dawn, the sun – the light, endless days of summer stretching ahead of her where she would ride her bike, go to the sea, sit on the beach and watch the sunsets.

By early May she had been through two hospitals, twenty mammograms, twenty breast biopsies, CT scans, bone scans, MRIs, PET scans. They ended with a chest core biopsy that pierced her back to get to the lungs without hitting her aorta. A little something, a suspicious mass showed up in a scan near the heart. She was offered five months of chemo, a double mastectomy she refused. Ais had a habit all her life of knowing everything better than everyone else. Doctors, surgeons, would prove no different. She would do it her way. The biopsy came back clear.

In June Maeve went out to her to help. The tumours grew apace, as they will do. Three weeks with someone looking after her, helping her, allowed her to see she was in deep denial with what was happening. She rang her team in UCSF, the hospital she was attending, and told them she would in fact do the chemo. She knew, by starting this at the age of thirty-eight, any hopes of having children were destroyed. She would go into instant menopause. The tumour measured 25 cm.

An MRI in July showed the tumour reducing, even as it tried to push through her skin. In September her hair began to fall out. She was tired, her bones sore, she imagined this was what ageing must feel like, the inability to type or open jars. She spent a lot of time considering why some people get sick and others don't. She was on a steep learning curve, where life as she knew it was slipping from her grasp.

She knew to survive she had to lean into her cancer, embrace it, accept it, know her adversary. She wrote . . . *you have to learn to forgive what you are holding onto, to just let go. We carry so much stuff around in our hearts and then wonder why we feel less than happy, it's ridiculous, isn't it? Well, maybe not, it took cancer for me to see that. I want to heal every facet of my body, mind and soul so that I can be of help to others going through this and shine a light onto what can be a very dark time but needn't be, it can be joyful, meaningful and if you try and make it so, illuminating.*

By November she was, in her own words, *bald as a baldy coot. I look like a cancer patient now, or a baby gerbil, or Duncan Goodhew without the swimming muscles.* She likened her treatment, a double chemotherapy dose of Adriamycin and Cytoxan to *a lovely vintage with a musty bouquet of the*

*70s, with distinct noxious undertones that bring to mind the grassy meadows of Chernobyl on a summer's day . . . . delicious.* The double dose proved a little too much for her tired bones and sent her into hospital with neutropenia – not enough white cells in her system to fight infection.

Maeve went out to San Francisco again that December to help Ais through her surgery, a double mastectomy. Three days later it was Mam's first anniversary – it seemed years since she died, but it had been only one. Ais flew through the surgery. Christmas was tough that year.

The results came through in January, and they were positive. The pathology after surgery indicated clear margins around the tumour, with nothing left behind. All lymph nodes biopsied came back negative, even the one removed. Skeletal ribs and pectoral wall both tested negative. Breast skin also tested negative. Of the tumour removed, less than 2 mm of the necrotic mass was cancerous. She was, as far as they were concerned, cancer free.

She took this diagnosis and ran with it. Sprinted with it, far, wide and long into the future. But that small, suspicious mass beside her heart? It hadn't gone anywhere. She was offered radiation treatment and refused it. All she could hear, take in, believe, were the words cancer-free.

\* \* \*

That June we decided to throw a massive party in my house. I was living in a bungalow with a huge garden, beside a canal, and had the most room to host the family coming: all the Bunburys, Thunders and Mulcahys we could gather. There was a lot to celebrate. Ais was home on holidays for a few weeks, and this was a chance to see all her aunts and uncles, all her cousins in one swoop, without running around to see everyone.

She would be 40 later that summer, in August, and would not be home for it. Rossa had been promoted to lieutenant colonel, a massive achievement. But promotion meant a trip abroad, and Rossa already knew where he would go – Afghanistan. Any time he left the army base where he would be stationed in Kabul, it had to be in an armoured car or a tank. He spent months doing courses before leaving, travelling all over Europe.

Maeve and Ian were celebrating their engagement – they planned to marry in September in a small Spanish wedding with only a few relatives invited, so this was a chance to see everyone and share this lovely, happy news. Me, I was a year on from the split, starting to date, not meeting anyone, writing every minute I got; this day was my achievement, throwing a party for sixty people and getting everyone together when it wasn't a funeral. There were children and toddlers on bouncy castles, dads playing football with their kids in our huge garden, teenagers walking around the house trying to find the best WiFi – the sun blazed down on us; it was a gloriously happy day.

After the food, the desserts, the coffee, the songs began; we sat around the tables scattered under the apple and birch trees, drinking wine. We were, I think, like something out of Tolstoy; we were the happy family as Patsy, Mum's oldest brother, led the singing, followed by his daughters and grandsons. Then the Thunders sang, Brian with his strong baritone and assured ballads; everyone had a crack at a song, and it was like Mam was still there, in the centre of us all, biding her time until someone, usually Tony, commanded her to sing 'Summertime', and she did, closing her eyes and strumming her guitar, holding us all spellbound in her magical, melodious voice, as she sang the words we have been reared on, *your daddy's rich, your mamma's good-looking, so hush lil baby, don't you cry*. Aisling sang Ella Fitzgerald, 'Someone to watch over me', a poignant paean of longing and impossible love.

Unbeknown to us all, death was there too, hovering over and skirting the full summer trees, watching and waiting.

# 15. A WEDDING IN COMARES

*Tarantism (n.) – overcoming melancholy by dancing*

DURING HER FEW WEEKS at home, Ais notices a pea-sized node above the clavicle and is constantly stretching her arms, rotating her shoulders, trying to stretch the pain away. The lump triples in size until it protrudes from her neck. When she gets back to San Francisco, she is seen quickly by her team and they give her devastating news – it's back. She spends the morning getting a biopsy, doing labs, then drives out to the beach and yells and roars and screams at the ocean. Then it starts again, the dreaded round of phone calls where she tells us the worst news.

There are two tumours, above and below the clavicle, on the same side as the tumour that surgery removed. It is the same aggressive triple-negative lobular cancer, extensive in the chest wall, the tumour at the base of her neck spreading out of the breast area that is of concern. It grows fast and is staged at 4. She starts months of chemo, with a break planned in September for Maeve's wedding in Spain

\* \* \*

Maeve and Ian chose Comares, the tiny Spanish hilltop village north of Malaga to be married in. This was where Mam had spent a month in April 2009, after Dad died. The house is the one where she played guitar, and it belonged to John and Esther, uncle and aunt of Maeve's best friend Alice from her schooldays. They ran a scheme called WOOFing, working on an organic farm. You paid a reduced rate, did some work, learned some skills. It was not just an escape for Mam, but a return – this part of Spain is where she and Dad had spent their honeymoon.

Going there felt like the closing of a circle between mother and daughter. Mam and Dad could not be there, so Maeve went to where Mam had been, to sleep in the room she had slept in, swim in the pool she had swam in every day. After months and years of darkness, going south to the sun and the light felt right.

We gathered the night before the wedding, Ais looking beautiful as only Ais with a shaven head could. Maeve was completely stressed, making paper decorations and arranging flowers. It was a DIY wedding, and the next morning was busy, setting up the tables, doing the flowers, arranging the bar. The lads spent all morning arranging a shelter up the mountain. It reminded me of a giant sail coasting over a sea of rock and stone.

The bridesmaids came and took Maeve away to get ready. Guests, friends and family arrived, and the time came to send everyone over to the sail-chapel. Aisling was the pagan priestess, the witch minister, and had spent the morning writing links between the poetry and songs for the ceremony. The house was finally clear.

I went upstairs to tell them to come down. Rossa waited below to walk Maeve over and give her away. All brides are beautiful, but she was tremendous in her beauty – her floating white dress made her dark skin and hair even more striking. She moved before us like an angel. Maeve was happy and afraid, and Rossa, steady and sure, helped her pick her way over the rocky ground. Ian nearly collapsed when he saw her.

The words, the poetry, the songs that day were all about love. Our loss was keen and sharp, but it was blunted by the waves and the sea of love flowing around us that day. We were buoyed by the presence of Mam and Dad's sisters and brothers, our cousins, their best friends, as if the rolling valleys and arid hills and mountains were not made of rock but of saltwater and we were being tossed and held by deep, surging waves.

At the table after the meal, Rossa rose to give his speech. Dad, not there, but absolutely there, as Rossa's words carried us all away on a river of hope and certainty and love. He has always had the most uncanny ability to capture everything about a person and put it into words.

He described Maeve that day, her wedding day, as our glue. Not the baby of the family, but the strongest of us all, the one that bound us, roped us together when we scattered apart and reminded us constantly of how important we were to each other. She hates dissension and conflict and was particularly upset by the distance between Ais and I. But something there was already changing. In Comares Ais and I shared a room, had lots of laughs and good chats. With Mam gone, a space opened in our relationship, and we could breathe again. We were dealing with each other as adults, not children.

Spain was a milestone for us, our first major family event without our parents, and we not only got through it, we had a brilliant time. They were missed acutely by everyone there who knew them. We envied Ian and his parents, but honestly, we envy anyone who still has their parents. That never goes away. But long conversations with their best friends helped – the Hurleys and the Studderts. There is something so beautiful about a long chat with one of their friends. I treasure these times. Mam and Dad come back in a way with the people who knew them best, as they hand us over stories and memories to hoard away and take out as needed.

* * *

We returned home from Spain to yet another hammer blow – once Aisling had returned to San Francisco, another tumour was discovered. This time, no surgery was offered, instead we heard words like *life expectancy*, *terminal*, *five years*, *palliative care*. Would the pain and suffering never end? Would death ever take a fucking break and leave us the hell alone? What had she done, what had *we* done to deserve this? Six years since Dad had died, two years since Mam.

I hate and loathe and always have done, ever since Mam lay, strangled with tumours on her deathbed, the fighting words, the aphorisms and metaphors surrounding cancer. I cannot abide, having seen it twice at close quarters, the idea cancer is a battle to be fought, and that by dying from it, a battle is lost. Instead of shrouding it in fighting talk, cloaking our fear in battle phrases, how about we turn instead, defenceless and naked, and face our enemy?

Why can't we be stronger and braver, look hard at the death that is coming and in doing so, make the most of the life that remains? This loved one, this child, sibling, parent, lover, friend, husband, wife – they are still here with us. They should be supported, held and loved, adored beyond all parameters, limits and boundaries. We should be opening our hearts to the fathomless love that exists within all of us and wrapping that person, enfolding them in that love. Should we be fighting or loving, battling or living, struggling or simply dying?

Acceptance of death is the hardest thing, the most impossible hurdle in our society. We run from it when we should be turning towards it, always knowing it, always seeing it, acknowledging and accepting its inevitability. Death is waiting for all of us. Isn't it better to live in the light of that knowledge rather than hiding in the shadows?

\* \* \*

This time around, Ais concentrated on what she wanted to do. She got a housesitting gig in the hills in Bolinas, above San Francisco. She lived in a yurt, the very unusual staff quarters away from the main house. There was a wolf to look after – yes a wolf – and coast rides to be taken in her car, and plenty of meditations and meetings with her women's group, also up in the hills. Frances McDormand was her neighbour, and sightings of Frances at the village store, over the fences between the properties, were excitedly relayed to us via text.

Her left arm began to swell up, making cooking, driving, even typing difficult. The tumours were growing, twisting through her neck and bubbling up under the skin. She sought out shirts with high collars to hide it or wrapped her neck in scarves. In the spring of 2015 she began to have blinding headaches and dizzy spells. Driving was now not safe. One day the whole of one side of her body went numb, and her friends took her to the ER. More tests, more scans, more devastating news – only this time it was far worse than anything we had previously heard: brain tumours, multiples of them.

In Ireland, we don't offer patients surgery at this stage. It's palliative radiotherapy, to shrink the size of the tumours and prolong the lifespan for as long as possible, but really, it's only weeks. Brain tumours are swift and decisive fuckers, making the patient extremely sick, changing the personality as they merrily thrive in the different cortexes, subtracting movement, speech and personality as they grow.

But America is different. There, science is greater than death, more powerful, and brain surgery was offered. Not only would the tumours be removed, brachytherapy implants would be inserted into the tumour sites, providing a constant dose of radiation to prevent their reoccurrence. Oh, America and your hubris!

I rang Mike, my doctor friend, and gave him the latest. I was livid, furious with the San Francisco surgeons who fed her an eternal rope of hope, stopping her coming home. *You are dying*, I wanted to scream down the phone to her, but I never did. *Come home*, I wanted to beg, but didn't. This was her decision and no one else's. *Six months*, said Mike. She wouldn't see Christmas.

It's just not possible to stay on top of everything when a person you need is leaving. You are in the world of the living, they are moving to the world of the dying. And you don't know it yet, but you are about to leave the world you inhabit, this chaos, this stress, this pressure is the siren call, the swansong for life as you know it. When they die, you are travelling too.

Hours every day are spent on calls – calls to her, or catch-up calls. Whoever had spoken to her last called the rest of us and gave us updates as to how she was: rapidly losing power in her arms and legs. There were calls where we tried to figure out how to get her home, rounds of calls where we argued, rounds of calls to apologise for the arguments, calls where we did nothing but cry, calls to and from relatives, family friends, Newbridge friends, college friends, army friends, Kerry friends, work friends – it was amazing any of us got any work done at all. By the time one round of calls had been worked through, a fresh crisis had hit and word had to be got out again.

There were dynamics and tensions and problems with Aisling dying that had simply not been there with Mam and Dad. Losing a sibling is completely different to losing a parent. We all had unique, precious relationships with her that were intertwined with us as family, but we also stood apart, alone. You can be deep, best friends with a sibling in a way you can never be with a parent. Experiences, history, good and bad times cleave and twist you to each other, a little like the tumours twisted and climbed around the host organs. We extend our tentacles into each other as children and never quite are able to let go. There's no excision or surgery for this.

It felt like Ais was using me as her punchbag during the final months. There was no partner, no parent there for the days when she needed to spew and vent and exorcise all the anger, the pure cold fear of her life slipping away, the unquenchable devastation that death was waiting for her. There were nights when she picked up the phone and gave it all to me, unable to do this with her housemates, her friends, with Rossa or Maeve. It was like being punched, hard in the stomach, over and over, body blows I could not dodge that left me reeling, exhausted, wiped.

We were dealing with a lot. We needed to get Ais home so we could care for her, mind her, get her into hospice, but she refused. She was following a treatment plan she would not abandon as she was convinced she was getting better. Her absolute refusal to see what was happening incensed and infuriated me – that she could not see, would not see that she was dying. But of course that refusal was pure Ais, right to her core – the party was not ending, not yet, not on her watch. There was still drinking and dancing to be done, laughs to be had.

The tumours pressing on her brain were of course part of it too. They affected her decision-making and her personality. Could I have been a bit kinder, more patient, more forgiving? Less demanding that everything run the way I wanted it to, not the way she needed it to? We were still, as her vitriolic phone calls proved, the fighting, bitching children, and the support both of us needed was thin on the ground. We were both single, doing it all alone; there was no partner around for either of us to help or support.

But no one can truly be there, not in the way you want them to be. No one can really help, because you need someone to come in with a magic wand and wave this cancer away, to turn it from your door as it knocks, repeatedly, until it has worn away the timbers with its mortal persistence. Death and cancer shredded our doors, destroyed our children's ease and innocence. Their tiny worlds were hammered again and again and again. When it should have been cinema trips and shopping and discos, it was hospitals and graveyards and grief.

We staggered through the days, doing the bare minimum, doing the necessary, relying on wine and coffee and tunes, sugar, dance parties, dark, gothic humour between ourselves to pull us through. Ian and Lorna were as stitched into this as the three of us. We were six facing death, altogether. Outside this perfect circle, a desert stretched. No one could cross it to get to us.

# 16. CATHAIR AISLING / AISLING'S FORT

*You are not enclosed within your bodies,*
*nor confined to houses or fields. That which is*
*you dwells above the mountain and roves with*
*the wind – Kahlil Gibran*

IN NOVEMBER I FOUND myself once more in Dublin Airport collecting my sisters. This time Ais came through the arrivals gate in a wheelchair, Maeve following with about twenty bags. Ais never travelled light.

She stayed with me for a couple of weeks, then I drove her to Maeve, who, with Ian, looked after her in Cork. At the start of December she was in Kerry, in a cottage called Tadhg House, beside Rath. It overlooked the secret beach, and there was a path to it through the garden. You opened the doors and the windows and breathed in the sea.

It was quite incredible to have her home, that she'd made it back. She was at the advanced, terminal stage of cancer and should have been in hospice. She was seriously sick, far too sick to be left on her own, and one of us had to be with her all the time. Getting to Kerry in December for a week meant an army of helpers had to be installed at home to cover everything. My friends and relatives rallied; I drew up a roster. I will never forget all those who helped me get that time with Ais.

The car was packed with food, drink, togs, warm clothes and Juno, the mini schnauzer pup I finally accepted in late October, riding shotgun. I pulled into the house hours later and Maeve ran out to meet me, her face haggard with exhaustion and worry. Seeing Ais after only a few days, I was floored by her deterioration. Cosied up beside the fire, wrapped in blankets and scarves, she was perpetually freezing and wore cute knitted caps. The cottage reeked with oils: the strong ointment she would slather on her tumour, still believing in fairies and magic and the effects of potions; the sweeter note of the oils she burned; scented candles; the underlying hum of soup.

I never saw Ais walk into a space she would stay in and not try to change it. She surrounded herself with stones, feathers, crystals, bones and shells – talismans from her life in San Francisco, treasures from her beloved beaches in Kerry. She had sent Maeve to the caravan to gather up all the lamps and candles as Tadhg House didn't have enough. She embarked on a frenzy of online shopping, spending hundreds on homewares, convinced she was turning a rented house into her forever home.

I don't know if that was mostly tumour or fear, but Ais was convinced by doing something she had always done well and extremely beautifully – making a house a home – she could defy death and keep it away. You knew the minute you entered her house who she was. There was nothing ambiguous about her décor. All she was missing was the broom and the cat. Once Maeve left, we were on our own, and I worried about how we would get on.

I walked to Rath with Juno as the day gathered in and had a swim, plunging from the pier into the dark water as the evening fell around me. The horizon bled, until I could not tell land from water, mountain from sea. I fought the waves crashing against the dark, black hulk of the pier – no one should swim like this, on their own, in December, with not a soul around to raise the alarm, in cold water, in falling darkness. If I got into trouble there wasn't a hope of anyone noticing.

But I wasn't alone. They were with me, swimming around me, protecting me, talking to me, telling me things. And I talked to them, telling them we were here, close by and she was so sick, telling them to mind her, to mind all of us. But I made no prayer or invocation to save or spare her; I knew it was futile. Instead I begged them to carry us through the darkness ahead, to lift us all and stop us from going under, to get Rossa home in time.

In the space of a few short days, Tadhg House healed so much for us, and for that alone I will always treasure that little cottage. We worked and talked through decades of hurt and pain. She brought things to me, challenged me, called me out on things she hated about me, as only sisters can. I gave it all back to her.

But we weren't fighting, we were exploring, chatting, laughing, drinking. We drank the days away. I had no children to mind, and she was dying, so why not? Baileys coffees, wine in the evenings, finishing the days with whiskey by the fire. Her drinking made me laugh. She took supplements and herbs all day, ate the purest, vegan food – then wiped it out with alcohol at night.

We talked about our childhood and where the hatred had started, the roots of our fighting. A lot of it had been misdirected jealousy, a warped perception of Mam having favourites. Ais ran Mam down; I defended her. Ais ran through how persistently unseen she had felt, the feeling that nothing she did was ever good enough for Mam. And she was demanding of us, for sure. There was always a sense of competition with everyone else's sons and daughters. Degrees had to be first class. Careers to be stellar. Sons-in-law to boast about. (Fail, fail, fail.)

I explained to Ais how becoming a parent wipes you clean. It drains you in ways you can never imagine, sucking all your energy and power away. But it also resets and transforms us, wipes a whole lot of the bullshit we have been carrying away. There's just not the room for it anymore. And when you survive your first bout of sleepless nights – the terror, the endless work and anxiety of your firstborn – when you realise this baby was gifted and granted to you with no checks or licences or tests, and you have done it, you have not killed the tiny human entrusted to your care, your thoughts begin to turn to repeating the insanity, because you have forgotten the pain.

Somewhere in that roaring river you have crossed, somewhere in the maelstrom of forgotten nights and haggard dawns that bled into days that never seemed to end, you knew something – so completely and profoundly, it changed everything. You finally got it. You realised everything you have done, every nappy changed and feed delivered, every Babygro and vest washed, every time you cleared the kitchen floor of the day's play, *they* did this, all of this, for all of you.

Your parents fought the same battles every day. You are finally, intensely grateful, and all the shit has been wiped away as cleanly and efficiently as you wipe the baby's bottom. You don't care anymore about anything, because you recognise parents for the absolute heroes they are. And hopefully you tell them you finally know. The babies grow, into surly teenagers, defiant students, oblivious twenty-somethings, and you hold on, waiting, telling yourself, someday, someday. They will go through the fire of broken nights and babies screaming, obliterating you to your very core but remaking you at the same time. We not only give birth to our children, but to new versions of ourselves, and it takes years to realise it.

This is what separated Aisling and me; this is the screaming gulf we teetered on, liable to fall into at any minute. A word, a wrong look could start a row between us, and here was the root of it: that Mam had favourites.

I made more tea, we sat at the kitchen table, looked at the grey sea dancing itself onto the rocks. We heard it as it pounded and winter-thrashed, and I laid it all out for her. The truth. I built a wall of words, low, squat and incontrovertible, just like the stone walls in the fields and roads around us.

I started with one of my earliest, strongest memories, the day she was brought home from hospital, how Mam focused on her to the oblivion of all else. Their black heads bent together, eyes shining at each other, so tight my four-year-old self could not separate them, no matter how hard I tried.

How Mam breastfed her, when Rossa and I had been bottle-fed. The sadness and grief Mam carried. Her mother had died the year before Aisling was born. It was exactly what I'd had with Doireann after Dad dying. I told Ais how powerful she was, how much strength she gave Mam, how she pulled Mam through her darkest time. What it's like to lose a parent and, in the same year, give birth to a child – how it saves you. It propels you forward and teaches you grief cannot be surrendered to. Grief is a wave we must surf and ride.

All the love, all of it – the ever-present, never-ending love that grows and never abates. Days build on days, nights are stacked up, endless and painful, but the love grows and grows. How there are no favourites, there never could be – you love your children in different ways, easier on some, tougher on others, because you as parent are the ultimate arbiter. If anything the more work they are, yes, then, maybe the more you love them – how it breaks you in two when you are angry with them. It never leaves you, the shame when you lose it. You carry it around like a dark bruise that fails to fade.

All the things Mam wanted and never got. The money that was never there for clothes, to make the house nicer, to buy a second house. How livid she got when we broke things, coloured glass from the Middle East slipping through our clumsy fingers – she knew it could never be replaced. She wanted to be elsewhere, back working in the bank, surrounded by the cool, imperturbable logic of money, figures, accounts of things that could be tallied and resolved and made sense. Not enmeshed in a haze of endless, never-ending tasks. She stared longingly at her Spanish guitar and played Mozart and Brahms in her head while we slept, and she wrung out buckets of nappies, and that made her a great mother by putting our needs first. She gave us everything we needed. More than anything, she loved us equally and could never have chosen between us. She did her almighty best in the face of years of grief and pregnancies, of babies and babies that never were.

That evening Ais wanted to go to the sea, and I drove her to Derrynane. Everything took ages. Getting her wrapped up enough to get out was a struggle. As I parked at the harbour, darkness was descending. We walked to the end of the pier and breathed in the sea, the disappearing light, the stones, the mountains. She spoke about Kerry magic, how good she felt, how being here healed her. She spoke about the spirits in everything, how all the inanimate things surrounding us were alive, responding to our energy, taking ours in and giving it back to us, a vast landscape of emotional seas, streams, rivers, mirroring us back to our infinite selves.

We walked slowly and for her, painfully, down to Abbey Island Beach. The light was gone, the sea foamed with the breaking brightness of the waves. Everything was dark, inky, navy, occluded. I walked to the waves and dipped my hand, saying hello to the sea. I turned and couldn't see her anywhere.

Then I heard her laughing, hysterical, giddy, compulsive. I followed her laugh and found her, lying flat down on the sand, making sand angels, trying and failing to make wings with her impotent left arm. I couldn't see where she was. It was like the sand, the earth, the rocks of Kerry had already enfolded her.

I lay beside her and did the same, pushing the damp sand, doing what we had done all our lives, through all our childhood, our countless days on the beach in Carne – our relentless creation of thousands of castles and houses and buildings and towns, our sand-sculpting, our intent engineering, our moulding of the most transient of materials, the most resistant to permanence: sand into little houses. Cottages with chimneys and doors and windows, and tiny, paper-thin sand walls protecting them. We were always building walls to keep the bad things out.

And that's all Ais was trying to do, in her rearranging of Tadhg House, in her frenzy of online shopping, in her adorning of anything that stood still with fairy lights. She was making a house to keep the bad things away. Ais was building her fortress, her castle, she was raising her walls and ignoring the cannonballs lobbed at her. She was under siege, trapped, surrounded, and she was still laughing. The party would not end yet.

It got darker and darker as we lay there and laughed. The cold seeped through me, the sand soaked my jeans, but she would not leave. Hours after we left the beach, the breaking waves continued their surge and ate the beach up, wiping our transient angels. But I see them – angels, sisters, soldiers – every time I'm on that beach, winter or summer. I hear her laughing, I see her making her indentation, and there was nothing temporary about it. Ais inhabits that beach, and all the beaches she loved, she's there in the rocks and the stones and the sand; they took her magic in and absorbed her and mirror her back out to us. We just have to know where to look and how to listen.

I will never forget her that night, our last time together on Derrynane – her hilarious, addictive laugh, her defiant, heroic sense of fun and craic that she met cancer with and never flinched from. I thought at the time she was in denial, running away. I see now she met cancer with every single breath, accepted it, and refused to let it define and dominate her. Her aggressive desire to hope, to live, to cheat death was her fighting it. Hope, humour, laughter and love raised her walls so high she could not even see cancer on the other side. Those weeks in Kerry, attempting to create a home, were spent doing what she loved best, where she loved best. She was queen of her castle – her cathair, her fort – and cancer was not taking that from her.

The next day I left and drove home, knowing I would never see her in Kerry again. I left her, a witch beside the fire, wrapped in whiskey, scarves, blankets and laughter, in astounding courage and grace that to this day still blinds me and takes my breath away.

# 17. LAST CHRISTMAS

*Oh, write of me, not,'Died in bitter pains,'*
*https://www.poeticous.com/helen-hunt-jackson/emigravit*
*But 'Emigrated to another star!' –*
*Helen Hunt Jackson*

FOR THE FIRST TIME in my life, I wake alone on Christmas morning. The kids are with their dad and even Juno is gone, to the Studderts. I have to go to Cork, to Marymount Hospice, but I cannot leave the house. I repack bags, considering every piece of clothing I bring – is this what I will be wearing when she dies? I empty and clean the fridge, not sure when I will be back. I consider the fridge too – surely every other fridge in the country is overflowing, and mine is empty. I cut more Christmas cake, pack more shortbread. I'm not able to leave my house because I'm painfully aware the next time I come back to it my sister will be dead.

Eventually I catch a hold of myself, get in the car and drive. It's two hours from Kildare to Cork, all motorway, but I'm going a lot further than 200 miles. I'm spinning through the years, decades of Christmases past unspooling before me as the car eats up the miles. Dad's insistence on not allowing us into the sitting room before eight. The crazy, sweet things he would find to put into our stockings to surprise us. How much he loved it, how much he loved every minute of Christmas Day. He was truly in his element, tears streaming from his eyes with happiness when we finally broke through the sitting-room door and fell upon our presents. Within them, there was always something we had not asked for and had not even imagined we wanted. Those would turn out to be the things we cherished and held onto long after the others disappeared or wore out.

Mulcahy Christmases were happy and joyful and packed with stupid traditions like spending all of Christmas Eve polishing brass, silver and glass so that everything in the house shone. Fighting over the location of the tree, though it ended up in the same corner of the sitting room every year. Lighting a candle in the hall window and singing Silent Night together, before we split away, mortified, as teenagers – now one of our most sacred memories. Escaping for pints and trying to get through Midnight Mass without disgracing ourselves.

Hundreds of childhood memories wash over me as I work through the counties, and she is laughing in all of them, her cheeky grin and squinting eyes, her irrepressible, contagious laugh spilling out of her and into all of us. It's a beautiful and rare gift, to make people laugh the way she did, to bring fun to any situation, no matter how serious – to be able to ramp up the fun times, the good days into unforgettable nights.

I didn't know what kind of reception awaited me. The previous weekend I had gone up and down in a day, and when I arrived she raised an arched eyebrow at me, told me to get out of her room, which I did, returning a little later only to be asked, *What the hell are you still doing here?* It was impossible to know what behaviour was hers, which belonged to her fear or the brain tumours.

When I got to her room, the party was in full flow, Baileys poured liberally into coffee. The lady with the Christmas drinks trolley was told to come back again soon, as we would need her. Ais directed everything from her bed. She was with and not with it, struggling to stay with us in this world as the next one called her. She asked repeatedly for Dad, Rossa and Bruno, her favourites. Maeve and I told her repeatedly Dad was on the way up from Kerry, Rossa was flying home – he was in Kabul that Christmas morning, waiting to get a flight from Afghanistan to Schiphol; he needed an armed escort to get to the airport, it would take two days to get to Cork – and Bruno, well, dogs weren't allowed into hospices.

She picked at her turkey and looked for more booze. *I don't mean to be difficult*, she said to Maeve after lunch, her eyes huge, *but could I have some more champagne?* We were munching my shortbread, cherry and almond, the treat Dad loved and ate so much of. Ais said something so funny I inhaled a chunk as I laughed and immediately started to choke. I ran to the bathroom, trying to cough it up, miming to the girls I needed my back thumped.

Ais leapt out of the bed, dragging her drip with her, and hit me powerfully on the back between my shoulders. She hit me until I was pushing her off me, but she persisted, delighted to have an excuse to legitimately beat the shit out of me. Maeve ran down the corridor to the nurses' station, shouting, *Help, my sister is choking!* The nurses responded, running to her room with a crash cart, oxygen, and they saw me, shortbread dislodged by Aisling's thumping, tears streaming down my face. Everyone fell around laughing. No one found it funnier than Aisling, exhausted by her exertions, before she was helped back into bed.

Again and again, the acute, awful injustice of it all floors me. If I stopped to think about it then, I ran the risk of stopping completely so I didn't. Miriam Hurley came into see us, and I sat with her in the canteen under institutional lights and trees and decorations and cried and got the strength to go back upstairs and face what cannot be faced.

You leave the room because you have to; you can't breathe. Death is sucking all the oxygen, all the life out, and there is no way to stay in there. Death's imminence, its force dominates and presses down on every molecule and atom in the room. It infuses every breath: hers as she starts to struggle and ours as we start holding them from tension and fear. This is only going one way, there is no circumventing the finality of death.

The minute you step outside, as soon as you leave, you are panicky and jittery because anything could happen in the seconds, in the slipped minutes you have gone. There is absolutely nothing like a break. Breaks do not exist. Your mind is completely, totally focused on the person on the other side of that heavy fire door; the person who is dying. You think of what they are going through, what you need to be doing to help them, to ease these brutal hours for them.

In this waiting room, when you don't know how or when death is coming, the last thing you are able to do is remotely process what you are going through, the sheer horror of it. The cancer show is in town once again, grotesque and livid, as vile and inescapable as the tumour twisted round her neck. Its tentacles reach all over her body, secondary fingers, malevolent sister tumours pressing down on her precious brain, taking up space, altering her behaviour, thought processes, memory.

*Where's Dad?* she kept asking. *It's Christmas, he should be here. Where's Bruno, where's Rossa?*

*On his way, Ais. You know we can't bring Bruno in here, the nurses would kill us. On his way, on his way, on his way.*

\* \* \*

I spent Christmas night with her, the nurses wheeling in a camp bed for me as she slept. She constantly jerked and

161

thrashed with the pain. Sometimes she cried softly in her sleep, a gentle whimpering. Once or twice she breathed; *this sucks, this sucks*. And everything you need to know about my sister is in those words.

My sister, my beautiful, wild, fiery Ais was dying of cancer. Brain tumours were crushing her cerebellum and causing her tortuous headaches. She was leaving this world, a world she adored and loved. She was leaving family and friends behind who worshipped her. She was leaving behind her future – a future she craved and desperately longed for – full of love, family, children, travel. She never, ever complained. The most she ever said was *this sucks*.

And it did. Massively, enormously.

This was a Christmas night like no other. She moaned all night, and I tried to sleep but couldn't because I'm a complete princess when it comes to beds and pillows. About three in the morning, she reared out of bed, shouting at me, *What the hell are you doing here? You know I can't stand you sharing a room with me!*

*All the other beds are taken, Ais. I have to sleep here*, I told her.

*Well don't you dare snore*, she said then lay back, before shooting up again, *Dad?* she asked. *Rossa? Bruno?*

*On their way, sis, on their way, I promise.*

She subsided back into a fitful sleep and I thought of all the Christmas nights we shared, the lovely feeling of hopping between each other's rooms, comparing our hauls, snuggling down with a new book, stuffing ourselves with chocolate.

It was the last conversation we ever had. The following morning the doctors came and we were put out of the room as they assessed her. The morphine pump had to go on, the pain was too great for her to bear. We knew what this meant from Mam: a swift slip into unconsciousness and from there, an easy, painless death. A gentle, medical assist onto the far side. Yet again, another round of explaining to the nurses that our brother was in the air, he would be there tomorrow, the day after Stephen's, his absolute need to get to see her, how she kept asking for him. The doctor and nurses listened but the decision was made. Maeve and I left the room as the pump went on, around eleven in the morning. When we came back, the awful tension in her face was gone.

We sat there in the quiet room, and our phones buzzed with texts. We said very little in reply. It was not looking good. We texted other, close family that the end was coming. We lit her candles, burned her oils, read her prayers from her books, read her poetry, we sang her songs, played her favourite music, and told her over and over and over again how much we loved her. Love is the only word anyone needs to hunt for.

The hours advanced, and Rossa was flying. We held her hands and entreated her, begged her to hold on, to hang on, to wait for him. He had to see her. But as surely as Rossa was flying home, Ais was at the airport, checking in for her final flight.

She died at 4.30 am, the day after Stephen's, the 27th of December. Rossa was still in the air, close to Holland. Maeve and I witnessed all the candles in the room go out as she took her last breath, exhaled, was finally still. It was the hour before dawn, the darkest part of the night, the veils between the worlds so thin she carried the light around her from our world to the next one. She carried the light to accentuate and increase the power of her own, a reminder of us. Just as we lit the candle in the Christmas Eve window as an ignition of magic, Ais brought light with her. Our fiery girl, gone to set fire to new worlds. Ais never failed to make an entrance, and surely she had to rob some light from this world to announce her blazing arrival in the next.

Fifty per cent of our family, gone. It sucks.

Half an hour later, the nurses come to get me. It was Rossa, calling from Schiphol, calling as soon as his plane landed. I had to tell him she was gone; they'd missed each other. Maeve went up to the room to sleep. I stayed with Ais. I sat with her for hours, told her things I need to say that she can no longer hear.

Maeve came in, tears in her eyes. *I saw her Mir,* she said. *I was asleep and she came right up to me, laughing, her, face so happy and she looked at me intently then she disappeared into a ball of blue light and fizzed away.*

*That figures*, I thought. She had flown away as a piece of light. She was gone, she had pierced the veil, moving with ease between this world and hers. Ais the traveller was off again.

# 18. AISLING'S ASHES

### The Song of Amergin

*I am the sea breeze*
*I am the ocean wave*
*I am the surf's thunder*
*I am the stag of the seven tines*
*I am the cliff hawk*
*I am the sunlit dewdrop*
*I am the fairest flower*
*I am the rampaging boar*
*I am the swift-swimming salmon*
*I am the placid lake*
*I am the excellence of art*
*I am the vale echoing voices*
*I am the battle-hardened spearhead*
*I am the God who gave you fire*
*Who knows the secrets of the unhewn dolmen*
*Who understands the cycles of the moon*
*Who knows where the sunset settles*

THERE ARE SONGS SUNG of the Milesians who came to our
shores when the Tuatha de Dannan held sway, millennia

ago. How they landed at Inbhear Scéine, where Amergin's wife Scéine died in the attack, and Amergin adjudicated between the De Dannan and the Milesians. The Milesians agreed to retreat back to sea, beyond the ninth wave, a magical boundary.

When they attacked again, the De Dannan raised a mighty, magical storm to keep them away from the shore. Amergin began to sing, an invocation, a paean to the island they were trying to conquer, a bargaining plea, a poem of worship, a call to the soul of Ireland. The waves parted and the boats made land. There was a bloody, fierce battle with heavy losses on both sides, but the Milesians triumphed, killing the three kings of the De Dannan in single combat.

Inbhear Scéine, where the Milesians came in over nine waves, is outside Kenmare. It is, as we stand on Rath in the gathering dark, about forty kilometres east of us as the crow flies. The Milesians sailed past Rath on their way to conquering Ireland five thousand years ago. The sea that surges into this beach holds the memory of the battle – the waves carry the echo of Amergin's battle cry, his words. It is no wonder to me that everything about this place carries magic. This sea, this water, these waves carried our ancestors.

After the battle, the Tuatha De Dannan went under the ground and became the Sídhe, the fairy folk. Who knows what kingdoms unravel and twist below our feet, what chambers of wonder and ancient magic are buried beneath the mountains? Where else, if you were fairy, would you want to be for eternity, if not beneath these mystical mountains of Ivereagh?

Aisling felt it, she knew they were here, she always felt the magic of this place. And this is where we leave her behind us, to enter the earth, to join her fellow Sídhe folk, our magical fairy girl of fire.

\* \* \*

Cremation is completely different to interring a body. It's fraught and drawn out, without the fog of shock and the cushion of alcohol that normally accompanies death and an Irish funeral. But it was what she wanted, and we understood. The thought of Aisling being buried in Newbridge was ridiculous. She had always hated the town.

In some ways the similarities to the funeral are there – the coffin disappears, the crowd disperses, some accompany you back to whatever event has been organised, until the undertaker calls to tell you the ashes are ready for collection.

The ashes are in a large, green plastic tub, about the height of a two-litre water bottle but much wider. There's a whole body in there. The contents are astonishing. The bones are crushed and milled, mixed with the finer ash of the coffin and her clothes. Grey and dark grey, with tiny fragments of darker black, white, sand, beige – it resembles the groaning clouds of a rain-laden Irish sky.

For a girl who was completely in denial about her death, her instructions concerning her ashes were explicit. One third on Rath, where everyone will walk and play and be over her for eternity. One third to San Francisco, where her friends will take her up the mountains where they did ceremony together and set her witchy spirit free. Final third to the Skelligs, to a place on Skellig Michael precious to her.

None of this surprised me. This girl was never afraid to ask for what she wanted in life, to go after things, to take what she wanted even if it meant upsetting people. Part of me loved she was still demanding things of us. Time was once again against us – Rossa only had a couple of weeks at home before he had to return to Afghanistan to complete his mission. So we went to Rath in the middle of January.

We rented two houses, one of them Tadhg House where Ais had spent her time in December. We cooked and sat around fires. I went for a walk on Derrynane with the man I always wanted to love me but who could not be for me. I slipped on winter-wet rock, fracturing my wrist. Lorna strapped me up and immobilised me, filled me with paink-illers. At the end of it, we walked to Rath as evening fell, and the mountains dissolved into the early winter dark.

Contrary to her wishes we took her low, not high. Rossa and I were acutely conscious of the probability of her being eaten by dogs or babies if we left her on the dry white sand above the high-water mark. The tide was out. We walked to the shifting, sucking sand at the corner of the pier, beside the steps where she loved to sit, smoking, flirting, dreaming. We scooped handfuls from the box and rubbed her into the sand and said silent prayers for Mam and Dad to mind her, to take her, to keep her with them, knowing such prayers were futile. She had already absconded on her own wild travels.

Maeve had fashioned a tiny boat from scraps of driftwood, wound together with bits of twine. She put some ashes into it, lit a candle and set it on the water. The insistent tide, the gently lapping waves pushed it towards us then pulled it back out, and the little boat danced around the rocks. Only when it had been taken out around the corner, out of sight, did we turn and walk back over the beach.

I thought about Dad and what he had always said about every seventh wave being stronger and more powerful than the others, like the sea was collecting itself, only to deliver an astonishing display of its beauty, power and secrets, to announce itself, as if we had forgotten: *Here I am, this is who I am, this is what I am capable of. Heed my strength, my might, my unheralded ability to crush you mere mortals who dare to enter my domain.*

\*    \*    \*

The second dispersal of ashes was more down to earth. I had divided the consignment of ashes into thirds: one in a wooden box, one into a sturdy plastic circular container, the kind of thing you'd put soup in to take to work, the rest in the original tub. The night I divided the ashes, which I had done in my garage, with the door open, it had been wild and windy, and as I poured the ashes from the tub into the box, into the container, the wind suddenly picked up and whirled the ashes away from me, depositing them over my garden, lifting her over the bank to the canal, a place she loved to walk.

I snapped the garage door shut, too late. Some of her would remain in Kildare after all.

The day before my sister's ashes were sent back to the States, the undertaker texted to confirm details: *Your sister is on her way to the airport.* I cracked. How could they use this language, as if she were still alive? The next morning, early, I got the text: *Your sister is on board flight EI61 from Dublin*, and then three hours later, *Your sister is in flight over the Atlantic.*

*What are they doing,* I thought, *tracking the flight?* I sat at the kitchen table, called Maeve, and we both bawled at the absurdity. I thought of all the other times Ais had flown, years of coming and going across the Atlantic. It was surreal, even as the final text arrived: *Your sister has landed at SFO.*

In San Francisco Aisling's friends took her ashes (not Ais, but her ashes) up a mountain where they frequently went at weekends to do ceremony: light fires, camp out, go swimming in lakes. It was part of her not only to be close to nature, not just to be in nature, but to actually be nature – to rejoin the earth she loved so much.

The final part of her dispersal was delayed by a happy announcement – Maeve was pregnant. The season that boats can go to the Skelligs is extremely short: from April through to the end of September, and we would not be able to go that year. Art was born the following March, and while we were thrilled for them, that the baby was healthy and well, we were keenly aware of the gaping void of Mam, Dad and Ais not being there to meet their grandson and nephew. Art would grow up without the pleasure and joy of knowing them.

It was August 2018 before we managed to make it. Nothing made me happier than the tumult of the blue around me on the boat to the Skelligs – the ever-shifting floor of the sea, spotting seals basking on the rocks, and looking out for dolphins. Dolphins carry an extraordinary energy with them, possibly because they are mammals of the sea, not fish. They move between the world of land and ocean. They are a bit in both as they fly through the air then pierce the depths again. It is their speed and playfulness we respond to and obsess about as humans, I think. They remind us of our fundamental desires, to play and be free. Any time I'm in a boat and dolphins appear, people start laughing from absolute joy. That is what they do to us.

We saw no dolphins on the day we went to the Skelligs.

We landed and disembarked easily, then took the winding, twisty road around the base of the rock, past the helicopter pad. When we got to the steps, we pushed past the crowds and the guides giving talks. At the lighthouse buildings, the sea had done its best to take them back. I could imagine the winter waves and storms mounting the walls and breaching through the lighthouse left alone, with no keepers to tend it since the light had become automated. We wandered, and I touched the white stone building with my hands, imprinting it on me again. I hung over the wall and watched the ceaseless march of the waves against the jagged rocks below. Maeve pulled me away. We had ashes to scatter. Me revisiting the lighthouse was not why we were there that day.

We went back to the base of the steps and started climbing the uneven stairs. We stopped at the wailing woman stone, a place Aisling had particularly liked. We walked through to the garden, and a guide shouted and harried us, *You're not supposed to be there!* But we ducked under the wall and buried part of her in the garden.

Aisling believed in previous lives and was sure she had been a monk on the Skelligs. She believed in the theory of ley lines, and the placement of various spots along these alleged energetic lines infused them with power. I did not share her belief in those theories, but I knew the power of the islands – anyone who visits there cannot help but know it. And for those of us lucky enough to have any kind of connection to them, we do not have to be convinced of it – it's very simple. The islands radiate power, force, mysticism. The *Star Wars* fans in their cloaks and lightsabre know it. The workers on the island know it. The guides know it. The boatmen who spend their days fishing as they wait for the tourists to return to the landing know it.

We climbed to the beehive huts, and Maeve moved through them until she came to stop in one I knew would have been the abbot's cell, the biggest and best. *This is where she lived,* Maeve told me, almost apologetically. At this stage, the day was so fantastic, I said nothing. If Maeve and Aisling believed she had been out here before, in a previous life, who was I to argue? Not then, not that day, when this was something so precious to Maeve. She said prayers and lit candles. I absorbed the power of the ancient stones.

I remain transfixed by the miracles of engineering on the Skelligs and always will be. That men had the courage and the sheer gall to create homes where none should ever have been created. That lighthouse families endured years here on posts – families with servants and teachers, a community as solid and vibrant as the monks centuries before, two tribes at either lighthouse, scratching vegetables from meagre scrap-plots of grass nurtured by seaweed, tending cows that fell over cliffs to their doom below, all their water falling to them from the sky and held in hollowed-out tanks of stone as ancient as the steps to the monastery.

A miracle of survival, that's what the Skelligs mean to me. Life lived in the face of cruel, weather-worn hardship and privations.

There were still ashes left after the wailing woman, the garden and the beehive hut. I took the tub from Maeve and went into the abbot's garden, remembering a place I had loved on previous trips. At the edge of this tiny stone

triangle, the side of the Skellig falls steeply away. I stood
on the wall and emptied the last of her there. Over the
rocks, on the wind, she fell and settled on the sea. But I
knew this was the greatest fallacy of all, the notion that
bringing her ashes here and scattering them would imply
some sort of permanence on this rock in the Atlantic. Her
bones might rest among the stones and thin grasses
temporarily, but I knew the mighty winds that howl around
this holy rock. How mercilessly she would be moved on
again – but what was Ais if not a girl destined to keep
travelling? So I shook her out, over the rocks, over the
grasses, down to the inlet below where the seals liked to
climb on the rocks and moan. I let her be caught, if only
momentarily. I knew every part of what we had scattered
would end up in the sea, in the currents, in the waves.

Back on the boat, we turned and watched, mesmerised
as the Skelligs receded, getting smaller and smaller, until
they disappeared – but ever in our hearts, always in
our souls.

*Ais, fire-girl*

*She is the sea,*
*She is the wave,*
*She is the surf,*
*She is the cliff, the crag, the rock.*
*She is the sun who shines,*
*She is the woman who wails,*
*She is Skellig.*

*She is battle-hardened,*
*She is fire.*
*She knows the secrets of the earth,*
*She knows the cycles of the moon,*
*She sees where the sunset settles.*

# 19. DOCTORATE: A CARTOGRAPHY OF GRIEF

*Futile – the winds –*
*To a heart in port –*
*Done with the compass –*
*Done with the chart! – Emily Dickinson*

EVERYONE HAS THEIR PARTICULAR fascinations, and mine is maps. I grew up with stacks of *National Geographics* in the 1970s that often had beautiful, large maps within their glossy pages. I could pull these out whenever I wanted, pore over historical maps of the Mediterranean, Greece, Mesopotamia, double-sided portraits of wonder and magic, with a map on one side and a legend, an explainer, on the other. I could spend hours lost in the pages of a supersized *Britannica* atlas that depicted the continents in painstaking detail, both geographic and geopolitical.

At school, bored, I would spend hours staring at the huge maps covering the classroom walls, heathen Russia drawn in startling red. The best books of my childhood, Ursula Le Guin's *Earthsea* quartet, began and ended with maps. I craved books that would contain this magic at their beginning, with strange lands and seas – like our world but utterly removed from it.

As army brats, maps were all around us. Dad kept well-thumbed route books in the car, highlighting in yellow paths the journeys undertaken. On one wall of the caravan was a yellow, fading Ordnance Survey map of Wexford, showing every beach, marsh and plain around us in fascinating detail. When it came to secondary geography and learning how to map-read, I knew it already, how to do this, how to recognise all the symbols, how to turn the map in the direction you intend on going.

Dad was quite the navigator, and he taught us this skill at an early age. It was something he dropped casually into walks and drives. I remember him taking me outside our first caravan in Wexford, after the sun had set behind the hayfield, and pointing the constellations out to me. Ursa Major and Minor, Cygnus, Cassiopeia, Lyra, Pegasus – he knew them all and, at a very young age, he taught me how the sky above our heads was another world, but a world that had been mapped. He pointed out Polaris and said, *If you can find that star, you'll never be lost.*

In the car, he would toss a map to us in the back and tell us we were going from New Ross to Kilkenny, and we had to tell him how to get there. He taught us how to establish ourselves with directions, how the sun goes daily from east to south to west. You know north by how the moss grows.

On walks through the Wicklow Mountains and the glens, he taught us how to look for drier ground and avoid the bog, how to walk through bog if you had to. As kids we did a fair amount of orienteering, and here, finally, was a sport I could get behind, that I could enjoy, where a geek like me had a chance against the sporty kids. Here was a race I might not come last in, despite my astonishing lack of athletic ability, unlike my siblings.

At the start of every race, a map was placed in my hands, and to finish the course in good time, I had to navigate. I loved it, loved the speed at which we had to assess the map, figure out the course, then use our spatial abilities to overlay the map on the terrain around us. Like my father taught me, stay calm and find the way. Panic ruins everything.

\* \* \*

The time after Aisling is bad, very bad. I face a January alone, broken-hearted, with a broken wrist. I can't drive or do much around the house. I struggle to get dressed every day and do the simplest things, like cooking and laundry. Slicing vegetables and preparing dinners becomes an ordeal.

The funeral is over. The children, stunned, are back at school. I spend my days wandering through the house, half-heartedly picking things up. I am in a fog, a daze of misery and heartbreak.

Yet always in the midst of grief, some strange thing is silently, seriously handed to us, draped over our shoulders, placed on our head like a well-fitting hat, strapped across our chests, a sword we do not even know we have or need. The strange thing never fails you. The strange thing keeps us climbing through the treacherous, slippery trenches of grief, gifts us an unknown tenacity that keeps us from surrendering, a spark that drives us forward, armour that we strap on to keep us alive in the battle.

As surely as our dead have left our world, to the world we cannot follow them to, we too have left our world and gone to another, inhabited by millions like us, the bereaved, the bereft, the lost and the broken, crawling on our hands and knees through the days.

Sometimes you look back and see the shiny, happy, normal world you once lived in, the unknowing you used to inhabit, before death and grief rewired your brain and rejigged your personality. That world is closed to you now. Instead, you are in a new land, nebulous and vague with chronic mists and murky swamps and sucking seas. There are sharp, fierce mountain ranges of loss to navigate around. Eventually you realise these peaks of devastation are unclimbable – you will spend the rest of your life going round them, endlessly circling the foothills, their lonely, forbidding heights looming over you forever.

We know that to survive, to live, we have to be aware of the craters that are everywhere now, in this land of grief. We are citizens here and must make our peace with it.

Death has made us so, handed us our passports and ushered us onto the ferry when our loved ones died.

After Dad died, I came across Elizabeth Kubler-Ross's theory, widely peddled, about grieving. I looked in disbelief at these stages she mentioned – denial, bargaining, acceptance – and wondered what was wrong with me, that my grief was not following that trajectory. My grief was not linear. It was wild, chaotic and unpredictable. I could not say from one minute to the next how I would feel. Anger, rage, deep sadness, heartbreak, inertia and an inability to do anything – these were my markers, the contours of my grief. Sleeplessness, exhaustion, anxiety entered my life with a resounding bang. Honestly, the anxiety has never truly left.

On digging deeper into Kubler-Ross's seven stages, I discovered that she had written these stages about people who were dying, not people who were grieving. Her stages had been packaged up and neatly presented – that is to say, misappropriated – over many years by the hospice movement and various organisations, in a misguided effort to help people. There seemed to exist no handbook, no cartography of grief. I thought of the hundreds of books written for life – about parenting and babies and childhood development. Where were the books for death?

Where was the manual, the guidebook, the travel guide to steer me through this place I found myself in, half my family gone and only three of us left? My children had lost their grandparents and their aunt who they adored. Their absence was a crater, a void. How was I supposed to tell them how to make sense of this loss when I could not untangle it myself?

* * *

When we cleared the house in College Park after Mam died, Rossa came down from the attic with a pile of the old *National Geographics*. I kept as many as I could, and found within their magic, faded pages, plenty of maps. I framed some, and one, 'The Heavens' – a beauty of navy and yellow detailing and hundreds of stars, all the constellations – still hangs above my desk. It shows the maps and routes of the planets from the years 1970–73, my first years. I can look at this map whenever I want and know this is what the skies looked like when I was born.

Maeve and I call each other frequently, trying and failing to understand what happened. She is gone, and we are left behind. The crowds of people who surrounded us at the funeral, the wake, the cremation are now gone and silent. We are left to struggle through our grief alone.

Now, with Ais gone, the only thing that makes sense to me is being outside. I can only breathe outside the house and not inside it. I take the boisterous, joyful puppy that arrived last October and finally start paying her some attention. Juno arrived at the worst time, the most chaotic, deranged time in my life, and now it is time to make sense of everything again.

Most days it feels like I can't get out of bed, but I do.
My supreme achievement at that time is getting the kids
up and out the door every morning. They don't want to go
to school, and I make them go. I come home from the
school run, put Juno on the lead, wrap myself up and head
out. Some days we walk for hours and for miles, through
January rain and wind, underneath skeletal trees and over
brown grass.

There are days I want to follow Ais, into the maws of
death, use her passing as a slipstream I can share. Living,
existing just feels impossible. But I can't. There are four
depending on me, tenacious, delicate threads of steel,
hooking me into the future. Five now, with this tiny dog.
Juno pulls me on the lead, down the canal, across the
Curragh, pulls me into the future, pulls me back into life.

* * *

Once we get used to the treacherous landscape, we develop
an ability to walk a tightrope, balancing the pull between
toppling into the voids and holes and teetering at the edges.
Often life becomes a lot simpler and softer. We possess a
clarity of vision, a laser-focus of knowledge on what matters
and what doesn't. Survival is doing this to us, remaking us
the way becoming a parent did.

We come back from the brink changed. A little deeper, a
little darker, a tad more appreciative of everyday things –
beating hearts, lungs that work, functional limbs. We are

marked by an unholy pain and are more considered in everything we do. We are slower to be spontaneous because, coursing with anxiety, we are used to being on high alert. We are slower to judge or criticise because pain has schooled us to be kind, to realise most of the things people worry about are not worth it.

We become really good at some things. Resting. Doing exactly what we want, saying no to people. Cutting toxic people from our lives. Life has to be simpler and easier, because we're just not able for most of it. Because in this world, over the roads and motorways, are giant, huge signs on gantries everywhere, flashing out the words in capital letters: *LIFE'S TOO SHORT FOR THIS SHIT.* We read those words and layer them over every aspect of our lives, we suck and absorb them deep into our bones and radiate them back out with everything we do.

We go deeper on a lot of things. And everywhere, we can see the holes.

We think about the things we have forgotten and want to do again before we leave this life. We go back to sailing, or take up hockey, go to the rugby games. We buy a keyboard and continue the piano lessons we abandoned as a child, yet the scales and arpeggios are still there, locked into our hands. We pick up a paintbrush, put some colour on a page and remember how much we love painting. We look up old, forgotten, important friends from college and organise a reunion. We need a lot of laughter now.

We move through this difficult, treacherous landscape with precision, intent, and laser-like focus. We tell our children and all the important people in our lives how much we love them, constantly. Our children bear it because they can see it in our eyes, love is all that matters to us now. How this land and living here is teaching us there is only one word that truly matters, and it's love.

# 20. COMPASS POINTS

*Let sea-discoverers to new worlds have gone,*
*Let maps to others, worlds on worlds have shown,*
*Let us possess one world, each hath one, and is one.*
  *– John Donne*

BOOKS ARE THE FIRST thing people notice when they come into my house, probably because I have an excess of them, scattered through the rooms in piles, my already read and to-be-read. There are shelves everywhere, with books piled in front of them. My books are my treasure. As Cicero said, *A room without books is like a body without a soul* and this is a maxim I adhere to a little too strongly. I have no trust or faith in people without books in their houses. At night I'm alone, but not lonely, accompanied by the millions of words I have read, words that have ignited my imagination and kept it burning, through all my troubles.

When I read 'The Good-Morrow' by John Donne after Mam dying, there were three lines in it that I returned to over and over again, trying to make sense of: Every line stopped everything in me with a stunning recognition. Sea-discoverers, that's what my parents were. Maps, that's what

I was searching for. Worlds on worlds – that's what life feels like to me now. That I'm living in the world that everyone else is, but at the same time in a completely different one, one that only the other bereaved understand and get.

The line about possessing worlds, the idea we are all savagely, ultimately alone and we are going through this world solo, how deeply can we ever understand and be understood by another person – those three brief lines encapsulated everything I was going through. The clarity and modernity of Donne's writing blew me away – we talk about Hemingway's hard prose, I thought, why aren't we worshipping the poetry of Donne, writing in the sixteenth century? Donne was famous for his ambiguity, for his ability to cloak the universal in the personal, like the line about lovers finding a new world in each other, 'my face in thine eye, thine in mine appears' but each firmly staying in their own.

I wanted, needed books like that, books with perfect worlds it would not be easy to step away from once I was pulled in and Mantel does that so perfectly with her depiction of the Tudor courts and castles, the details of Cromwell's home, his wife and daughters who die, a man who lives on with his grief and does not let it stop him.

I reread Ursula Le Guin's *Earthsea* quartet, her ideas about shadow selves, our fears, running away, then turning and hunting down what terrifies us made perfect sense to me. Her Earthsea is another world, perfectly delineated in a map I studied again and again. Years later I read how and when she had created those maps: in her kitchen, on a roll of butcher's paper, surrounded by children. She wrote those worlds to escape to, and in doing so handed down a perfect world to generations of readers.

So much of what Le Guin is writing about, the power of words and language, her idea that magic can only occur when the true word of a thing is named or applied, was stunning to me. The idea that under language as we know it is another, deeper language, that words have weight and meaning and power beyond what is imaginable.

Duality in books was a big thing for me, this idea of there being a shifting layer under what was visible, because this is what life has always been for me, a sense of other worlds pushing in and intruding on this one. The absent / present that underpins Camus' *L'Étranger* made complete sense.

Existentialism, the idea of one life to be lived as intensely as we can, the theories of the absurd and the defiance necessary in the face of it, was easy to understand. I had lived with the idea of absent / present all my life. The ideas were immense and towering but it was his style, how he wrote, getting to the essence of things quickly and cleanly, in a direct, pared-back stripping of language I adored.

At the end of first year I went to the south of France to au pair, bought all of Camus' books and read him in French, on beaches, in bars, on trains and terraces, in silent rooms at night, shutters barred against mosquitoes. I came across a verb, *bouleverser*, it means to turn something on its head. And Camus did that for me, in one perfect little book, which I was lucky enough to read and examine at the perfect age of eighteen. Life was not to be endured, life was to be lived. *The Outsider* centres on the sun, the sea, the primal, all-encompassing necessity of sex and this pagan trinity sang to me, head, body and soul.

Camus gave me searing hot sunlight and possibility and courage rather than fear, sown into me from birth by the Church. He allowed me to shrug off my Catholicism like the hairshirt it was and embrace philosophy as my new religion. I sucked up his words like a bee takes in nectar, on packed and crowded beaches, on the terrace under the shade of fig trees, I read beside the swimming pool while the child I looked after slept, I read on boats and islands and beaches on my days off, stopped, looked up at the Mediterranean shining in front of me and knew across that shining expanse of water, that sunlight, lay Algeria, his world, where he had lived and loved, played football, smoked, thought, plotted, wrote, worked.

More than anything, books conspired to weave themselves together into pathways and bridges over the gaping holes and sucking swamps, magic carpets of paper and text that allowed me not to sink in. And in the very worst of times, when grief flung me back into the holes, with their treacherous, slippery sides, books were a ladder, physical and mental. I take the piles and classics in case of emergencies and put them to use, stacking them up three at a time, and build a ladder, a stepstairs of books to lead me from the holes. They remake a world of solidity beneath my feet when there's nothing but air and gaping voids, in inspiring and fantastic patterns, a tapestry of wisdom, a constellation of stars by which to navigate.

My books make me and keep me happy, and despite my many failings as a parent, I'm comforted by the knowledge I have given my four a legacy more valuable than any fortune. They have the boundless, limitless, infinite world of the imagination. They know to escape requires nothing more difficult than holding slices of pages in your hand.

I saw most clearly how alone I was at Aisling's funeral. Ian was with Maeve at every moment, through every difficult day, and every time I saw Rossa and Lorna together, she had her hand on his shoulder, his arm, his on her back – they were visibly, concretely supporting each other.

I wanted someone there so desperately, so badly, and maybe that deep longing is what drove men repeatedly away. I was a cracked and broken vase, taped together and lightly glued – it took nothing to undo me. Rejection, relationships not working out were sometimes as devastating to me as the deaths I had been through; it took very little to fling me back into the crevasses of grief.

Despite the repeated heartbreak, the pain of things not working out that ran so deep, I had to carry on. It did not matter to the children that a man they had not met had broken up with me. There were school runs to be done, meals to be cooked, work to be finished and the loneliness when there was no one to talk to in the evenings was brutal and terrifying.

I spent years after my mother died trying to write a book explaining grief, looking for the meaning of it. How to cope with death, how to survive it when you are left behind, laid waste and flattened by it. I'm writing every day once my wrist is out of its cast. I'm trying to write and failing, a book about loss and grief and death and family but it spins wildly out of control as I keep writing it, through all the deaths and all the years; it's patchy and uneven and like my head and heart, all over the place.

Yet writing it all down keeps me sane. Writing it is everything I want to say to the partner, to the person I want to be there and is not, and sometimes I feel that is the cruellest loss of all, the absence of someone to love and be loved by, that I have to go through all of this on my own is impossibly hard, my Sisyphean task.

\* \* \*

There's a responsibility that comes with being a single parent that others find hard to understand. You're a lone soldier defending the walls; there are four of them to look after, on your own, and you not only have to keep yours safe, but fed and watered, looked after and loved. This work takes everything from you, leaving little energy for the other work that must be done, the work that earns money and pays bills.

You're one worker on a perpetual double shift. There's a constant pressure nobody outside of your situation can understand, because all of your friends are married and have two incomes, two sets of arms for the work, two heads to solve problems.

*How do you do it?* people sometimes ask me, or more often: *I don't know how you do it.*

*I try my best,* I might say if they stopped to listen. *I do it because they are wonderful kids and they make it easy for me.* These four beautiful kids were as hammered by all the death as I was, suffered through the years of me being, like my mother, both absent and present. Meals were cooked, houses sorted, laundry done, but I was mostly lost in a haze of misery and grief. They have to cope with their parents being split up, and it injures them, all the time.

My consolation prize: *Imagine how bad it would be for you if we still lived together.* It's a poor one, and it fails to comfort. Just as I look to other couples, jealous of their combined strength and constantly, acutely aware of my own lack of it, they too look to families who are together. In friends' houses they see dads coming home from work and mothers not wrung out by exhaustion.

An unheralded benefit to running and being part of a single-parent family is how close we are, but more so, how

191

close they are. I see them on the rare occasions now when they are together, when the older two are home from college, and how they communicate. Silently, with shrugs and looks and raised eyebrows. How they laugh together, how they get and support each other. They possess, in spades, Beckett's strange thing that never fails: a golden glitter, a determination to keep trying that makes my heart sing.

The five of us are like a compass, I think. They are the directions, and I am the arrow. I place Doireann in the north – she likes things to be cold, inaccessible, frozen. Dark skies and rainy days are her preferred weather, and I tell her how she should emigrate to Canada, Sweden, Denmark, to live in a land where they know how to be quiet. Oisín, my eldest and my artist, is in the east, currently there in Dublin, degree in art finished.

Rebecca, our youngest, our knotted cord, is in the south, with searing heat and light and sun. She will travel, and already speaks of doing architecture, which I can see. She is twelve, obsessed with Lego, still happy, still innocent, still a child. Like the anchor of the family, she plumbs the depths and finds a home for the anchor and steadies the boat, pointing us towards the sun. When Aoibh was a tiny eight years old, she stalked the promenade in Salthill in Galway with ferocity and intent and announced she would return to live there. She kept her word, so she is my west, living in the city and studying in the university, where she haunts the library and lays down all the medical words she will need for her career.

I am the arrow, swinging between them and pointing the way, pulled always to the south-west, to Kerry, where I long to be. My parents taught me how to swim through anything, in any weather or sea. One stroke, one breath building on another, one more kick and you will reach the shore. By diving to the depths and spending time in deep green cathedrals of wonder, I found and understood that there were other worlds. That to be in them, all we must do is listen and be quiet and still and the words will come, this strange thing that never fails us will be gifted to us here in these aquatic kingdoms.

My experiences of grief are the contours, the grids, the waymarkings and directions of the map I now carry within me and can share with anyone. Grief is not a feeling to be stopped, it's a route to follow and discover. Just like long hikes teach us about our strengths and dimensions, how far we can go, what we can cope with, so too does grief. It's blowing the horn on the underpasses of motorways and ancient bridges and shouting *Up the Muls!* We've got this. We can do this.

The children are my compass points, my four directions, four walls that I am constantly building and strengthening until they stand on their own. I'm not the kind of parent to stand in their way if they want to leave; my aim, someday in the future, is to be rattling around a tiny caravan in Kerry for half the year and spending the winter like my mother, in an empty house, surrounded by candles, music and books. They are my four directions and I want them to do what my family has always done, to leave where they are and land somewhere else, making new lives for themselves.

This summer Aoibh flew to Boston with a gang of her friends to work for the summer. I will miss her, her sisters will miss her more keenly, and of all of us, Aoibh will miss Juno the most. I've been telling her about Aisling's years on Nantucket, how she can get a ferry to the island from Boston and Maeve will tell her all the places to visit, the bars Aisling drank in, the restaurants she worked in, the beaches she loved. Eight years after her aunt died, Aoibh will get to walk the streets she cycled on, pass the gardens she worked in; she will see Aisling's skies, her beaches, her sun, her sea.

Just as Aisling did, she lights up an entire room with her smile, her laugh and her fun. Just like Aisling, she is surrounded by great friends and will travel far, the farthest of all of us, so far west the sea runs out and turns to sand.

\* \* \*

For a long time, writing this book, I focused on the power of words, thinking about the hundreds of times I had heard the phrase *There are no words*. I thought that was the answer: *I'm a writer, words are who I am and what I do*. I would find the words and give them back to all the people who stood in front of me and told me they did not exist.

This approach, this way to writing the book, led me in the wrong direction for many years. I went so off-course that I was far beyond the borders I was trying to chart. I felt often, as I wrote, frustratingly close to knocking through the door that the real essence of the book lay behind, but I could not find it. I knew what I wanted to do, what I was trying to do, which was to use our awful, terrible experience and somehow package it up, explain it and present it to others as a guide on how to get through the worst time in their lives.

I wanted to explain death to people, to those who did not understand it. Part of it, I realised, was buried in existentialism, the idea of one life to be lived as intensely as we can, its theories of the absurd and the defiance necessary in the face of it. I wanted to take our greatest fear, our worst terror, and wrap it up in language so fine and beautiful that the reader would be carried along and be comforted by how I fell – how far, how deeply, how completely lost I was – and how I rose again with all the things that sustained me: books, music, art, friends, love, swimming, the sea.

People, when they lose someone, look for a timeline, a reason, an answer. Here's the answer: there is none. There is no time where this will get better. It eases and fades, gradually, over the years. The bag of stones you are carrying gets more comfortable. The shape of your shoulders and back changes, moulding to it.

But then come days you could never expect. Days when you realise, despite it being years since your loss, imagining you are over it is only that: imagining. There will be days when the plaster is cruelly ripped off, revealing the festering wound underneath. When this happens, when you are flung back into that other, battered landscape, with mountains you cannot climb and impassable bogs, deserts and rivers that cannot be crossed, you realise how pitiful and minimal your progress has been, how damn superficial it is and you wonder, are you cursed? Are you marked forever? Doomed to be unhappy and sad and lonely for ever? Will you ever be truly happy again?

The pain runs so deep. It runs deep because it is part of who you are now, and you will never shake it off. This pain has marked you, this pain has made you who you are now. Anyone scored by grief, by tragic loss, is marked and somehow set apart from others. It's everywhere in us, how we move our eyes, how we speak, how we listen to others. The pain of grief can cause you to become the quiet one in the room, the one who is overlooked and not accounted for. Funny people crack fewer jokes. Garrulous talkers listen more often. It's not that we have less to say, it's just that we have got used to having conversations with ourselves, or with our dead. We have long, drawn-out chats with them in our heads – and they don't talk back.

We know and accept people don't want to listen to our stories of heartbreak, loss and loneliness. Others don't want the knowledge that we have days where we are utterly unhinged. We are on our own in this. Their eyes glaze over, their focus shifts, they want to be rid of us. No one wants

to hang out with someone stinking of grief. It's all so difficult, so messy, so raw. It's like talking to someone who is
bleeding out in front of you, heedless that blood is pouring
from their arteries, unstoppable. We should be over it by
now, it's been months. We should be moving on with things.

But we are moving on with things. We answer the damn
alarm every single morning when we want to throw it at
the wall. We shower, when honestly, not washing ever again
seems like a pretty feasible option. We get our kids up and
out the door to school. We work all day, then we cook and
feed and clear up and put children to bed. We might step
out of the river of life for a few hours or days, but we are
pulled back in by life, by work, by children. Much as we
want to, we cannot sit on this riverbank and passively watch
the world; we are of the world and must return to it.

You open the laptop and type, slowly, it takes years, a
decade, forever, all about your loss and death and grief
and all the knowledge you now possess but struggle so
hard to put a boundary around. All your intimate knowledge of the craters, the voids, the crevasses, even though
it nearly kills you again in the writing of it, bringing you
back to those days and nights when you lost them, the
seconds they left and slipped away as visceral now, years
later, as they ever were.

You come at it sideways, like a diligent crab, stacking
thousands and thousands of words up that will be lost in
the end, but you had to write them to find the others. You
know they are inside you, and it is your job, your work to

get them out. Even if writing sometimes nearly stops you breathing.

There are the words to be found if only we have the strength to look for them.

I found the words in deep, wild, secret places where no words are spoken. I heard them in the silence of mountains and the roar and pounding and the quiet breathing of the sea. I often found the words where no sound is possible, in the green depths of underwater. I saw the words, read them in the light and colour of great paintings hung on gallery walls. I looked at photos of my dead parents and sister and saw the words in their eyes, shining at me. *Live*, they tell me, *live hard and happily, swim deep and long, swim hard.*

*Love, Mir. Love with every damn fibre of your being.*

People think, and insist on the most ridiculous of fallacies in the face of the incontrovertible truth that exists in any collection of books: *There are no words.* Nay, sir, they exist in their happy millions.

*       *       *

Last summer in Kerry was our last in the caravan, after thirty years it is time for a new one. I spent hours staring at curtains she made, at cushions she sewed, at cups and plates in use for five decades. My sense of a second home is shattered now, forever gone. There is no permanent refuge for me, no keys to handle and dream of opening doors with again. I took most of the books, books that had sat there through thirty winters and summers and will now join mine on my shelves. I asked for a share of the shell collection – I will carefully dispense it into a glass jar and put it somewhere in the kitchen, on the table probably, always in my eyeline and there with every cup of coffee, every meal. I leave my kayak and its red paddle there so I can always get out on the sea.

My time there will be measured now, in a way it never has been. I will spend every day I have there on the beach. I will swim when the days are silver and when they are blue and golden, when they are perfect. It will never be too cold for a swim and every swim will be worth it, a sacred talisman of salt and minerals and wave to imprint and tattoo on my soul to carry me through the winter. I will keep hoping for a change in fortune that will allow me to get my own place there, but really, my place there is already assured. All I have to do is turn up at Rath, shed my clothes, don my togs and enter the water, dipping my shoulders in decision and resolution. I leave the sandy floor and strike out through the green, past the pier, beyond it, to where I know they are. I wave to Ais, preening on the pier, smoking, ready to flirt.

The strokes lengthen and the trills of cold shoot up and down, radiating over my skin to kickstart my heart, warm up my soul. I stop and tread water, look at the mountains of Beara in front of me, turn and see the mountains of Caherdaniel behind me. Sentinels, soldiers. I dip my head and dive, touching the white sandy floor and scooping some in my hand, doing what I have done all my life, I look up to the circle of light above my head, and surge towards it.

I hear them under the water, in the sea, whispering to me, all the things I need to hear: *Another year down Mir, well done.* And I've got a map of the way through that nobody else possesses. Its grid references are love, strength, graft and determination.

Life will never be the same again. The only certainty is the worlds to be uncovered are endless. *And someday, Mir,* they whisper from the deep, *you'll meet him.* Not on dating apps or in bars. You'll find him on a beach, on a pier, coming out of the water, at a wake, exiting a graveyard. He'll be unhurriedly unfolding his map of his world and might call you over to have a look. You will know him by his kind eyes, his sure touch, his capable hands, hands that can hold a map steady, hands that know the power of a book in them.

I leave the sea reluctantly, my extremities tingling, and shake the magic water from me, trailing my hands through the water, kicking water into waves like I did when I was a kid, because I can. I feel the sand and stones beneath my feet, choose one and walk out, knowing, after a swim like that, how strong I am. How much I can do, on my own: the things I can and will achieve alone. I am strong enough for water, for sea like this, I am strong enough for anything.

# 21. THE ROAD TO RATH

*Querencia (n) (Spanish) – a place from where one's strength is drawn, where one feels most at home; the place where you are your most authentic self*

MY FIRST MEMORY OF the sea is from this beach. A tiny arc of grey sand, bisected by a torrid mountain stream that freezes the water but also lends it clarity – bookended by ancient black rocks, it gives us everything. A pier to jump from when the tide is high. A stony surface to endlessly beachcomb on when the tide is low, adding to our lifetime collection of sea-urchin tiles, periwinkles, seastones, seaglass. A placid backstretch of sand to leave boats and kayaks on safely. I never leave this beach without something in my pocket, and I do my best never to leave it without a swim.

The names in this place are like a necklace of precious stones, glittering and priceless. These words, rooted in Irish, are an incantation to me – they stir something in my soul. No name is so loaded for me, so complete, as Rath. A tiny land, a fiefdom within a kingdom, a tiny road that leads to a tiny beach with a tiny pier. The road to Rath is just another boreen, a narrow road where cars have difficulty passing each other. It goes nowhere, petering out halfway up a small mountain. But for us it is the road we are dreaming of through the long dark winters when we are far from here, it is the road we turn into, the road that marks the end of our long drive south, bounded by low stone walls and thick with fuchsia and montbretia. The children's excitement rises to feverish levels, and before I have gone through the barrier to the campsite they are gone, tumbling out of the car, running down the hill, looking for their friends. It's Easter, or May or July, and my first time here since last summer. My eyes drink in the sea before me and turn into the caravan. We are here, where we have longed to be all year. And as soon as we can, we'll be on Rath again.

It's less than ten minutes' walk from the campsite to the beach, and it's a walk of unsurpassed beauty. To the north, the mountains of Beenarourke, Farriniaragh, Coomnahorna, Cahernageeha and Coad form a natural boundary, along which the Ring of Kerry route runs. Derrynane lies the other side of Lamb's Head, to the west, the east is the Beara peninsula and the Kenmare river, and to the south is Dursey Island, the Cow, the Bull and the Calf and open water. And in the quiet centre of all this astounding beauty, holding its own, is the beach and pier at Rath. The road is a sliver of heaven, a narrow grey canyon through a vast expanse of nature gone wild, rough fields hewn painstakingly from the mountain, created with back-breaking toil, seaweed and hope.

These unpredictable patches are bounded by stone walls and hedges of fuchsia, through which all kinds of wildflowers thrive and bloom. The road is a riot of colour, scent and gentle sound in summer: the red of the fat fuchsia bells, the fiery orange of montbretia with its heads dipping low, bent under the weight of its prodigious success, the yellow honeysuckle and the infinitely pale pinks of the Kerry lilies. The air is sweeter than any air should ever be, laden with the scent of thousands upon thousands of wildflowers, thriving in the wet, boggy ground.

There is an abundance of quiet sound, the birdsong of thrushes, larks and robins, the low call of the cuckoo, the thrum of worker bees, the swish of the summer wind through the reeds and rushes. The verge is sometimes punctuated by the strong sharp blue of the sheep's-bit, a tiny wonder of a weed that is particular to this corner of Ireland, a wildflower that looks like a dandelion dipped in cobalt, and infinitely precious to me; it's my favourite flower, a blue weed, and I only find it here.

Walking down this road is my praying. It is a sacred space to me – it is a thousand other days and walks woven together into a tapestry of happiness that nothing could ever unravel because it is tattooed onto my soul. If the sun is shining, the sky above is an impossible vault of blue, throwing the hulking shadow of Eagle Hill at the end of the road into sharp relief. It's a congregation and confluence of colour and natural beauty I cannot imagine being bettered.

We walk this road as often as we can, coming to the beach most days. The kids pick the fat red fuchsia bells and suck the nectar out. The road gently twists, we come to the cross, where the road forks and rises to the top of Eagle Hill. We turn left, downhill again, lured by the blue sea – always on our left.

We pass the wall, the one that Rossa broke through with Mam. Once, when you came this way, you pushed through a fuchsia bush, hopped over a boggy patch of mud and walked a few steps up a short hill to be presented with the most stunning view: an arc of white beach dissolving into the blue sea, the black pier punctuating the water beyond the rocks. Now, there is only a wall nobody can climb. I think of the Selfish Giant every time I pass it.

At the end of the road is Peggy's Field, a rocky scrap of land above Rath beach. It is a hilly field carved out of the end of a mountain at the end of a tiny boreen, and that is it. No facilities, nothing bar a single tap. It is rough, challenging, but for four decades the same families spent summers here. Why do they do this, especially when there is a spanking new, state-of-the-art campsite only a few hundred metres away? Because of the sea.

In Peggy's Field there is no division between caravan and tent and beach, they are all one. You sleep at night lulled to sleep by the waves, all day you breathe in great intoxicating lungfuls of sea air. It's paradise to anyone who loves the sea. Stand here and stare at the crashing waves, be mesmerised by the constant roll and ebb, a sight that always hypnotises me.

This is the road my parents walked every time they went for a swim. They often came early, in the morning, before breakfast, carrying the bare essentials of togs and towels. They walked, and chatted and waved or nodded to everyone they met, stopped outside houses to talk to friends, and were entranced every day by the stunning beauty of the place. They saw the changes of the seasons, coming in April when the fuchsia hedges were still bereft of their red jewels, when the montbretia were only tiny green shoots peeking through the claggy earth.

They walked here in high summer, when the road was busy with walkers and cyclists, intent with cars flying up and down, and they enjoyed it in autumn when everyone had left and it was serene again, the colours on the mountains turned. They loved swimming and they loved swimming here.

I wonder a lot why we love Rath so much – is it because we are happy here or because our parents were so happy here? We know this place, it is in our bones, our hearts, our souls. Is it the light? The memories? The associations with childhood? Is there anything more magical than building sandcastles with your children on the same beach your parents did with you?

Or is it the sea? Because here, it's never the same. It is different after rain, after a few days of sun. It is another world of high tides and extravagant ebbs during a full moon, and after a storm it's like a beast. I think the sea is where all our souls really long to be. Spread your hands and look between your fingers. The traces of our amphibious ancestors are still there, waiting to be used, waiting to pull water through them and keep you afloat. We go to the beach every day we can, even when it is overcast and cloudy and threatening rain, because this is Ireland and no one ever knows when the clouds will separate and the sun will come through, blazing and gloriously hot.

But we are not really here today and now. We are here, in an ever expanding, never ending loop of time, a warp, a weft, today is not really today. This day is every day you have spent here, for some since they were babies. Many adults sitting on the beach, rising from their rugs or battered beach chairs to greet old friends, have spent forty, fifty, sixty summers here. And each day is an enrichment, a continuation of all the days we have spent here before. We sit on the beach and remember other days, days like this when the skies were overcast but we were in shorts and the kids ran around in togs. I remember being pregnant and walking in the water, the tide at its lowest ebb, the pier exposed, a dark monolith encrusted with barnacles, dotted with anemones, and someone called from the rockpool at the far side of the beach, *starfish*!

And I walked carrying my children, one in my arms, one inside me. Someone had uncovered a battalion of starfish, and I placed one in Oisín's chubby hand and his eyes ignited in wonder. Sea-discoverer. I remember coming here for the first time with Oisín, six weeks old, and I walked down the road in glorious sunshine in between the interminable and never-ending feeds, and he was tiny in his sling and his scrap of a sunhat, and I dipped his feet in the water, a pagan baptism, kissing the silky whorl of hair on his head and whispering the magic words to him about the sea, initiating him into my tribe of swimmers.

I remember days spent with Mam, lying on the beach in the days before children, and reading books, their spines cracking with sand, enjoying endless swims. Bringing the boat out with Dad, the joy of hours of fishing, helping to gut the fish on the pier, slicing off the mackerel heads and tails, tossing them to the seagulls that crowded the water, waiting for their bounty.

It was easy, companionable, delightful, and I miss them painfully and viscerally, glad of my sunglasses that hide the tears that threaten to spill when I see other families, three generations like ours used to be, gathered in gossipy circles, beach chairs turned to the sun, throwing beers to each other from the cool box.

Every time Mam walked down the road to Rath, every time she got changed on the pier and descended the steps and got into the water, she taught me how to be in the face of grief. With every step, with every swim, with every toss of her head in the water and her slow, gentle breaststroke, she remade the map that had been ripped from our hands when Dad died. Here, she was saying, this is all you need. The sea will always hold you. It will keep you afloat in your worst times.

Being on Rath without them is so hard, but it's also the place they come closest to us. They return and reappear, in memory and the heart, when I plunge in the water and take the swim, they are here whispering to me from the green water, telling me to swim out further, to the deep, where I will leave other people's noise and chatter and hear what they are saying to me again.

I cut through the years of loss as I move through the sea and I am out, past the pier, where the dark rocks and kelp interrupt the white sand and the searing green and here they are, swimming round me again, Mam, her blonde hair, her gold flashing in the sun, always tossing her head, and Dad, his dark head slick with the deep, he went down to rise and that is all he wants to do, dive, return, dive again, in every swim he is trying to recover the secrets of the sea and explain them.

They are telling me things, things I cannot understand. That I am doing my best and they are proud of me. That they cannot believe how things are progressing, that all the years of hardship and graft were worth it; we have beaten the odds, we are winning. That the older two are doing so well. That Doireann and Rebecca are beautiful and precious, and I need to teach them the sea. To keep writing and to tell all the stories burning within me. That they are close, as close as it is possible to be – that if there is a veil between the living and the dead, here on Rath our veil is opaque and I can nearly pierce it if I swim.

I only have to be quiet and listen to the sea.

# ACKNOWLEDGEMENTS

When you have been writing a book for a decade, there are a lot of people to thank. Rossa, Maeve, without your generosity of spirit and open hearts, this book would never have seen the light. Lorna and Ian, for being as much a part of the team as any of us, your constancy, faith in us and unerring good humour will never be forgotten. Caoimhe and Laoise, for always making dark times a lot brighter. The wider Mulcahy, Bunbury, Thunder and Tucker families who were with us every step of the way and never left us behind. Our other, army family who never faded away – Studderts, Wyers, Madigans, Goslings, Mangans, Youngs and Quirkes.

Celine, Niamh, Helen, for three decades of friendship and many chats about the ideas in this book at all the right times. Nick, lifelong member of a select two-person book club. Seoirse for preaching acceptance and many arguments about souls. Annie for always reminding me I was a writer, even when it seemed impossible to believe.

Mike, for always giving me the words, even when they were the hardest to hear. Finola, for a chat on a hard day and a line you threw away that became the central key of the book. Brian for relentless cheerleading, hope and faith.

The Hurleys, Sean and Brenda, John, Catherine, Miriam, Liam and Paul, who brought us to Kerry and welcomed us back every summer, showed us that true riches consist of a boat, a line, a bite, a feed of mackerel, and gave me the finest gift of all, Juno.

The Wavecrest crew, especially Greg and Mairead, Eddie and Lynsey, Ruth and Tony, Gillian, Helen, Catherine, Mary for late night chats, laughs, sometimes tears and years and years of swims, kayaks and long beach days. To all of the O'Sheas, past and present, and the incredible job you do welcoming us every year to the most beautiful campsite in Ireland.

Noel, Sandra, Katie, Jerry, Brian, Vinny, Helen, Davey and Joan, John in Oz, Dave, Ena and Traolach – all my friends in the Blind Piper and Caherdaniel who permit me to labour under the delusion that I am connected to the place. Thinking of John Murphy and Paddy Breen who showed me the power of a good story, truth optional.

The Writing Group where a lot of these essays were first written and false notes called out, Imelda, Sinead, Annie, Viv, Don, Mike, Sharon, Mairead. John Lenihan, Eddie Kelleher, Matt Padwick, Miriam and Catherine Hurley, Ailbhe Thunder for being this book's very early readers; Ed O'Loughlin for being its last. Celine Kiernan and Eileen Carroll of Kildare and Newbridge libraries for support. Niamh Creighton for excellent advice.

Mentors and editors who helped me become a writer: Frédéric Royall for sending me on an odyssey of European literature in the UL library and stretching my brain; Nick Mulcahy for teaching me sentences, Lucille Redmond for paragraphs; Patsey Murphy for sending me to a storm-lashed rock in the Atlantic then giving me the space to tell the story; Rachel Collins for making me tear up stories and start again; Damian Cullen for publishing pieces that changed my life; Ronald Quinlan for heroic polishing of copy. Justine White and Fiona Candon for actually paying me to write about castles and kings for Fáilte Ireland. Desmond Morris who taught me his golden rule of 'simplification without distortion' and allowed me to fight with him over his letters.

To my publisher Deirdre Nolan, who caught a shadow of what this book could be and refused me until I had done enough work to bring it into the light. To my agent Ivan (no relation) Mulcahy who is a delight to work with and a much- appreciated presence in my corner. To my brilliant editor, Amy Borg, who threw all the pieces of this mess of a book into the air, confident she would catch them as they fell, with sure hands and an unerring eye. Leonie Lock and the team at Bonnier; Declan Heeney and all the team at Gill Hess; Alex Kirby for exceptional book design.

Always remembering Dave Bourke, European Studies 89, with whose untimely death my apprenticeship in grief began.

To my compass points, Oisín, Aoibh, Doireann and Rebecca, everything, always is for you. Thank you for your brilliance, resilience, kindness and love and please never stop teaching me things.

What's Wrong with

# Dispensational
# Eschatology?

Charleston, SC
www.PalmettoPublishing.com

*What's Wrong with Dispensational Eschatology?*
Copyright © 2023 by Stephen M. Vipperman

Library of Congress Card Catalog Number
Unless otherwise indicated, Scripture quotations are from the Holy
Bible, New International Version (NIV), 1983.

Paperback ISBN: 978-1-7374008-3-7
eBook ISBN: 978-1-7374008-4-4

ε σ χ α τ ο ν

What's Wrong with
# Dispensational
# Eschatology?

Stephen M. Vipperman

*This book is*
*dedicated to God's Infallible Word.*
—John 1:1–5

# PREFACE

This work is an offshoot of *Revelation: One Apocalypse, 7 Unveilings*, which I published with Palmetto Publishing in 2021. It was my first attempt at writing, and no sooner had it been printed than I wanted to make improvements upon it. That book included (1) six different methods of interpretation for the book of Revelation, (2) an apologetic response to the dispensational interpretation, and (3) my commentary on Revelation. Instead of simply writing a second edition, I intend to rewrite the one book into three smaller books; together they will form a second edition. *What's Wrong with Dispensational Eschatology?* is the first of those three books.

Accordingly, some of this book can be found in *Revelation: One Apocalypse, 7 Unveilings*, and I have acknowledged this in the footnotes, but most of the book is a complete rewrite. It is intended to address a particular and widespread misunderstanding of the doctrine of end times.

Doctrine is an interpretation of what the Bible teaches. The Bible is the infallible, inerrant Word of God. We can manipulate Scripture to arrive at a predetermined conclusion. Such a contrived doctrine (teaching) does not merit the label "infallible," but when a doctrine has been successfully marketed, it may be mistakenly merged with the Word of God.

Dispensational doctrine was first developed during the 1800s.[1] At some point during the Niagara Bible Conferences (1878–1909), belief in dispensational doctrine became blended with believing the Bible. I contend that dispensationalism is an unwarranted and unsupported addition to Scripture.

---

[1] According to Weber, John Nelson Darby introduced dispensational eschatology at the third Powerscourt conference in 1833. Timothy P. Weber, "Dispensational and Historic Premillennialism as Popular Millennialist Movements," in A Case for Historic Premillennialism: An Alternative to "Left Behind" Eschatology, ed. Craig L. Blomberg and Sung Wook Chung (Grand Rapids: Baker Academic, 2009), 10. Also see Stephen Vipperman, Revelation: One Apocalypse, 7 Unveilings (Charleston, SC: Palmetto Publishing, 2021), 36–40.

# TABLE OF CONTENTS

# CHAPTER ONE

## An Introduction to the Problem

The very mention of the secret rapture of the church excites the minds and hearts of many Christians, especially those within the Baptist tradition. Many Baptists love and embrace everything about the rapture. Their hearts skip a beat every time it is mentioned. The *Left Behind* series of books, by Tim LaHaye and Jerry Jenkins, whose fictional stories are set in the aftermath of the rapture, has become something akin to an addendum to the Bible for many Christians. It seems these Christians can never get enough of the rapture and the things that some believe will take place on earth after the rapture.

If the central focus of the untold millions of God's people is the rapture of the church, it behooves us to look very closely at the Scripture undergirding this teaching. If we find that the foundation of the secret rapture is sure, then let us strongly embrace it, but if the foundation crumbles under the microscope of God's Word, then we must respond courageously to correct our thinking and convictions. Woe unto us if we intentionally close our eyes to false teaching.

The doctrine concerning the secret, invisible, pretribulational rapture comes from dispensational eschatology. Dispensationalism arose in the 1800s. These scholars looked at Scripture in a brand-new way and began to interpret Scripture through a new lens. They found seven distinct epochs in the Bible. In every age God dispensed some revelation by which man could be saved, but six of these dispensations failed to bring salvation.

Because dispensationalists wrongly compartmentalized the Bible into these seven dispensations, they were compelled to draw some conclusions that would also be wrong. For these interpreters, a successful dispensation is when the kingdom of God is manifested on earth with Israel ruling the world from Jerusalem. The belief that Israel must rule the world from Jerusalem is called Zionism.

Instead of the cross, Zionism is the focal point of dispensationalism. It is driven by Zionism: dispensationalists are looking for Old Testament (OT) promises to be fulfilled in the future as the nation of Israel rules the world from Jerusalem. Dispensationalists look for Israel's kingdom to be a distinct and separate plan from the church. They keep Israel separate from the church, yet they maintain that Israel, as a national entity, is still on the path to salvation and glory.

Zionism has caused dispensationalists to construct a convoluted doctrine of the end times (eschatology) in which Israel will rule the world. The convoluted eschatology is known as pretribulational premillennialism. Premillennialism teaches that there is a future one-thousand-year kingdom on earth at the end of time, when Jesus and Israel will rule the world from Jerusalem. Jesus returns prior to the millennium. Pretribulation teaches that there will be a seven-year tribulation prior to the millennium, and Jesus will return to rapture the church prior to the tribulation.

It is somewhat difficult to accurately summarize dispensational teachings because their doctrine is still developing. It is hard to hit a moving target. The progressive dispensationalists (1980 and forward) are scrambling to respond to the criticism advanced against classic dispensationalism (1833–1979). The progressive scholars try to minimize the distinction between Israel and the church. At the same time, they keep enough of a distinction between the two in order to maintain pretribulational premillennialism and Zionism. Progressive dispensationalists maintain the name "dispensationalist" but rarely speak of the dispensational ages. There is another group of scholars that rejects the dispensational ages and refuses the moniker of "dispensationalist," but this group maintains the convoluted eschatology known as pretribulational premillennialism.[2]

Below is an overview of the eschatological events according to some classic dispensationalists.[3] Not all dispensationalists will approve of the following outline, as they are not uniform in every detail, but if you search the writings of dispensationalists, you will find these teachings.

**Dispensational Teachings**
1. Jesus's First Coming
    a. Classic dispensationalists teach that the First Coming of Jesus was a failed dispensation. Jesus offered the kingdom of heaven to the Jews, which would have enabled Israel to rule the world from Jerusalem. They declined the offer.

[2] See, for example, Paige Patterson, *Revelation* NAC (Nashville: B&H, 2012).
[3] Anthony A. Hoekema, *The Bible and the Future* (Grand Rapids: Eerdmans, 1979), 186–193. *Revelation: One Apocalypse, 7 Unveilings*, 26–28. See also the books labeled "Dispensational" in the annotated bibliography.

WHAT'S WRONG WITH DISPENSATIONAL ESCHATOLOGY?

    b. Dispensationalists believe that Jesus postponed his plans with the Jewish people and inaugurated a parenthetical age with the church, one not foreseen in the OT.

2. Jesus's Second Coming, or Parousia,[4] Stage One: The Rapture
    a. Dispensationalists believe that the Second Coming of Jesus will be in two stages. They call the first stage the rapture. Jesus will come down from heaven to rapture the church. He will not completely descend to earth. Christians all over the world will suddenly and secretly vanish from the sight of unbelievers and rise to the marriage of the Lamb in heaven.
    b. The Holy Spirit will join the church in heaven to attend the marriage of the Lamb. Church members who have died will be resurrected to participate in the rapture.

3. The Seven-Year Tribulation
    a. The church is gone from earth. The Holy Spirit is gone from earth. The parenthetical age is over. Dispensationalists believe that multitudes will be left behind by Jesus to suffer through a tribulation.
    b. During the tribulation, they believe 144,000 Jewish people will be saved, who in turn will lead an innumerable multitude to salvation. Israel will rule the entire world from Palestine.
    c. They believe that the wrath of God will fall upon the earth in various forms, and many people will be destroyed, as described in Revelation 6–18.
    d. They believe the enemies of God will gather on the battlefield of Megiddo to fight the battle known as Armageddon.

---

[4] *Parousia* is a term that comes from the Greek New Testament (GNT) and means "coming" or "appearance." It refers to the second coming of Jesus.

4. Jesus's Second Coming, or Parousia, Stage Two: The Millennial Kingdom

   a. Dispensationalists believe that after God spends seven years destroying the earth and the church spends seven glorious years in heaven, Jesus returns to earth with the church, in a reversal of the rapture.[5]

   b. They also believe that Jesus sits on a throne in Jerusalem and inaugurates a one-thousand-year earthly reign known as the millennial kingdom.

   c. They believe the devil will be bound and cast into the abyss for one thousand years. Everyone on earth will enjoy great prosperity.

   d. They believe OT saints will be resurrected to join Jesus in his millennial kingdom.

   e. They believe that Jews who died in the tribulation will participate in the resurrection and join Christ in Israel for the millennial kingdom.

   f. They believe that any Israelite who did not come to faith during the seven-year tribulation will come to faith when Jesus appears.

   g. They believe "sheep and goat" judgment will occur; sheep will enjoy the millennial kingdom, and the goats will go to hell.

   h. They believe the millennial kingdom will fulfill the OT promises made by God to Israel.

   i. They believe the temple in Jerusalem will once again exist. Sacrifices will be offered in the temple as memorial offerings.

---

[5] Some dispensationalists believe the church remains in heaven, so Israel may have exclusive control of the earthly kingdom.

5. The Loosing of Satan
   a. Dispensationalists believe children born during the one-thousand-year period may or may not become believers. These new unbelievers will be gathered by Satan when he is loosed at the end of the one-thousand-year period.
   b. They believe this final revolt will be crushed by Jesus, and Satan will be cast into hell forever.
6. New Heaven and Earth
   a. Dispensationalists teach that the believers who died during the one-thousand-year period will participate in the resurrection.
   b. God will create a new heaven and a new earth for the abode of all his people.
   c. Dispensationalists teach that there will exist some sort of eternal distinction between redeemed Jews and redeemed Gentiles.[6]

Dispensational eschatology does not hold up to biblical scrutiny. The Bible does not actually support or warrant dispensational eschatology, yet it is widely received in my Southern Baptist denomination. Dispensationalism has been marketed as an infallible doctrine. Some dispensationalists say you do not believe the Bible if you do not believe dispensational doctrine. Some dispensationalists say you must believe dispensational doctrine and view the Bible through the lens of this doctrine, or you will not be able to understand the Bible.[7] The well-known pastor and committed dispensationalist John McArthur

---

[6] L. S. Chafer, *Systematic Theology*, 8 vols (Dallas: Dallas Seminary Press, 1947), 4:47. According to Chafer, the church would inhabit the new heaven, and Israel would inhabit the new earth. Some progressive dispensationalists have backed off this claim.
[7] Charles Ryrie, *Dispensationalism Today* (Chicago: Moody Press, 1970), 31.

says, "Amillennialism is a defection from the clear and straightforward meaning of Scripture and so is postmillennialism."[8]

It is wrong to presume that Scripture must be viewed through the lens of dispensational doctrine. This faulty premise corrupts the reading of Scripture. It causes dispensationalists to read the Bible with this faulty notion: "Anything I read in Scripture that contradicts dispensationalism must be twisted and modified until it agrees with dispensationalism."

Some people are hesitant to debate eschatology, but Baptists have a reputation for being people of the Book. As a general rule, Baptist preachers tell it like it is without equivocation or fear of hurting someone's feelings. Eschatology should not be an exception to the rule. Let us look at a few of these dispensational doctrines of the end times and compare them to the Word of God. May our doctrines bend and conform to the infallible Word. May the Holy Spirit guard us against bending his Word to our doctrine.

---

[8] John McArthur, "Why Every Calvinist Should Be a Premillennialist, Part 6 (Selected Scriptures)," Grace to You, March 30, 2017, YouTube video, 1:02:50, see 6:45.

# CHAPTER TWO

## Dispensational Doctrine: The First Coming of Jesus— "A Failed Dispensation"

One of the more egregious aspects of dispensationalism is that the First Coming of Jesus was a failed dispensation. Dispensationalists believe Jesus tried and failed to establish the kingdom of God with Israel during his First Coming. They believe he was completely rejected by Israel, and thus, Jesus had to resort to a contingency plan: the cross and the establishment of the church.[9] Contrary to dispensational doctrine, Scripture clearly teaches that Jesus successfully established the millennial kingdom, and that will be discussed in chapter five. Jesus came to earth to be King (**John 18:37**), and he reigns on his throne today (**Heb. 1:3**), but dispensationalists fail to understand the nature of the

---

[9] See, for example, Herman Hoyt, "Dispensational Premillennialism," in *The Meaning of the Millennium: Four Views*, ed. Robert Clouse (Downers Grove: InterVarsity Press, 1977), 84–88.

kingdom. Dispensationalists also diminish the importance of the cross when they call it a "contingency plan."

The idea that Jesus came to be a political leader and liberate Israel from Roman oppression was an early misconception of some followers, but how could Jesus be a failed political leader when he never attempted to be a political leader?

### Zionism and the Glory Days of Israel

I do not know how many ladies feel this way, but I know many middle-aged men who daydream about their "glory days," when they were young, healthy, strong, and fast and had good heads of hair. Unfortunately, we do not circle back around to such times, but we move onward toward new adventures like having grandchildren.

When Daniel realized the seventy years in captivity were ending and it was time to return to Israel (**Dan. 9:1–3**), I suspect Daniel dreamed of the glory days of Israel. He probably envisioned the days of David and his mighty men, who conquered all the enemies of God and took Jerusalem as the capital of Israel. Daniel probably envisioned David leaving the throne to Solomon, who was known for great wealth and great wisdom and for building God a great temple. Eventually Solomon's pagan wives led Israel astray, but before that problem reached maturity, the nation was healthy, wealthy, and wise. The nation worshipped the one true God together in the temple. While Daniel might have dreamed about these glory days, the bulk of the revelations from God told Daniel that severe tribulation was coming for Israel.

The Jews in **John 6:15** who wanted to make Jesus king were probably thinking of Israel's glory days. Jesus eluded them because the literal, physical kingdom built by David is inferior to the spiritual kingdom built by Jesus. The spiritual fulfillment found in the New Testament

(NT) is infinitely greater than the physical shadow of the OT, and Jesus would not settle for an earthly Zion.

*After the people saw the miraculous sign that Jesus did, they began to say, "Surely this is the Prophet who is to come into the world." Jesus, knowing that they intended to come and make him king by force, withdrew again to a mountain by himself.*
—John 6:14–15

Before the disciples were filled with the Holy Spirit, they also struggled with dreams of the return of Israel to its "glory days." In **Acts 1:4–8** the disciples asked Jesus about the restoration of Israel, but Jesus rebuffed them and told them to wait for the Holy Spirit and to focus on witnessing. The disciples obeyed Jesus, they were filled with the Holy Spirit, they witnessed, and they never again spoke of the "glory days" of Israel.

Modern-day Jews still dream of the restoration of Israel. They are waiting for a political messiah[10] who will return Israel to its "glory days" in which all their enemies are conquered while Israel enjoys health, wealth, and admiration from the world. They wait in vain for this messiah because they rejected the Messiah who established a spiritual Israel.

During the last days of the Apostle Peter, in **2 Peter 3:10–13**, Peter says that we are looking forward to a new heaven and a new earth. Peter does not say that we are looking forward to the restoration of Israel and a future millennial kingdom.[11] Peter indicates that the coming of the

---

[10] See, for example, Ben Shapiro in "Why BEN SHAPIRO Doesn't Accept JESUS as the MESSIAH," Fook SJW, August 2, 2018, YouTube video 5:34, see 3:50.
[11] Bruce Waltke, "A Response," in *Dispensationalism, Israel and the Church*, eds. Craig Blaising and Darrell Bock (Grand Rapids: Zondervan, 1992), 355.

Lord will be the destruction of heaven and earth, not the beginning of a millennial, earthly Zion.

*The day of the Lord will come like a thief. The heavens will disappear with a roar: the elements will be destroyed by fire, and the earth and everything done in it will be laid bare.*

—2 Peter 3:10

Dispensationalists are like the unbelieving Jews: they are waiting in vain for a messiah to restore an OT Israel, and they denigrate amillennialists who proclaim the advent of spiritual Israel and the heavenly Jerusalem.

## The Spiritual Nature of the Kingdom

An earthly kingdom, ruled from a throne in Jerusalem, was not the original intention for the incarnation of God the Son. A worldly kingdom would be too small a kingdom for God. God's kingdom is spiritual.

*Once, having been asked by the Pharisees when the kingdom of God would come, Jesus replied, "The kingdom of God does not come with your careful observation, nor will people say, 'Here it is,' or 'There it is,' because the kingdom of God is within you."*

—Luke 17:20–21

If Jesus intended to rule this world from a throne in Jerusalem, then why did Jesus tell Pilate, **"My kingdom is not of this world"** (**John 18:36**)? Those who handed Jesus over to be crucified alleged Jesus's kingship to be a threat to Caesar (**Luke 23:2; John 19:12**), but Jesus was not competing with Caesar for tax dollars. Instead, Jesus was competing with Satan for the souls of humans (**Mark 12:17**). Jesus did not deny his royalty and sovereignty, but when he said that his kingdom is not of this world, he alluded to a misunderstanding of his reign. Many kingdoms are defined by border or perimeter walls marking the geographical lines of the kings' realms. God's kingdom is not defined in this manner. It is not a matter of real estate but a matter of subjects. When God the Son broke into the world via the incarnation, he built a bridge with the cross. This bridge solved humanity's greatest dilemma: How can sinful people approach a Holy God? Without the cross, the King would forever be separated from his subjects. The establishment of this bridge inaugurated the millennial kingdom. The millennial kingdom is one in which God presently reigns in the hearts of believers on earth (**Eph. 3:17**) and the souls of the martyrs reign in heaven, seated upon thrones next to Jesus (**Rev. 20:4**). The millennial kingdom is a kingdom that spans both heaven and earth.

**When Did God Decide the Purpose of the Incarnation?**
Dispensationalists describe the cross and the establishment of the church as God's "plan B," but notice the purpose of the coming of Jesus in the following verse: **"For even the Son of Man did not come to be served, but to serve, and to give his life as a ransom for many"** (**Mark 10:45**). The cross was God's intention from the very beginning, which rules out any notion of God altering his plan. The angel told Joseph, **"She [Mary] will give birth to a son, and you are to give him the name Jesus, because he will save his people from their sins"** (**Matthew 1:21**).

Early in his ministry, Jesus spoke to Nicodemus and said, **"Just as Moses lifted up the snake in the desert, so the Son of Man must be lifted up, that everyone who believes in him may have eternal life"**

(**John 3:14–15**). From the outset of his ministry, Jesus was telling people like Nicodemus that he was going to the cross. This message surprised them because it was not what they expected from the Messiah, but it was no surprise to God.

Jesus was chosen to shed his blood for us before the world was created (**1 Pet. 1:20**). Jesus did not come to condemn or overthrow the Roman Empire for their oppression of Israel: **"For God did not send his Son into the world to condemn the world, but to save the world through him"** (**John 3:17**). Without the cross, there would be no salvation for the world. The cross was not plan B. The cross was the original intent of the Father even before he sent the Son. The necessity of the sacrifice has been known to God since the dawn of creation, as evidenced in the verse below:

> *All inhabitants of the earth will worship the beast—all whose names have not been written in the book of life belonging to the Lamb that was slain from the creation of the world.*
>
> —Revelation 13:8

When Jesus, Peter, James, and John came down from the mountain, Jesus told them not to tell anyone about the transfiguration, which they had witnessed until after he had risen from the dead (**Mark 9:9**). The disciples were perplexed and could not comprehend the meaning of "rising from the dead" (**Mark 9:10**). In Mark's Gospel, Jesus would often perform a miracle, and then he would forbid the people to publicize it. This element in Mark's Gospel has become known as the Marcan secret. Jesus did not want them to miscommunicate his purpose as Messiah. Until his disciples could accept a crucified and resurrected Messiah, they were not able to accurately proclaim the Messiah. The cross and resurrection were integral parts of the purpose of Jesus.

There is no indication in the Gospels that Jesus adjusted his ministry from becoming a geopolitical leader type of Messiah to a "plan B" crucified Messiah of a parenthetical age. It seems that it took the disciples quite a while to grasp that Jesus was destined for the cross, but there is no indication that God had to pivot from one plan to another, and it contradicts Scriptures like **Mark 10:45** and **Revelation 13:8**.

Dispensationalism teaches that in the future, Jesus will sit on a throne in Jerusalem for one thousand years and that will be the millennial kingdom that he intended with his First Coming. This doctrine creates an insurmountable problem: If Jesus was supposed to sit for a millennium on an earthly throne in the flesh, then how could he die upon a cross? Without the cross, how could there be any propitiation for sin? How, then, could we be saved? Walter Kaiser says, "The most serious objection against the postponed kingdom to the Jews in the first century runs directly counter to the necessity of Messiah's sacrificial death before Messiah can enjoy 'the glories that would follow.'"[12]

### Daniel's Prophecy

Dispensationalists use the term "parenthetical" because they believe Jesus did not establish the millennial kingdom when Daniel predicted it would be established. According to Daniel, the kingdom should be established with the First Coming of Jesus (**Dan. 2:44–45**). Daniel predicted the rise and fall of four earthly kingdoms: the Babylonian Empire, the empire of the Medes and Persians,[13] the Greek Empire,

---

[12] Walter C. Kaiser Jr., "Kingdom Promises as Spiritual and National," in *Continuity and Discontinuity*, ed. John Feinberg (Wheaton: Crossway, 1988), 298.

[13] Some critical scholars like to separate the empire of the Medes and Persians. See, for example, John J. Collins, *Daniel, with an Introduction to Apocalyptic Literature*, FOTL (Grand Rapids: Eerdmans, 1984), 52. However, the Medo-Persian Empire is seen as one empire in the book of Daniel. See Daniel 6:8, 12, 15, and 8:20.

and the Roman Empire. Daniel predicts the formation of God's kingdom during the time of the fourth kingdom, the Roman Empire.[14] God's kingdom is a rock (or stone) that is not formed by human hands; it is of supernatural origin. Daniel predicts that this kingdom will grow perpetually. The stone serves two purposes: building and crushing.

*Jesus looked directly at them and asked, "Then what is the meaning of that which is written: 'The stone the builders rejected has become the capstone'? Everyone who falls on that stone will be broken to pieces, but he on whom it falls will be crushed."*

—Luke 20:17–18

*For in Scripture it says: "See, I lay a stone in Zion, a chosen and precious cornerstone, and the one who trusts in him will never be put to shame." Now to you who believe, this stone is precious. But to those who do not believe, "The stone the builders rejected has become the capstone," and, "A stone that causes men to stumble and a rock that makes them fall." They stumble because they disobey the message— which is also what they were destined for.*

—1 Peter 2:6–8

The cornerstone has been laid. The kingdom of God has been established. His kingdom grows. Every person who answers God's call

---

[14] Walvoord says the fourth kingdom is the Roman Empire, but since the Roman Empire was not crushed in military conquest by the First Coming of Jesus, then the kingdom of God described in Daniel 2:44 has not arrived: "Daniel's prophecy passes over the present age, the period between the first and second comings of Christ or, more specifically, the period between Pentecost and the rapture of the church." In other words, there are parentheses between Daniel 2:43 and 2:44. John F. Walvoord, *Daniel*, rev. ed. Charles Dyer and Philip Rawley (Chicago: Moody, 2012), 85.

chooses to have his carnal nature broken to pieces over this stone. The Christian surrenders his life to the lordship of Jesus. As the Apostle Paul said, **"I have been crucified with Christ and I no longer live but Christ lives in me" (Gal. 2:20)**. The Christian's carnal nature is broken over that stone so that the spiritual nature may build the house of God. For those who refuse the message of salvation, the cornerstone has been laid, and already, the death sentence has been pronounced (**John 3:18**). The unrepentant will be crushed by that stone.

Classic dispensationalists believe we are still waiting for this stone, this kingdom of God, but Daniel mentions no postponement between the fourth kingdom and God's kingdom. It is a matter of historical fact that the Roman Empire was the fourth kingdom from Daniel's starting point, and Daniel says the kingdom of God would come during the time of those kings, (**Dan. 2:44**). Progressive dispensationalist Stephen Miller says, "The kingdom of God in view here did not begin at Christ's first coming but will be inaugurated at his return."[15] This discrepancy between Daniel and dispensationalism compels us to reject dispensationalism or to consider Daniel to be a false prophet.

Dispensationalists are some of the greatest advocates for the authenticity of Daniel's prophetic nature. Dispensationalists should be commended for their vigorous defense of an early date for the authorship of Daniel against liberal theologians. They do not want to label Daniel a false prophet, but neither do they want to believe that the kingdom of God was established with the First Coming of Jesus. In an effort to alleviate their lack of coherence with Daniel, dispensationalists insert parentheses into the timeline. By their reckoning, the time between the First and the Second Coming of Jesus does not count; it is merely

---

[15] Stephen R. Miller, *Daniel*, NAC (Nashville: B&H, 1994), 216.

parenthetical. At the end of the "church age," the parentheses will also end, and Jesus will finally establish the millennial kingdom, just as Daniel foretold.[16]

Dispensationalists must believe this postponement was not foreseen by the OT, since Daniel makes no mention of the parentheses. Is that how we should construct doctrine? If our extrapolation of Scripture contradicts Scripture, may we invent parentheses to fix the problem? Or should we bend our doctrine to Scripture? There is an alternative to the parentheses: Jesus did not postpone his kingdom; he established his kingdom.

**Was the "Church Age" Unforeseen?**
Dispensationalists say the establishment of the church (i.e., "the church age") was an unforeseen, parenthetical contingency plan, but this is not correct. Isaiah foresaw, **"But he was pierced for our transgressions, he was crushed for our iniquities"** (Isa. 53:5). The psalmist foreheard Jesus say, **"My God, my God, why have you forsaken me?"** (Isa. 22:1), and the psalmist foresaw them casting lots for his garments (Isa. 22:18). The suffering Messiah who establishes the church was foreseen by the OT.

The OT also saw Israelites worshipping together with Gentiles: **"In that day the Root of Jesse will stand as a banner for the peoples; the nations will rally to him, and his place of rest will be glorious"** (Isa. 11:10). Israel was only one nation, yet Isaiah foresaw nations (plural) rallying to the Root of Jesse. Isaiah prophesied, "Come, all you who are thirsty" (Isa. 55:1); "Let no foreigner who has bound himself to the

[16] See, for example, John F. Walvoord, *The Rapture Question*, 2nd ed. (Grand Rapids: Zondervan, 1979), 25–31.

LORD say, 'The LORD will surely exclude me from his people'" (Isa. 56:3). Isaiah foresaw that God's house would be a house of prayer for all nations (Isa. 56:7). The OT saw the church, consisting of both Jews and Gentiles, centuries before Jesus established the church.

## Conclusion

The OT did not fail to foresee the cross. It did not fail to see the worship of both Jews and Gentiles as one body of believers, which is the church. Daniel did not foresee a parenthetical age, because Jesus did not inaugurate a parenthetical age. Dispensationalists who invent the parentheses fail to grasp the spiritual nature of the millennial kingdom and thus fail to see that Jesus has already inaugurated this kingdom. We do not yet see the full glory of God's kingdom and the pervasiveness of his reign, but the kingdom has been established already.

> *Thou hast put all things in subjection under his feet. For in that he put all in subjection under him, he left nothing that is not put under him. But now we see not yet all things put under him. But we see Jesus, who was made a little lower than the angels for the suffering of death, crowned with glory and honour...*
> —Hebrews 2:8–9 (KJV) [emphasis mine]

No parentheses are needed. Daniel's timeline is correct. Jesus is on the throne. Jesus reigns already. The kingdom will grow until it fills the earth (**Dan. 2:35**). Jesus, God the Son, will hand the millennial kingdom over to the Father at the end of the millennium. At the end of the millennium, time will end, but the kingdom will not end. The kingdom will be transformed. God's kingdom is eternal. The verse below is evincing the kingdom has been established and is progressing to its full glory:

> *Then the end will come, when he hands over the kingdom to God the Father after he has destroyed all dominion, authority and power. For he must reign until he has put all his enemies under his feet.*
> —1 Corinthians 15:24–25

# CHAPTER THREE

## Dispensational Doctrine:
## Parousia, Stage One—"The Rapture"

Dispensationalism teaches a pretribulational rapture, meaning the church will secretly and invisibly rise to meet Jesus in the air while life on earth continues into the seven-year tribulation. Some dispensationalists have had fun with this doctrine, employing bumper stickers that warn of unmanned vehicles in case of rapture. It is true that the church will rise to meet Jesus in the air when the Lord himself comes down, but the bumper sticker warnings are superfluous because there will be no one left on earth when the church rises to meet Jesus.[17]

The Bible does not use the word "rapture" in any verse. The following verse is the one that comes the closest:

---

[17] Many of the arguments in this chapter can be found in my prior work, *Revelation: One Apocalypse, 7 Unveilings*, 44–52.

*For the Lord himself will come down from heaven, with a loud command, with the voice of the archangel and the trumpet call of God and the dead in Christ will rise first. After that, we who are still alive and are left will be caught up [raptured] together with them in the clouds to meet the Lord in the air.*
*And so we will be with the Lord forever.*
—1 Thessalonians 4:16–17

Clearly, it is biblical that the church will rise to meet Jesus in the air, but dispensationalists insert "will be raptured," replacing "will be caught up." The scholars who have translated the Bible do not use the word "rapture" in Thessalonians or anywhere else. Check your Bible. Dispensationalists use the word "rapture" because it has become so entangled with dispensational doctrine that the word has come to mean much more than what the Bible says.

The problem with the dispensationalists' doctrine of the rapture is that they have life on earth, continuing with an innumerable multitude of people being saved during the seven-year tribulation. Dispensationalism is wrong because when Jesus returns, it will be too late to be saved. The Bible makes no allowance for salvation after the Lord himself comes down. It is a dangerous and heretical manipulation of Scripture to teach a doctrine of salvation that promises and predicts salvation of the masses after the Lord himself comes down.[18] Today is the day of salvation. When the Lord himself comes down, it will no longer be today.

---

[18] According to John F. Walvoord, "The Scriptures clearly indicate that a great multitude of both Jews and Gentiles will trust in the Lord after the church is caught up to glory." *The Revelation of Jesus Christ* (Chicago: Moody Press, 1966), 139.

*Therefore God again set a certain day, calling it Today, when a long time later he spoke through David, as was said before: "Today, if you hear his voice, do not harden your hearts."*

—Hebrews 4:7

*For he says, "In the time of my favor I heard you, and in the day of salvation I helped you." I tell you, now is the time of God's favor, now is the day of salvation.*

—2 Corinthians 6:2

In **Matthew 25**, Jesus tells a parable of the ten virgins. Five virgins carried lamps and oil, but five virgins carried only lamps. They waited for the bridegroom, and at the last minute, the five virgins without oil had to run out to purchase oil for their lamps. The bridegroom came while they were gone, and the door leading to the banquet was shut. They begged for the door to be opened, but the bridegroom responded, **"I tell you the truth, I don't know you."** The central proposition of this parable is that once the bridegroom (Jesus) appears, there is no longer time to get ready. Dispensationalism contradicts this Scripture by teaching that after the bridegroom comes to receive his bride and ascend to heaven for the marriage ceremony, there will be seven years of opportunity to accept Jesus as Savior, and during those seven years, all Israel will be saved.

### In the Days of Noah

When the flood came in the days of Noah, it was too late to seek salvation. Noah's family entered the ark a week before the flood (**Gen 7:1–16**). Jesus compares his Second Coming, where people are left behind, to the days of Noah: **"As it was in the days of Noah, so it will**

**be at the coming of the Son of Man…" (Matt. 24:37–39).** The *Left Behind* series has caused us to believe that the church is taken first, and the unbelievers are left behind. However, according to Köstenberger, "In this example, you would want to be one of the ones left behind because the ones swept away were taken away in judgment or, as Luke describes it, destroyed…These verses are often used to support the idea that Jesus will come to take away his people before judgment comes, but the point in both Matthew and Luke is that when the Son of Man comes, it is God's people who will be left while all others will be taken away in judgment."[19] In the days of Noah, the wicked were swept away in judgment, and Noah's family was left behind. The wicked go to their eternal punishment first.[20]

**Second Thessalonians 1**
Look at how the church in Thessalonica was encouraged during their time of tribulation. They were told that when the Lord comes to bring relief to the church, on that same day, the wicked would be punished with everlasting destruction. There is no seven-year tribulation between the coming of the Lord to relieve his church from tribulation and the everlasting destruction of the wicked.[21]

---

[19] Andreas Köstenberger, Alexander Stewart, and Apollo Makara, *Jesus and the Future: Understanding What He Taught about the End Times* (Bellingham, WA: Lexham Press, 2017), 83. Also see Craig L. Blomberg, "The Posttribulationism of the New Testament," in *A Case for Historic Premillennialism: An Alternative to "Left Behind" Eschatology*, eds. Craig L. Blomberg and Sung Wook Chung (Grand Rapids: Baker Academic, 2009), 78.

[20] Previously, I contended that those left behind were lost people going to hell in *Revelation: One Apocalypse, 7 Unveilings*, 45, but I would like to amend that statement to agree with Köstenberger and Blomberg.

[21] *Revelation: One Apocalypse, 7 Unveilings*, 47–8.

*All this is evidence that God's judgment is right, and as a result you*
*will be counted worthy of the kingdom of God,*
*for which you are suffering. God is just:*
*He will pay back trouble to those who trouble you and*
*<u>give relief to you who are troubled [tribulation]</u>, and to us as well.*
*<u>This will happen when the Lord Jesus is revealed from heaven</u>*
*in blazing fire with his powerful angels.*
*He will punish those who do not know God and*
*do not obey the gospel of our Lord Jesus.*
*<u>They will be punished with everlasting destruction</u> and shut out from*
*the presence of the Lord and from the majesty of his power*
*<u>on the day he comes</u> to be glorified in his holy people and*
*to be marveled at among all those who have believed. This includes*
*you, because you believed our testimony to you.*
—2 Thessalonians 1:5–10 [emphasis mine]

Dispensationalists divide the Second Coming of Jesus into two stages: first Jesus comes part of the way down to rapture his church, and then seven years later, he comes all the way down to separate the sheep and the goats and to inaugurate the millennial kingdom. They add this division of the Parousia (appearance of Jesus) for the same reason they add the parentheses to the timeline: it must be added to accommodate doctrine that they believe to be infallible. They need two Second Comings to accommodate their misunderstanding of the millennial kingdom. They need a millennial kingdom in which Israel is saved as a nation, so they need the church to exit earth during the first stage of the Parousia so that Israel may be saved during the tribulation and ready for the millennial kingdom.[22]

But does the Bible divide the Second Coming of Jesus into two stages? Anthony Hoekema says, "There is no sound Scriptural basis for the position that the Second Coming of Christ must be divided into these two phases."[23] Are we allowed to create this division in the Lord's coming? Should we add something to the Bible to eliminate a discrepancy between Scripture and a doctrine that has enjoyed great marketing? Or should we bend our doctrine to Scripture?

### Final Trumpet Verses [24]

The following two quotes from the Bible are known as the final trumpet verses. Dispensationalists refer to the first passage as the rapture of the church, and they claim the second passage describes the coming of Jesus, which they believe would take place seven years later, after the tribulation:

> *Listen, I tell you a mystery; We will not all sleep, but we will all be changed—in a flash, in the twinkling of an eye, at the last trumpet. For the trumpet will sound, the dead will be raised imperishable, and we will be changed.*
>
> **—1 Corinthians 15:51–52**

---

[22] According to John F. Walvoord, "The interval between the translation and the Second Coming is absolutely necessary for the creation of a new generation of believers in Christ, composed of both Jews and Gentiles who retain their national identification..." *The Rapture Question*, 92. See also Stephen Miller, 257.

[23] Anthony Hoekema, *The Bible and The Future* (Grand Rapids: Eerdmans, 1979), 165.

[24] *Revelation: One Apocalypse, 7 Unveilings*, 46. See also, Vern S. Poythress, *Understanding Dispensationalists*, 2nd ed (Philipsburg, NJ: P & R Publishing, 1994), 71–77.

*At that time the sign of the Son of Man will appear in the sky, and all the nations of the earth will mourn. They will see the Son of Man coming on the clouds of the sky, with power and great glory. And he will send his angels with a loud trumpet call, and they will gather his elect from the four winds, from one end of the heavens to the other.*
—Matthew 24:30–31

Dispensationalists must believe in two last trumpets. The last trumpet sounds when Jesus comes for his church (**1 Cor. 15:51**), and the other last trumpet sounds when Jesus comes at the end of the age to bring judgment upon the earth (**Matt. 24:30–31**). Dispensationalism teaches that there will be a seven-year tribulation between these two last trumpets.

But the question must be asked: How can there be two last trumpets? Does the angel Gabriel have two trumpets labeled "last trumpet"? I hope he does not get them mixed up. Perhaps the angel Gabriel blows the last trumpet for seven years? I hope Gabriel has good lungs. Is the Bible in error by having the last trumpet blast at the rapture but then sound again seven years later? Or are dispensationalists in error because they have created a two-stage Parousia, which does not exist in Scripture? What will dispensationalists add to Scripture to eliminate this discrepancy between their doctrine and what Scripture says concerning the last trumpet? These are not two trumpet blasts but one because when Jesus comes for his church, on the same day, he will bring judgment to the lost.

## Conclusion

When the Lord himself comes down to receive his church, that is not the end of a parenthetical age. It is not stage one of the Parousia. It is the Parousia (the Second Coming of Jesus). It is the end of time. It is Judgment Day. The first load leaving earth will go to eternal damnation, and on the same day, the bride of Christ will rise to meet her groom.

# CHAPTER FOUR

## Dispensational Doctrine:
## The Seven-Year Tribulation—
## "Israel Saved apart from the Church"

Tribulation is the translation of the Greek NT word θλιψις=*thlip-sis*. The word "tribulation" can be tricky because it means different things to different people. People will twist the meaning of the word to conform to the doctrine of the person using the word. Here are three opposing understandings of the word *tribulation* according to amillennialists, dispensationalists, and postmillennialists.

1. Tribulation is the suffering of the people of God. It is pressure put upon them by the world to deny Christ. This is the amillennial view.

2. Tribulation is a seven-year period of the wrath of God upon the world found in Revelation 6–18. There will be horrific destruction upon the planet, the annihilation of many people, and the salvation of all Israel. This is the dispensational view.

3. Tribulation is the wrath of God upon Israel for rejecting Jesus as the Messiah, which led to the destruction of Jerusalem and the temple in AD 70. This is the postmillennial view.

A false argument common from dispensationalists: they prove that the church will not suffer the wrath of God because Jesus took this wrath for us on the cross, which is true, but then they falsely conclude that the church must be raptured prior to the tribulation. This fallacy is known as "missing the point." Wrath is for the lost. Tribulation is for the church. The Great Tribulation is the persecution of the church by the world. When you conflate wrath and tribulation, you miss the point. The fact that the church will not suffer the eternal wrath of God does not prove the church will not suffer tribulation from the world.[25]

Dispensationalism teaches that once the church is removed in the first stage of the Parousia, then God may return to his original plan for Israel during the time of the seven-year tribulation, which they also call the Great Tribulation. No one denies that tribulation exists. No one denies that tribulation can be severe. No one denies the amillennial view of tribulation—that the church suffers tribulation for the cause of Christ. But the dispensational understanding of tribulation is disputed. Their understanding of the tribulation is a recent (nineteenth-century) development.

Before addressing why dispensationalists need the Great Tribulation, there are two aspects of the dispensational, seven-year tribulation that I wish to denounce. First, I reject the doctrine that teaches that this tribulation takes place between two stages of the Parousia. I have already addressed the error of the two-stage Parousia in the previous chapter.

---

[25] For an example of this false argument, see Paul Feinberg, "Pretribulation Rapture," in *Three Views on the Rapture: Pre-, Mid-, or Post-Tribulation*, ed. Gleason Archer (Grand Rapids: Zondervan, 1984), 50–72. See Hoekema for a good response to this false argument, p. 170.

If the Parousia is not in two stages, then there can be no seven-year tribulation between those hypothetical stages.

Second, I wish to denounce dispensationalism's doctrine of Israel's salvation after the appearance of Jesus. We have already established that the Bible teaches that today is the day of salvation, but dispensationalism teaches that all Israel will be saved during this seven-year tribulation. Why does dispensationalism want Israel to be saved during the seven-year tribulation? In order to accommodate doctrine that they believe to be infallible, Israel must be saved in the absence of the church so they can rule the world from Jerusalem.[26]

**Two People / Two Purposes Theory**[27]
Dispensationalism teaches that the church and Israel are two distinct groups of people that cannot be conjoined. This doctrine is often referred to as the two people / two purposes theory.[28] Dispensationalism needs to insert this seven-year period between two hypothetical stages of the Parousia so that God may complete his work of saving Israel apart from the church. These Zionists are focused on OT promises being fulfilled through the nation of Israel ruling the world from Jerusalem.

---

[26] Stephen Miller says, "The tribulation will be dreadful, but one purpose of it will be to bring the Jewish people to an attitude where they will receive Jesus as their Messiah," *Daniel*. NAC (Nashville: Broadman & Holman, 1994), 315.

[27] For further discussion, see *Revelation: One Apocalypse, 7 Unveilings*, 53–59.

[28] According to Charles C. Ryrie, "A dispensationalist keeps Israel and the church distinct… this is probably the most basic test of whether or not a man is a dispensationalist." *Dispensationalism Today* (Chicago: Moody Press, 1965), 44–45. Progressive dispensationalists have watered down and relabeled "two people / two purpose theory," but they maintain enough of a distinction between Israel and the church so as to justify the pretrib view. They say that Israel and the church are "different redemptive dimensions of the same humanity." Craig Blaising and Darrell Bock, "*Dispensationalism, Israel and the Church*: Assessment and Dialogue," in Dispensationalism, Israel and the Church ed. Craig Blaising and Darrell Bock (Grand Rapids: Zondervan, 1992), 384.

The fundamental doctrine that gave birth to dispensationalism is that there are seven[29] dispensations in the Bible. Each dispensation is a new revelation from God and carries with it the distinct possibility of salvation. Classic dispensationalism teaches that the promises made to Israel must be fulfilled with Israel. The promises cannot be transferred from one group of people in one dispensational age to another group of people in another dispensational age. Consequently, any OT promises made to Israel that are fulfilled during the parenthetical church age are not considered fulfilled, because dispensationalism does not allow the church to be considered Israel.

While the distinct dispensational ages are the reason classic dispensationalists keep separate Israel and the church, progressive dispensationalists have found new reasons. For example, Robert Saucy says Israel and the church must be kept separate because OT Israel was a theocratic nation and the NT church is not.[30] It is true that OT Israel was a theocratic nation, and the NT church is not literally a theocratic nation, but **1 Peter 2:9** says the church is a holy nation. While Peter was speaking of the church in the spiritual realm, it still undermines the argument of Saucy. Furthermore, his criterion is arbitrary. Why does the church have to be a literal, theocratic nation in order to be NT Israel? This chapter will show that the church is identified as Israel in the NT. Beale and Carson are experts on the NT use of the OT, and they say, "NT writers happily apply to the church, that is, to the new covenant people of God, many texts that originally referred to the Israelites, the old covenant people of God."[31] When the Bible identifies

---

[29] Dispensationalists argue among themselves as to the actual number of dispensations. See Ryrie 57–64 for an example of seven dispensations.

[30] Robert Saucy, "Israel and the Church: A Case for Discontinuity," in *Continuity and Discontinuity*, ed. John Feinberg (Wheaton: Crossway, 1988), 251.

[31] G. K. Beale and D. A. Carson, eds., *Commentary on the New Testament Use of the Old Testament.* (Grand Rapids: Baker Academic, 2007), xxvi.

the church as Israel, it is futile for any man to say, "No it is not! It does not meet my criterion."

## Romans 11:26: All Israel Will Be Saved

If there is any verse in the NT that might appear to support the future restoration of ethnic Israel as a nation and distinct from the church, it would be **Romans 11:26. Dispensationalism teaches, "All Israel will be saved" (Rom. 11:26)**. Obviously the statement is true because it is found in Scripture. But what does the statement mean? The pertinent question that we must answer: Who is Israel?

Dispensationalists vehemently argue that the church cannot be equated with Israel. Dispensationalists argue that the promises made to Israel must be fulfilled by the literal, physical descendants of Abraham. How can Israel be restored while the church is on earth without Israel becoming part of the church? As long as the church is on earth, any Israelite who comes to faith in Jesus, the Jewish Messiah, will become part of the church. Metaphorically speaking, they will be grafted into the same olive tree into which the church was grafted (**Rom. 11:23– 24**). The church and Israel will be conjoined.[32] As Riddlebarger says, "Paul's whole point was that while there were two kinds of branches, Jews (natural branches) and Gentiles (wild branches), there was only one root."[33] Dispensationalists do not have two olive trees to keep separate Israel and the church—hence the need for dispensationalism to create a time period where the church is absent: the Great Tribulation.

---

[32] Progressive dispensationalists believe "Jews and Gentiles are united in the same body of Christ but they are mutually dependent and ethnically distinct. Their identities, even in the church, do not merge." J. Lanier Burns, "The future of Ethnic Israel in Romans 11," in *Dispensationalism, Israel and the Church*, eds. Craig Blaising and Darrell Bock (Grand Rapids: Zondervan, 1992), 227.

[33] Kim Riddlebarger, *A Case for Amillennialism, Understanding the End Times*, exp. ed. (Grand Rapids: Baker Books, 2013), 219.

Is it biblical to say that the church is not Israel? The answer is, *no!* The letter to the church in Ephesus grants to the Gentile members of this church citizenship in Israel:

> *Therefore, remember that formerly you who are <u>Gentiles</u> by birth and called "uncircumcised" by those who call themselves "the circumcision" (that done in the body by the hands of men)—remember that at that time you were separate from Christ, excluded from citizenship in Israel and foreigners to the covenants of the promise, without hope and without God in the world. But now in Christ Jesus you who once were far away have been brought near through the blood of Christ. <u>For he himself is our peace who has made the two one</u> and has destroyed the barrier, the dividing wall of hostility, by abolishing in his flesh the law with its commandments and regulations. His purpose was to create in himself one new man out of the two, thus making peace, and in this one body to reconcile both of them to God through the cross, by which he put to death their hostility. He came and preached peace to you who were far away and peace to those who were near. For through him we both have access to the Father by one Spirit. <u>Consequently, you are no longer foreigners and aliens, but fellow citizens with God's people and members of God's household,</u> built on the foundation of the apostles and prophets, with Christ Jesus himself as the chief cornerstone. In him the whole building is joined together and rises to become a holy temple in the Lord. And in him you too are being built together to become a dwelling in which God lives by his Spirit.*
>
> —Ephesians 2:11–22 [emphasis mine]

This is not a short, obscure, difficult passage of Scripture to understand. It is boldly, blatantly, and methodically teaching that the Gentile church in Ephesus is part of Israel. You must refuse to believe in the efficacy of the blood of Christ in order to believe that the Gentile church in Ephesus is excluded from citizenship in Israel. To put it succinctly in one verse:

*This mystery is that through the gospel the Gentiles are heirs together with Israel, members together of one body and sharers together in the promise in Christ Jesus.*

—Ephesians 3:6

The two people / two purposes theory demeans and diminishes the work Jesus did on the cross. It is a heresy that denies that Jesus accomplished on the cross what the Bible says he accomplished—namely, the conjoining of two groups of people. Not only is the church in Ephesus saved by the blood of Jesus, but the church at large also is saved by the blood of Jesus, and by that blood, we are included as citizens of Israel. Progressive dispensationalists admit these verses (Eph. 2 and 3) teach that the promises made to Israel now belong to Gentiles who are in Christ, yet they still try to salvage the distinction between Jew and Gentile by saying that the Gentile Christians are only with Israel but not Israel.[34]

---

[34] See, for example, Carl B. Hoch Jr., "The New Man of Ephesians 2" in *Dispensationalism, Israel and the Church*, eds. Craig Blaising and Darrell Bock (Grand Rapids: Zondervan, 1992), 98–126. Hoch's argument does not pay attention to the plain, normal interpretation of the text, but rather it relies on the number of aorist verbs contrasted with the number of present tense verbs, as though this ratio nullifies the plain meaning of the text that says the two groups have become one in Christ.

So then, let us return to the question: When the Bible says, **"All Israel will be saved" (Rom 11:26)**, who is Israel? Let us answer the negative: Who is not Israel?

*A man is not a Jew if he is only one outwardly, nor is circumcision merely outward and physical. No, a man is a Jew if he is one inwardly; and circumcision is circumcision of the heart, by the Spirit, not by the written code. Such a man's praise is not from men, but from God.*
—Romans 2:28–29

The man who is descended from Abraham but does not have the faith of Abraham is not Israel. There are many such passages that refute the importance of being a literal descendant of Abraham: **Matthew 3:7–10, 12:46–49, 15:13; Mark 12:1–9; John 3:3, 8:39–47; Philippians 3:1–11; and Romans 9:6–8.** According to these verses of Scripture, there is no guarantee for the literal descendants of Abraham. Literal descendants of Israel, who are not inwardly circumcised, are not Israel. Inward circumcision is accomplished by the Spirit when a person repents and turns to the Savior (**Lev. 26:41; Deut. 10:16, 30:6; Jer. 9:25, 29:45; Rom. 2:29**). When dispensationalists insist that every biological descendant of Israel will be saved, they ignore these verses. According to Scripture, the church is the body of Christ, the bride of Christ, and the church is Israel, the seed of Abraham (the seed of Abraham would be the ancient equivalent of DNA):

*You are all sons of God through faith in Christ Jesus, for all of you*
*who were baptized into Christ have clothed yourselves with Christ.*
*There is neither Jew nor Greek, slave nor free, male nor female, for you*
*are all one in Christ Jesus.*
*If you belong to Christ, then you are Abraham's seed,*
*and heirs according to the promise.*

—Galatians 3:26–29

This church in Galatia is the seed of Abraham and is heir to the promises given to Abraham.[35] Dispensationalists teach that the promises made to Israel must be fulfilled with Israel. As shown above, the Bible considers the church to be the true Israel.

*Neither circumcision nor uncircumcision means anything; what*
*counts is a new creation. Peace and mercy to all who follow this rule,*
*even to the Israel of God.*

—Galatians 6:15–16

The Bible also teaches that through Jesus, the church inherits the promises of God regardless of when those promises were made. To the church in Corinth, the Bible says:

*No matter how many promises God has made,*
*they are "Yes" in Christ.*

—2 Corinthians 1:20

---

[35] Marten Woudstra, "Israel and the Church: A Case for Continuity," in *Continuity and Discontinuity*, ed. John Feinberg (Wheaton: Crossway, 1988), 235.

Dispensationalism tries to distinguish between heavenly and earthly promises, which the church may or may not receive, but Poythress says, "One cannot neatly divide between heavenly and earthly blessing because there is only one Christ, and we receive the whole Christ."[36] All promises made to Israel must be yielded to the church. Since the church received the fullness of Christ, then the promises to Israel are fully inherited by the church, both physical and spiritual![37] The fullness of the inheritance is indicated by the Scripture found in Colossians:

*For in Christ all the fullness of the Deity lives in bodily form and you have been given fullness in Christ, who is the head over every power and authority.*
—Colossians 2:9–10

"All Israel" refers to the church, which consists of both Jews and Gentiles. If the Gentile who believes in Jesus as the Messiah were left out, then all Israel would not be saved. If the Jew who believes in Jesus as the Messiah were left out, then all Israel would not be saved. This is why **Romans 11:26** says, "And thus all Israel will be saved" instead of "and then all Israel will be saved." All Israel is saved because the full number of Gentile believers have been included (see **Rom. 11:25**).[38]

---

[36] Poythress, 69.
[37] *Revelation: One Apocalypse, 7 Unveilings*, 58. Craig Blaising says some progressive dispensationalists will allow the church to receive the promises (covenant) from God to Abraham but not the Davidic covenant. Craig Blaising, "Development of Dispensationalism by Contemporary Dispensationalists," *Bibliotheca Sacra* (1988): 277–8. This illustrates what I said in chapter one—that trying to define dispensationalism is like hitting a moving target.
[38] Hoekema, 144.

Benjamin Merkle makes this same point by appealing to the words of James found in **Acts 15:16–17**. In these verses, James quotes **Amos 9:11–12**, which predicts the rebuilding of the house of David, but James equates this with the inclusion of the Gentiles: "He sees the salvation of Gentiles as part of the restoration processes of Israel. The house of David is being rebuilt—not just out of physical Jews but also out of spiritual Jews."[39]

**Supersessionism or Replacement Theology**

The doctrine that asserts that the church fully receives the promises made to Israel is known as supersessionism and is commonly labeled "replacement theology" by its opponents. This doctrine is not only found in Galatians and Ephesians, but supersessionism is also the entire point of the book of Hebrews. It is woven through the book so thoroughly that if you extracted it, very little would be left of Hebrews.

The author of Hebrews repeatedly brings up an OT type that is replaced by the NT archetype.[40] First, the OT type of messenger (angels) is superseded by the NT archetype messenger Jesus (**Heb. 1–2**). The OT type of prophet (Moses) is superseded by the NT archetype prophet Jesus (**Heb. 3**). The OT type of Sabbath is superseded by the NT archetype of rest found in Jesus (**Heb. 4**). The OT type of high priest is superseded by the NT archetype high priest, who is Jesus (**Heb. 4–5**). Every type that God implanted in the OT was fulfilled with a greater,

---

[39] Benjamin Merkle, "Old Testament Restoration Prophecies Regarding the Nation of Israel: Literal or Symbolic," *Southern Baptist Journal of Theology: Understanding and Applying Eschatology* 14, no. 1, (Spring 2010): 19.

[40] Bruce Waltke defines typology (type and archetype) as "prefigurations in the OT [type] of truths fully revealed in the NT [archetype]." Bruce Waltke, "Kingdom Promises as Spiritual," in *Continuity and Discontinuity*, ed. John Feinberg (Wheaton: Crossway, 1988), 276.

perfect archetype in the NT. The NT has a greater priesthood than the Levitical priesthood (**Heb. 7**), greater covenant (**Heb. 8**), greater tabernacle (**Heb. 9**), greater blood (**Heb. 9**), greater sacrifice (**Heb. 10**), and greater Jerusalem (**Heb. 12**).

The book of Hebrews speaks of the OT as a copy, shadow, or pattern (**Heb. 8:5, 10:1**). Jesus is not the copy, the shadow, or the pattern but the fulfillment of what was foreshadowed. He is greater than the OT pattern. The Jewish believers who are addressed in the book of Hebrews should not return to Judaism out of fear of persecution. How foolish to return to the promise of the coming Messiah when the Messiah has come.

Bruce Waltke says, "Not one clear NT passage mentions the restoration of Israel as a political nation or predicts an earthly reign of Christ before his final appearing. None depicts the consummate glory of Christ as an earthly king ruling over the restored nation of Israel. The Spirit's silence is deafening."[41]

NT days are not a parenthetical age waiting for God to return to a prior dispensational age. If you had a paper pattern for a suit, and the best tailor made you a suit from the finest material available, following the pattern, would you leave the tailor shop wearing the suit or wearing the paper pattern? Dispensationalists are eager for the paper pattern to be worn when the suit has already been made.

Merkle makes the same point when he says, "The OT presents a vivid and detailed picture of Israel's future restoration. We have seen, however, that these descriptions are not meant to be taken literally. Although it is true that these predictions and promises have a real meaning, the meaning is not expressed *in* the actual language, but *through* the actual language. By insisting on a literal interpretation, we are in danger of

---

[41] Waltke, 273.

forcing the text to mean something that God did not intend. The new covenant is characterized by the inner transformation of a person. This core was found in the old covenant but it was wrapped in an external shell. Now that the external shell has been shed, is it really God's plan to reinstitute it?"[42] When a Jewish person trusts in Jesus for salvation, that new wine needs to go into a new wineskin.

**Fulfillment versus Postponement**
Jesus said, **"Do not think that I have come to abolish the Law or the Prophets; I have not come to abolish them but to fulfill them"** (**Matt. 5:17**). Did Jesus fail to fulfill the OT promises? Was his First Coming a failure? No! Jesus did not postpone the promises of the OT; he fulfilled them. The NT days are not the result of a failed dispensation. The church is not a postponement of what God plans to do with his people. The church is a fulfillment of God's intention for his people.

The sevenfold promise made to Abraham (**Gen. 12:2–3**) is fulfilled in Christ. The promise made to David (**2 Sam. 7:16**) is fulfilled in Christ. The purpose of Israel's election is fulfilled in Christ: the blessing for all nations has come through Jesus, who is the quintessential Son of Abraham, the quintessential Son of Israel, the quintessential Son of David. True Zionism is found in the life of Christ, not the exaltation of ethnic Israel or a city in the Middle East. Kim Riddlebarger says, "The New Testament writers claimed that Jesus was the true Israel of God and the fulfillment of Old Testament prophecies. So what remains of the dispensationalists' case that these prophecies will yet be fulfilled in a future millennium? They vanish in Jesus Christ, who has fulfilled them."[43]

---

[42] Benjamin Merkle, "Old Testament Restoration Prophecies regarding the Nation of Israel: Literal or Symbolic," *Southern Baptist Journal of Theology: Understanding and Applying Eschatology* 14, no. 1, (Spring 2010): 22.
[43] Riddlebarger, 85.

## Conclusion

There is no need for the invention of the seven-year tribulation when Israel will be saved in the absence of the church. To be certain, tribulation will come, but anyone who is literally descended from Israel and wishes to be saved must come to faith in Jesus, the Jewish Messiah, and they must do so today. That person will be grafted into the same olive tree as the church. There is no need for the invention of the two people / two purposes theory, and there is no second olive tree to accommodate such a doctrine. The two people / two purposes theory is an invention that demeans and diminishes the unity accomplished by Jesus upon the cross.

"Our Lord clearly taught that when the Jews rejected him, God set aside national Israel as the distinctive, favored expression of his kingdom (Matt. 8:1–12; 21:43). Though many Jews are yet to be saved and become part of the one true people of God in Christ, the new man, God will never set them either apart from or above saved Gentiles in Christ or restore to them the 'weak and beggarly' shadows of the Old Testament."[44]

---

[44] Bruce Waltke, "A Response," in *Dispensationalism, Israel and the Church*, eds. Craig Blaising and Darrell Bock (Grand Rapids: Zondervan, 1992), 354.

# CHAPTER FIVE

## Dispensational Doctrine: The Parousia, Stage Two—"The Millennial Kingdom"

The reign of Jesus for one thousand years is mentioned only in Revelation 20. This reign is known as the millennial kingdom even though the phrase "millennial kingdom" does not appear anywhere in Scripture. It should not come as a surprise that the number one thousand is only used in Revelation to describe the kingdom of God, for Revelation is the only apocalyptic book in the NT, and this genre makes frequent use of symbolic numbers.

Before looking at the text, let us look at two rules of interpretation which are incorrectly taught by dispensationalists. First, dispensationalists teach that the student of the Bible should have one method of interpretation for all of Scripture. Second, dispensationalists say the literal interpretation is superior to the spiritual interpretation.[45] These two rules are horribly incorrect.

Despite what dispensationalists say, you should not have one method of interpretation. You could not even read a newspaper with one method of interpretation, much less the Bible. The front page of a newspaper is interpreted differently than the sports page, which is read differently than the classified ads. Your brain is so adept at switching methods of interpretation that you probably do not notice when it happens.

Every passage of Scripture has a literary genre. Every literary genre has its own rules of interpretation. There are narratives, poems, hymns, proverbs, parables, and many other genres found in the Bible. If you do not take the genre into account, your interpretation will be sure to take Scripture out of context. Alan Bandy says, "Meaning is intrinsically bound up in genre. The ensuing implication is that genre provides a context assigned by the author to communicate meaning…The book of Revelation belongs to the apocalyptic/prophetic genre and the apocalyptic genre by definition is highly symbolic. It is not intended to be interpreted in a literal manner."[46]

Despite what dispensationalists say, the literal interpretation of Scripture is not superior to the spiritual interpretation. The OT salvation narrative is literal. In the OT, the people of God were saved from bondage in Egypt by the blood of a lamb. In the NT, Jesus came to set the captives free, but his blood saved the people of God from spiritual bondage. A literal interpretation of "Jesus setting the captives free" is vastly inferior to the spiritual interpretation.

---

[45] See, for example, John McArthur, "Why Every Calvinist Should Be a Premillennialist, Part 6 (Selected Scriptures)," Grace to You, March 30, 2017, YouTube video, 1:02:50. Confer with *Revelation: One Apocalypse, 7 Unveilings*, 25.

[46] Alan Bandy, "The Hermeneutics of Symbolism: How to Interpret the Symbols of John's Apocalypse," *Southern Baptist Journal of Theology* 14, no. 1 (Spring 2010): 48.

Bruce Waltke says, "A detailed exegesis of Revelation 20:1–10 is a must. Revised [progressive] dispensationalists assume the Millennium as the 'not-yet' stage of the kingdom, but none validates it from the New Testament. This hypothetical assumption...enables them to maintain their cherished, literalistic interpretation of Israel's covenants and prophecies."[47]

Let us take a look at the one passage of Scripture, which mentions the one-thousand-year kingdom:

*And I saw an angel coming down out of heaven, having the key to the Abyss and holding in his hand a great chain. He seized the dragon, that ancient serpent, who is the devil, or Satan, and <u>bound him for a thousand years</u>. He threw him into the Abyss, and locked and sealed it over him, <u>to keep him from deceiving the nations anymore until the thousand years were ended</u>. After that he must be set free for a short time.*
*I saw thrones on which were seated those who had been given authority to judge. And I saw the souls of those who had been beheaded because of their testimony for Jesus and because of the word of God. They had not worshiped the beast or his image and had not received his mark on their foreheads or their hands. <u>They came to life and reigned with Christ a thousand years</u>. (The rest of the dead did not come to life until the thousand years were ended.) This is the first resurrection. Blessed and holy are those who have part in the first resurrection. The second death has no power over them, but they will be priests of God and of Christ and will reign with him for a thousand years.*
—Revelation 20:1–6 [emphasis mine]

[47] Bruce Waltke, "A Response," in *Dispensationalism, Israel and the Church*, ed. Craig Blaising and Darrell Bock (Grand Rapids: Zondervan, 1992), 353. While I do not offer a detailed exegesis, I will cover the pertinent verses and salient points.

Matthew and Luke often mention either the kingdom of God or the kingdom of heaven, and it should not be a foregone conclusion that this kingdom is distinct from the millennial kingdom. Matthew and Luke are not apocalyptic, but Revelation is. However, for the sake of argument, we could limit our discussion to an exegesis of **Revelation 20**. The dispensational exegesis argues that this millennial kingdom is in the future, and their argument rests upon two assertions that are easily disproven. First, they assert that since chapter 20 comes after chapter 19, then the millennial kingdom must come after Jesus's Second Coming, which is clearly described in Revelation 19. Second, they assert that Satan causes trouble, proving that he has not yet been bound and that binding precedes the millennial kingdom.

The first piece of evidence is based on the false assumption that the chapters of Revelation must proceed in a sequential or chronological order.[48] The chapters of Revelation do not proceed in chronological order; they recapitulate. The most obvious recapitulation is between chapters 11 and 12; there are at least seven major recapitulations in the book.[49] In regard to the millennium, the pertinent question is whether or not there is a recapitulation between chapter 19 and chapter 20. Chapter 19 unequivocally describes the Second Coming of Jesus, and chapter 20 begins with the binding of Satan, which leads into the millennial kingdom.[50]

---

[48] One progressive dispensationalist describes chapters 19 and 20 as sequential and argues this must be so because the binding of Satan speaks of "a complete cessation of the devil's influence in the world." Craig Blaising, "The Kingdom that Comes with Jesus: Premillennialism and the Harmony of Scripture," *Southern Baptist Journal of Theology: Understanding and Applying Eschatology* 14, no. 1, (Spring 2010): 7–8.

[49] For further discussion, see *Revelation: One Apocalypse, 7 Unveilings*, 71–73.

[50] For further discussion, see *Revelation: One Apocalypse, 7 Unveilings*, 61–64, 200–203.

In **Revelation 20:1–3**, Satan is bound and cast into the abyss. If the binding of Satan is a future event, then the millennial kingdom is a future event and cannot be attributed to Jesus's First Coming. Dispensationalists lean heavily upon the apocalyptic symbols in **Revelation 20:1** to interpret the binding of Satan in such a way that Satan could do no harm while bound, and thus, the binding could not yet have occurred since Satan still causes trouble.[51]

Apocalyptic symbols can be difficult to interpret, and sometimes we can only agree to disagree. This is not one of those times. When John, writing under the influence of the Holy Spirit, interprets the apocalyptic symbols, we are obligated to adopt his interpretation. John interprets these apocalyptic symbols by explicitly telling us that the binding of Satan means he cannot deceive the nations (**Rev 20:3**). Any interpretation beyond this exceeds the interpretation given by John.[52]

This binding of Satan is not an absolute binding, which would keep Satan from causing any trouble. **Revelation 20:3** describes it as the type of binding that is sufficient to allow the Gospel to be presented and to be received by people all over the world. This binding keeps Satan from deceiving the nations. If Satan cannot deceive the nations, then evangelism is possible; the Great Commission is possible. The explosive growth of the church found in the book of Acts is possible.

John is not only explicit when he interprets the meaning of the binding of Satan, but he also explicitly interprets the meaning of the

---

[51] According to John F. Walvoord, "The obvious teaching of the passage is that the action is so designed as to render Satan inactive. The intention is not to represent Satan as merely restricted but as rendered completely inactive." *The Revelation of Jesus Christ*, 291.

[52] Alan Bandy's second rule for interpreting symbols in Revelation is to "look for interpretation of those symbols within the vision." In other words, to embrace the interpretation given by John. "The Hermeneutics of Symbolism: How to Interpret the Symbols of John's Apocalypse," *Southern Baptist Journal of Theology* 14, no. 1 (Spring 2010): 50.

loosing of Satan. Satan will be able to deceive the nations when he is loosed. The binding and loosing of Satan are explicitly related to Satan's inability or ability to deceive the nations.

*When the thousand years are over, Satan will be released from his prison and will go out to deceive the nations in the four corners of the earth.*

**—Revelation 20:7–8a**

In **Matthew 12** Jesus speaks of the binding of Satan after healing a demon-possessed man. Satan is the strong man who must be bound so that Jesus can rob the house of Satan. Jesus clearly believes that the binding of Satan was instrumental in the miraculous healing. It is obvious from the Gospels that Jesus robbed the house of Satan repeatedly, a clear indication that Satan has been bound. It is obvious from the book of Acts that the message of salvation went out to the nations like never before.

It is true that Satan can still cause problems, but that does not prove that he has not been bound in such a way that he is hindered from deceiving the nations. The International Mission Board of the Southern Baptist Convention sends missionaries all over the world because we believe that Satan has been bound in the manner described in **Revelation 20:3**.

If Satan has not been bound in this manner, how were you able to understand the Gospel message? Why were you not deceived by Satan? Why would Jesus command his disciples to go and make disciples of all nations if Satan has the power to deceive all nations?

**Conclusion**

The binding of Satan, as described in Revelation 20, took place during the First Coming of Jesus. Since Revelation 19 describes the Second Coming of Jesus, then the binding of Satan is a literary marker noting a recapitulation. Revelation 20 does not follow Revelation 19 chronologically.

The millennial kingdom began with the First Coming of Jesus during the temporal reign of the Roman Empire, just as the prophet Daniel foretold. It will be handed over to the Father upon the Second Coming of Jesus.

The kingdom of God is only described as the one-thousand-year reign of Christ in the Apocalypse, but the kingdom of heaven / kingdom of God speaks of the kingdom where Jesus reigns. He is seated already at the right hand of the Father (**Heb. 1:3; Acts 2:33**), and he is crowned already with glory and honor (**Heb. 2:9**). The kingdom will grow, just as Daniel foretold (**Daniel 2:35**). King Jesus is not without a kingdom.

# CHAPTER SIX

## Dispensational Doctrine:
## The Temple Restored

Dispensationalism teaches that the temple in Jerusalem will be rebuilt and that sacrifices will be offered at the altar in memory of the sacrifice made by Jesus.[53] There are at least two serious problems with this dispensational assertion. Jesus gave us the Lord's Supper as a memorial for his offering (**1 Cor. 11:24–25**). What authority do dispensationalists have to change this memorial? Dispensational doctrine does not supersede the Word of God.

The more egregious aspect of this assertion is that it compels us to consider Jesus to be a false prophet. In **Mark 11**, Jesus sees a fig tree in leaf, so, from a distance, one might expect there to be figs, but it was not the season for figs. Jesus curses the fig tree, saying, **"May no one ever eat fruit from you again" (Mark 11:14)**. Jesus goes from the fig tree to the temple and clears out the money changers. In **Mark 13**, he

---

[53] John F. Walvoord, *The Millennial Kingdom* (Grand Rapids: Zondervan, 1959), 309–315.

tells his disciples of the coming destruction of the temple in Jerusalem. The fig tree was an object lesson on the way to the temple.[54] Just as the fig tree looked fruitful with its leaves, the temple looked glorious in all its golden splendor, yet the temple was unfruitful.

Is Jesus a false prophet? When Jesus said, "May no one ever eat fruit from you again," was he mistaken? I have no expectation of the restoration of the temple in Jerusalem. In the unlikely event that the temple in Jerusalem is restored, I am sure it will not produce the kind of fruit dispensationalists predict. It will not be used by anyone to draw near to God in worship. No one will ever eat of its fruit again. That much has been prophesied by Jesus, but dispensationalists say worshippers will offer sacrifices there in memory of Jesus's sacrifice. Because this false assertion compels us to consider Jesus to be a false prophet, the term *heresy* is appropriate for this dispensational doctrine.

Hebrews 8 also clearly refutes any notion of a future for the temple in Jerusalem. The leading spokesman of historic premillennialism and noted critic of dispensationalism, George Eldon Ladd, has worded the argument excellently:

"Any idea of a restoration of the Old Testament sacrificial systems, whether memorial or otherwise, stands in direct opposition to Hebrews 8:13, which unambiguously affirms that the Old Testament cult is both obsolete and about to pass away. Therefore Hebrews 8:8–13 refutes dispensational theology at two points: It applies a prophecy to the Christian church which in its Old Testament setting referred to Israel, and it affirms that the new covenant in Christ has displaced the Old Testament cult which is therefore doomed to pass away."[55]

---

[54] Köstenberger calls it an enacted parable and part of a "Marcan sandwich," which makes it an unmistakable reference to the temple and by extension, Israel, p. 111.

[55] George Eldon Ladd, "Historic Premillennialism" in *The Meaning of the Millennium: Four Views*, ed. Robert G. Clouse (Downers Grove: InterVarsity Press, 1977), 26–27.

OT scholar Richard Hess argues from the book of Ezekiel that the restoration of the temple must be literal and not spiritual. He argues that everyone who received the prophecy from Ezekiel on down, would have interpreted the prophecy in a literal fashion, which necessitates a "brick-and-mortar" building. Hess concludes, "If the words of the prophet are to be realistically fulfilled, as the early generations of readers of, and listeners to, the prophet certainly expected, then in its canonical context, it must take place sometime in the future but before the final appearance of the new heaven and the new earth."[56]

For the sake of argument, let us assume Hess is correct in saying *they* believed the prophecy should be fulfilled literally, not spiritually. Have *they* ever been wrong? Have *they* ever misunderstood God's Word? When God the Son said, **"Watch out for the yeast of the Pharisees,"** the disciples thought he said that because they had no bread (**Mark 8:15–16**), but they were wrong. They misinterpreted what God said. Jesus said to Peter, **"If I want him to remain alive until I return, what is that to you?"** (**John 21:22**). The disciples concluded that John would not die. *They* were wrong; *they* misinterpreted what God said.

Instead of relying on people who are fallible for an interpretation of Scripture, which predicts the rebuilding of the temple, we can rely on someone who is infallible.

---

[56] Richard S. Hess, "The Future Written in the Past," in *A Case for Historic Premillennialism: An Alternative to "Left Behind" Eschatology*, ed. Craig L. Blomberg and Sung Wook Chung (Grand Rapids: Baker Academic, 2009), 34.

*Jesus answered them, "Destroy this temple, and I will raise it again in three days." The Jews replied, "It has taken forty-six years to build this temple, and you are going to raise it in three days?" But the temple he had spoken of was his body. After he was raised from the dead, his disciples recalled what he had said. Then they believed the Scripture and the words that Jesus had spoken.*

—John 2:19–22

Hess admits he cannot reconcile his literal interpretation with these verses from **John 2**.[57] If Jesus equates his body with the temple, and the destruction of the Jerusalem temple was the penalty for rejecting Jesus, then how would the construction of a new temple honor God? Would it not be idolatry to choose a brick-and-mortar temple over the body of Christ? Why would anyone want a brick-and-mortar building for a temple when we have the body of Christ? The brick-and-mortar temple cannot accomplish for you what the body of Christ can accomplish. The body of Christ can make you righteous and acceptable before Holy God. Brick and mortar cannot do this.

**Conclusion**

The temple Jesus had spoken of was his body. Continuing with the metaphor, the church is the body of Christ. The church is the temple. The Lord's Supper is the memorial of his sacrifice. This has been established by the Word of God, and we cannot improve upon this. We alter it at our own peril. There is no need to rebuild a physical temple structure in Jerusalem. Such a temple would not produce fruit; it would only lead people away from the truth.

---

[57] Ibid., 35.

# CHAPTER SEVEN

## Conclusion

The First Coming of Jesus was not a failure. Jesus established the exact kingdom that he intended to establish. Jesus joined together Jewish and Gentile believers into one body, which is the church, the body of Christ, the temple. Jesus's Second Coming will not be in two stages: **"Christ was sacrificed once to take away the sins of many people; and he will appear a second time, not to bear sin, but to bring salvation to those who are waiting for him" (Heb. 9:28).** There is no third coming; you must be prepared for the Second Coming.

Doctrine does not supersede Scripture. Every doctrine that is contrived by man is subject to the scrutiny of Scripture. Scripture is the infallible, inerrant Word of God. Doctrines contrived by man do not enjoy such a moniker.

When we add something to the Bible (a parenthetical age or temple sacrifices, for example), we do not become more biblical. Jesus criticized the religious leaders for adding Corban to the Scriptures (see **Mark 7**). He explained to them that this addition had the effect of nullifying a verse of Scipture: **"Honor your father and your mother" (Mark 7:10)**. When we try to add to the Bible, the unintended consequence is that we delete from the Bible. We do not become more biblical but less biblical.

What's wrong with dispensational eschatology? It is not biblical. Dispensationalism has enjoyed great marketing. Many Christians teach from the Left Behind series as though it is an addendum to Scripture. Dispensational doctrine does not stand up to the scrutiny of Scripture. It should be left behind.

**Stephen's Eschatology:**

1. The history of salvation begins with God's promise after sin that created the need for a Savior: the seed of the woman (Eve) will crush the serpent's head. Contrary to dispensationalism, this promise revealed the plan of salvation (not one of seven plans), which does not change from one age to another. With further illumination of this revelation, we find that the Savior will be born of Shem, Abraham, Isaac, Jacob, Judah, and David. Eventually, the angel of the Lord provides illumination to reveal that the Savior is born of the Virgin Mary.[58]

2. What God did for his OT saints (Israel) and through them was a pattern in the physical realm, foreshadowing what he would do in the spiritual realm through Jesus. What God does for his people in the spiritual realm is greater than the shadow, which he did in the physical realm. For example, God saved Israel from physical bondage, slavery in Egypt, through the blood of a physical lamb. In the NT, God saves from spiritual bondage, slavery to sin through the blood of the Lamb, Jesus Christ.

---

[58] *Revelation: One Apocalypse, 7 Unveilings*, 66.

3. When Jesus voluntarily died on the cross and rose from the grave, he fulfilled the OT law and crushed the power of sin. He lived a sinless life as required by the OT law; therefore, death had no claim upon him. He died a death required by the OT law for our sins. He bound Satan in such a way that people might receive the Gospel.

4. Jesus inaugurated the millennial kingdom. The millennium is a lengthy period of time that is known only to the Father, but this kingdom is not eternal in the sense that it will be transformed at the time of the Second Coming. This kingdom is not about territory and taxes; such a kingdom would be insufficient for the King of kings. The kingdom of God consists of the eternal souls of the faithful. OT saints lived by faith, believing the Savior would come and bring salvation. NT saints live by faith, believing the Messiah has come. The OT pattern is obsolete—not because it failed but because it has been fulfilled.

5. The kingdom is growing, just as Daniel foretold (there are Christians around the globe), but the wheat and the chaff grow together. Tribulations and antichrists are to be expected, but every earthly kingdom and every cruel dictator will one day be crushed. The church will endure. The souls of those who die in the Lord will go to heaven and be with Jesus. Their bodies will sleep in the grave.

6. At the end of time, on the day appointed by the Father, Jesus will return. Just prior to Jesus's return, Satan will be loosed to deceive the nations. Perhaps the loosing of Satan will be for a period of seven days; perhaps it will be for three and one-half years. When Satan is loosed, everyone's eternal destiny shall be fixed, just as it was in the days of Noah when God closed the door to the ark.

7. Jesus shall return in triumph and glory. Satan will be cast into hell as a prisoner, not a ruler. The chaff (unsaved) will be separated from the wheat (saved) and collected for the fire. Then saints who are alive will rise in the air to meet Jesus, being transformed (receiving glorified bodies) in the twinkling of an eye. These saints will not precede the saints who have gone before them. The saints in heaven will also receive their glorified bodies.

8. The groom (Jesus) will present the bride to the Father: the millennial kingdom is handed to over to the Father, and it becomes the eternal kingdom.

9. This eternal kingdom exists in the new heaven and new earth. The meek shall inherit the earth.

# ANNOTATED BIBLIOGRAPHY

Archer, Gleason L., Jr., ed. *Three Views on the Rapture, Pre-, Mid-, or Post-Tribulation*. Grand Rapids: Zondervan, 1984. **Counterpoint Book**

Beale, G. K. The Book of Revelation, A Commentary on the Greek Text. Grand Rapids: Eerdmans. 1999. **Idealist Method Amillennialism**

Beale, G. K., and D. A. Carson, eds. *Commentary on the New Testament Use of the Old Testament*. Grand Rapids: Baker Academic, 2007.

Blaising, Craig A., and Darrell L. Bock, eds. *Dispensationalism, Israel and the Church: The Search for Definition*. Grand Rapids: Zondervan, 1992. **Progressive Dispensationalism**

Blomberg, Craig L., and Sung Wook Chung, eds. *A Case for Historic Premillennialism: An Alternative to "Left Behind" Eschatology.* Grand Rapids: Baker Academic, 2009. **Futurist Method Posttribulational Premillennialism**

Collins, John J. *Daniel with an Introduction to Apocalyptic Literature*. FOTL. Grand Rapids: Eerdmans, 1984. **Late Date,** *Ex Eventu* **Prophecy**

Clouse, Robert, ed. *The Meaning of the Millennium: Four Views*. Downers Grove: InterVarsity Press, 1977. **Counterpoint Book**

Davis, Dale Ralph. *The Message of Daniel, His Kingdom Cannot Fail.* The Bible Speaks Today. Downers Grove: IVP Academic, 2013. **Early Date, Reformed**

Duguid, Iain M. *Daniel.* Reformed Expository Commentary. Phillipsburg, NJ: P&R Publishing, 2008. **Early Date, Reformed**

Feinberg, John S., ed. *Continuity and Discontinuity, Perspectives on the Relationship Between the Old and New Testaments, Essays in Honor of S. Lewis Johnson, Jr.* Wheaton: Crossway, 1988. **Counterpoint Book**

Gentry, Kenneth L., Jr. *Before Jerusalem Fell, Dating the Book of Revelation.* 3rd ed. Fountain Inn, SC: Victorious Hope Publishing, 1998. **Partial Preterism Method Postmillennialism**

Goldingay, John. *Daniel.* WBC. Dallas: Word Books, 1989. **Late Date, *Ex Eventu* Prophecy**

Hendriksen, William. *More Than Conquerors, An Interpretation of Revelation.* Grand Rapids: Baker Books, 1967. **Idealist Method Amillennialism**

Hobbs, Herschel H. *The Cosmic Drama.* Waco: Word Books, 1971. **Historical Background Method Amillennialism**

Hoekema, Anthony A. *The Bible and the Future.* Grand Rapids: Eerdmans, 1979. **Idealist Method Amillennialism**

House, Paul R. *Daniel, An Introduction and Commentary.* TOTC. Downers Grove: IVP Academic, 2018. **Early Date, Reformed**

Johnson, Dennis. *Triumph of the Lamb: A Commentary on Revelation.* Philipsburg, NJ: P&R Publishing, 2001. **Idealist Method Amillennialism**

Köstenberger, Andreas, Alexander Stewart, and Apollo Makara. *Jesus and the Future: Understanding What He Taught about the End Times.* Bellingham, WA: Lexham Press, 2017. **Exegesis of the Mount of Olives Discourse**

Ladd, George E. *A Commentary on the Revelation of John.* Grand Rapids: Eerdmans, 1972. **Futurist Method Posttribulational Premillennialism**

_____. *The Blessed Hope.* Grand Rapids: Eerdmans, 1956. **Futurist Method Posttribulational Premillennialism**

Miller, Stephen R. *Daniel.* NAC. Nashville: Broadman & Holman, 1994. **Progressive Dispensationalism, Early Date**

Mounce, Robert H. *The Book of Revelation.* NICNT. Grand Rapids: Eerdmans, 1977. **Futurist Method Posttribulational Premillennialism**

Osborne, Grant R. *Revelation.* BECNT. Grand Rapids: Baker Academic, 2002. **Futurist Method Posttribulational Premillennialism**

Pate, C. Marvin, ed. *Four Views on the Book of Revelation.* Grand Rapids: Zondervan, 1998. **Counterpoint Book**

Patterson, Paige. *Revelation.* NAC. Nashville: B&H, 2012. **Futurist Method Pretribulational Premillennialism**

Poythress, Vern Sheridan. *Understanding Dispensationalists.* 2d ed. Phillipsburg, NJ: P&R, 1994. **Apologetic response to dispensationalism**

Riddlebarger, Kim. *A Case for Amillennialism, Understanding the End Times.* Expanded Edition. Grand Rapids: Baker Books, 2003, 2013. **Amillennialism**

Russell, James Stuart. *The Parousia, A General Inquiry into the Doctrine of Our Lord's Second Coming.* Hampshire, 1887. Reprint, UK: Bierton Strict and Particular Baptist, 1983. **Full Preterist Method Postmillennialism**

Russell, D. S. *The Method & Message of Jewish Apocalyptic, 200 BC–AD 100.* Philadelphia: Westminster Press, 1964. **Comprehensive guide to Jewish Apocalyptic Writings**

Ryrie, Charles C. *Dispensationalism* Today. Chicago: Moody, 1965. **Classic Dispensationalism**

Smalley, Stephen S. *The Revelation to John, A Commentary on the Greek Text of the Apocalypse.* Downers Grover: InterVarsity Press, 2005. **Idealist Method Amillennialism**

Sprinkle, Joe. *Daniel*. Evangelical Biblical Theology Commentary. Bellingham, WA: Lexham Press, 2020. **Early Date, Reformed**

Sproul, R. C. *The Last Days According to Jesus*. Grand Rapids: Baker Books, 1998. **Partial Preterism Method Postmillennialism**

Summers, Ray. *Worthy Is the Lamb: Interpreting Revelation in Its Historical Background*. Nashville: Broadman and Holman, 1951. **Historical Background Method Amillennialism**

Tanner, J. Paul. *Daniel*. Evangelical Exegetical Commentary. Bellingham, WA: Lexham Press, 2020. **Progressive Dispensationalism, Early Date**

Thomas, Robert. *Revelation 1–7: An Exegetical Commentary*. Chicago: Moody, 1995. **Futurist Method Dispensational Premillennialism**

_____. *Revelation 8–22: An Exegetical Commentary*. Chicago: Moody, 1995. **Futurist Method Dispensational Premillennialist**

Tsarfati, Amir. *The Last Hour: An Israeli Insider Looks at the End Times*. Minneapolis: Chosen, 2018. **Futurist Method Dispensational Premillennialism**

Vipperman, Stephen. *Revelation: One Apocalypse, 7 Unveilings.* Charleston, SC: Palmetto Publishing, 2021. **Historical Background Method Amillennialism**

Walvoord, John F. *Daniel*. Revised and edited by Charles H. Dyer and Philip E. Rawley. Chicago: Moody, 2012. **Classic Dispensationalism, Early Date**

_____. *The Millennial Kingdom*. Grand Rapids: Zondervan, 1959. **Futurist Method Dispensational Premillennialism**

_____. *The Rapture Question*. Grand Rapids: Zondervan, 1957. **Futurist Method Dispensational Premillennialism**

_____. *The Revelation of Jesus Christ*. Chicago: Moody, 1966. **Futurist Method Dispensational Premillennialism**

Wilson, Douglas. *When the Man Comes Around*. Moscow, ID: Canon Press, 2019. **Partial Preterism Method Postmillennialism**

# UNBLOCKING
# BLOCKCHAIN

# UNBLOCKING BLOCKCHAIN

## ENABLING YOUR DIGITAL FUTURE

### RAHUL PRAKASH

NEW DEGREE PRESS

UNBLOCKING BLOCKCHAIN
*Enabling Your Digital Future*

ISBN      978-1-63676-828-1  *Paperback*
             978-1-63730-214-9  *Kindle Ebook*
             978-1-63730-272-9  *Ebook*

*For Anubha, who makes it ALL possible*

# CONTENTS

———

# INTRODUCTION

___

Imagine that you wanted to sell counterfeit pharmaceuticals. How would you do it? You could start by manufacturing pills that look like brand-name pills, with the same coloration, shape, and markings. Because it is a counterfeiting operation, there is no need to spend much money on the actual ingredients to manufacture the medicine. You need to convince a buyer that nothing is amiss with your pills. Of course, if the drugs do not show up in the proper packaging, a buyer will think there's a problem. But that problem is easily solved. Just package your "brand-name" pills in matching boxes that look like the originals.

Now that you have created the product, you'll need to sell it without getting caught. Why not open an online drugstore based out of some remote corner of the world, with no effective drug regulation, away from the reach of regulators?[1] A ripe, new opportunity has shown up as the world deals with a global pandemic that has killed thousands of people

___

[1] Behner et al., "Fighting Counterfeit Pharmaceuticals"; Bulletin of the World Health Organization, "Growing Threat from Counterfeit Medicines."

worldwide. As vaccines and other cures start rolling out, it is only logical that people will look for all possible options to get their hands on them.[2]

Now suppose that it was your job to stop the counterfeiters. Finding them would be a tough task. How would you do it? You could start by buying samples of drugs from various markets, testing them to make sure they contain the right ingredients, and flagging those that do not. Considering that counterfeit pharmaceuticals make up $200 billion out of a $1.2 trillion market, you probably won't have the time or money to catch most of the bad guys.[3] Finding the harmful drugs is only one step in solving the issue. How do you go about finding where they are coming from in order to tackle the problem at the source?

You would have a tough job ahead of you. But maybe there is a smarter way to do it. What if you did not have to police all the online drug stores? What if you could empower buyers to know when they are victims of fraud? What if you could give them a tool to police their purchases and know when someone is trying to sell them fake pills? Blockchain may have an answer for you by making it possible to verify—with certainty—who made the pills.

FarmaTrust is attempting to do just that. To address some of these challenges in the pharmaceutical supply chain, Farma-Trust has introduced a blockchain-based solution. One aspect of the solution focuses on pharmaceutical tracking and data

---

2    Sun, "Be Equally Daunting."
3    Behner et al., "Fighting Counterfeit Pharmaceuticals"; Aitken et al., "The Global Use of Medicine."

services. This solution provides much-needed visibility into the journey of a product from the point of manufacture to the consumer. It helps with tracing the origins of the drugs and helps make sure that they are not counterfeit. Having a better understanding of inventory flow through the supply chain also helps the companies manage their stock accurately and reduce waste. In fact, FarmaTrust has attracted enough attention from the regulators in the US and Europe that trials are underway.

Another part of FarmaTrust's solution centers on Clinical Trial Services. The nature of clinical trials has progressively become global. Also, the trend of outsourcing trial services has increased recently. Because of these trends, we have a need for assurances that clinical trials are using the correct process. As more clinical trials are run worldwide, regulators need to focus on making sure that the quality of trials and the methods used to conduct them meet the standard.

**BUT, WHY USE BLOCKCHAIN?**
One of the most exciting qualities of blockchain, the data technology that we are exploring, is the immutability of stored data on the blockchain. We can trust the data because it cannot be tampered with due to this quality. Once you can ensure you have good data, it further facilitates data analytics and artificial intelligence applications. The immutability of data also helps regulators be comfortable with the information. They know that what they see has not been changed before it reached them.

The other aspect of blockchain useful for FarmaTrust is automating processes based on reliable data under certain business conditions. Some of the modules in FarmaTrust allow for automating functions like automatic purchase, automated ordering, automated regulatory reporting, automated payments, etc.

Blockchain also decentralizes control over the data. Centralizing your data under a single controlling authority leaves you vulnerable to the risk of being manipulated even if you have a distributed database. The data can be tampered with and changed to suit a particular purpose. A distributed data technology, like blockchain, has multiple controllers, making it difficult for any participant to indulge in nefarious activities for fear of identification.

The use of cryptography by blockchain is also crucial for the security aspects of the solution. We hear about all these high-profile hacks, not just on health records but also on financial documents. The use of blockchain helps protect against such attacks.

FarmaTrust's solution helps companies get more visibility in their supply chain. That, in turn, helps improve efficiency. End customers have increased trust in the medicines they are consuming. Companies also will tend to pass some of the cost savings to consumers in the form of reduced prices.

Online pharmacies help reduce the cost of operations and, in turn, reduce prices for customers. However, they are tainted by high rates of counterfeit drugs. A blockchain-based solution like FarmaTrust can help mitigate and prevent this problem. It allows companies to make data-driven decisions—with reliable data—and helps make the world a cheaper and safer place with the help of blockchain.

The key reasons to start using a blockchain instead of other existing technologies are the ability to feel comfortable with the system because data is not corrupt, multiple controllers that help detect any attempts to change the data, secure data storage, and automation using trusted data. Combining all these aspects makes it possible to operate more efficiently, reduce costs, and enable new value generation.

Yes, there are additional complexities because there is a transition involved in moving away from a centralized world to a decentralized world. We are so used to the centralized nature of doing things that anything different will seem like an added complication. The blockchain landscape is ever-evolving because it is an emerging technology. There are open questions about its speed, scalability, lack of standards, interoperability amongst different blockchains, and regulatory uncertainty. Users will need to gradually come to terms with the unfamiliarity of this decentralized paradigm. The shift to trusting the data will not be an easy transition.

Opportunities will explode once all the actors involved are comfortable. Once they understand that no one can change the data and that the data can be kept secure in this manner, blockchain's true potential will open up.

As Najib Rehman from FarmaTrust put it, "We can work with you, and we can show you what the difference is. What we want to do is work in parallel with your incumbent technologies. And then, as you see the real value of the distributed nature of the blockchain, that means that you can trust the data immutably. You can see why, then, you might want at some point, to turn off the old stuff and move over wholly.... There is now going to be a tipping point, I believe."[4]

*Unblocking Blockchain is an inquiry into that tipping point.*

My journey with blockchain started in the first quarter of 2019. As a new calendar year rolled around, we saw many articles on various topics reviewing the last year's happenings. These articles also gave the authors' views into expected progress in the coming year. One fine morning, an article flowed through my newsfeed: "Top 5 blockchain predictions for 2019."[5]

As I finished reading the piece, I repeatedly kept going back to a thought that stuck to me. The article highlighted the importance of non-technology issues in the success of blockchain projects. The relevance of business participation is valid to all technical projects, but why call it out specifically in the context of blockchain? I have always worked in the technology space from the business side of things, and this focus on non-technology issues caught my attention.

Lazily, with no real goal in mind, I started exploring blockchain. Then, one fine day, a direct message popped up. It was Jonathan Blanco inviting me to attend TF4. It turned out that TF4 was one of Seattle's premier blockchain conferences. Jonathan didn't have to offer me the $100 discount to

---

4    Rehman et al., "Blockchain & AI."
5    Casman, "Top 5 Blockchain."

attend; it was happening in Seattle that weekend. What was there to lose?

So, there I was on the thirty-sixth floor of Columbia Towers, overlooking the lovely view of the Puget Sound, surrounded by one hundred other people, listening to speakers talk about blockchain and cryptocurrencies. That event was my first introduction to blockchain. The conference positioning was for people who had already been working in the blockchain space.

For me, an absolute beginner, it was like drinking from a fire hose about all things blockchain. The sessions revolved around the application of the technology and were not heavily technical. My first introduction to a new blockchain language happened here—mining, tokenization, hash rate, and private permissioned networks, etc. And I was hooked.

The potential that the technology had was fascinating. The use of tokens could democratize investments in commercial real estate, infrastructure projects, etc. This application of blockchain could allow small investors to participate in these large-sized investments. The possibility of using the blockchain in voting—which could enable vote tallying to be real-time, accurate, and tamper-proof—would be so cool. The ability to track and trace—it has such potential.

If I could track where my donation money is going, I would be more likely to donate to people in need. Every time a natural disaster happens, all these options show up on Facebook and websites, asking for donations. But who knows where that money is going? For all I know, the moment I push that button to pay, it goes and just sits in somebody else's bank account. It seemed like this blockchain could provide a solution.

So many different possibilities were showing up. At least, that was the promise. There was a hint of what might be possible.

As I was trying to learn more about blockchain, I attended as many meetups and conferences as possible. However, much of the conversation was about cryptocurrencies and fintech. There was not much talk of the use of this technology in the enterprise space. This was perhaps because there has been more money flowing into cryptocurrency companies.[6] The conversation follows activity, which follows the money.

Communications coming out of enterprise customers mirror that conversation. As we can see below, the corporate mentions of the word "blockchain" dropped.[7]

## Funding to cryptocurrency companies has dwarfed funding to enterprise blockchain...

Annual VC-backed deals and financing, 2015 – 2019 ($M)

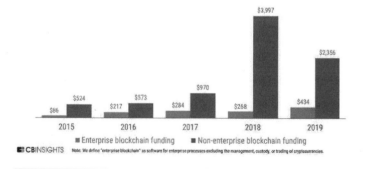

6    CB Insights, "The Blockchain Report 2020."
7    Ibid.

# Corporate mentions of "blockchain" dropped by more than half from 2018 to 2019

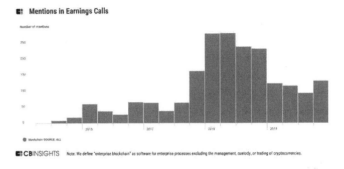

■¦ Mentions in Earnings Calls

¦¦ CBINSIGHTS    Note: We define "enterprise blockchain" as software for enterprise processes excluding the management, custody, or trading of cryptocurrencies.

Until now, it was all interesting at an intellectual level, but I could not figure out how I might be helpful in this space. All of that changed with the talk by IBM's Paige Krieger at the Hyperledger Seattle meetup. Paige's session was when my fascination with blockchain found a home.

Her talk was all about "enterprise blockchain." No cryptocurrencies here. And I just sat there and listened with all the possibilities taking form in my head. That session gave me my first taste of things that could create value for enterprises using blockchain. From there on, as I followed my curiosity, I discovered a fascinating new world of possibilities—a world where competitors worked together to generate value that was not possible before.

As my fascination grew, I looked to answer a personal question—whether or not it made sense to invest time and energy in this emerging technology. I could certainly sense the potential, but then, there was a conflict in the narrative. Furthermore, the truth of the matter is that today's business and technology leaders also face the same questions.

New technology is knocking on your door with the promise of an opportunity to do good for your company. You could increase revenue by unlocking new value and decrease costs by helping competitors turn into cheerleaders for each other. But—and there is that "but"—is there a business case worth pursuing? Even if the ROI is justified, is now the right time?

Suppose you act right away, and the technology does deliver what it promises. In that case, you can grab a competitive advantage by exploiting new opportunities before your competitors. But, if you are too late to the party, you are just catching up and trying to stay in the game.

What if it is just hype?

*Unblocking Blockchain is a journey to unravel that hype.*

Gartner has its Hype Cycles framework to help business and technology leaders frame emerging technologies and interpret the hype that comes with them.[8] In our case, blockchain is currently supposed to be in the "trough of disillusionment."

Per Gartner's description of the trough of disillusionment, "Interest wanes as experiments and implementations fail to deliver. Producers of the technology shake out or fail. Investments continue only if the surviving providers improve their products to the satisfaction of early adopters."

Well then, is the interest in blockchain waning?

---

8    Gartner, "Hype Cycle."

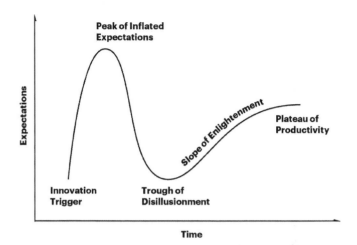

If you were to follow the money, it would indicate that block-chain technology's interest does not have enough tailwinds. Data by CB Insights seems to confirm that hypothesis. Looking at venture capital (VC) funding trends in blockchain, the report shows that in 2019, funding dollars fell over 30 percent, compared to the year before.[9]

## 2019 funding fell while deal activity held relatively steady

Annual VC-backed deals and financing, 2015 – 2019 ($M)

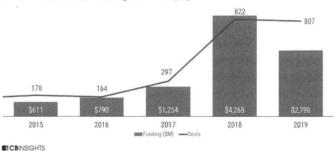

| | 2015 | 2016 | 2017 | 2018 | 2019 |
|---|---|---|---|---|---|
| Funding ($M) | $611 | $790 | $1,254 | $4,265 | $2,790 |
| Deals | 178 | 164 | 297 | 822 | 807 |

■ Funding ($M)  — Deals

CBINSIGHTS

---

9   CB Insights, "The Blockchain Report 2020."

On the other hand, headlines are going through my news-feed: "Why Mastercard's Blockchain Focuses on Practical Applications," or "How Walmart and Others Are Riding a Blockchain Wave to Supply Chain Paradise," or "Figure Technologies Raises $103M to Continue Blockchain-Based Lending."[10] There are also the big household names working on blockchain projects, such as Starbucks, Samsung, and more.[11] IT services companies are putting money and resources behind advisory services to support their clients with worldwide blockchain services: Accenture, IBM, Infosys, etc.

So, what is the truth? Is blockchain useful or not? Is it an emerging growth opportunity, or is it doomed to stay stuck in a trough of disillusionment, never to climb up the "slope of enlightenment?" Is it coming out of the trough? If not, when might it do so? How do we know that it is on an upward trajectory? Should business leaders and technology leaders invest their time and money into this new technology now? More importantly, where are we headed from here?

If you look at the press releases coming out, it is difficult to gauge how much of that is marketing hype and how much of that is reality. Will all the successful pilots survive a move to production and work at scale? All of these successful proofs-of-concept—do they have a valid business case behind them? Or are they getting started to check the box of "blockchain

10   Hines, "Why Mastercard's Blockchain"; Dimitrov, "How Walmart and Others"; PYMNTS, "Lending Firm Figure."
11   Kapilkov, "Starbucks to Let Customers"; Erazo, "Blockchain-Powered 5G Phone."

buzzword" and pacify investors and shareholders? This narrative entails much conflict.

When I was just starting my career as a young business consultant, I was facing a similar question. At that time, enterprise resource planning (ERP) technology was all set to revolutionize companies with its promise of a commonly shared view of reality across various company departments. And now, here we are, with blockchain and its promise of a commonly shared view of reality across multiple companies that are typically competing with each other. So, an ERP of ERPs? Maybe.

I wrote this book to share my insights with business and technology leaders who are asking the same questions. I hope to help them navigate these uncharted territories for their own organizations.

In this book, you'll learn what the adoption journey with blockchain could look like for your company. You start experimenting with the technology and take some time to learn about it, decide use-case to pursue, and run a proof of concept. In the process, you realize that blockchain is a team sport and to succeed, you need to play with others. Including more people to build the network and get them around the table makes this work hard. We also discuss how to be prepared for typical challenges. We then look at some advanced work being done with blockchain in supply chain and also in combination with other emerging technologies.

The book lays out a framework on how to take your company through its blockchain adoption journey. As it draws on early adopters' real-world experiences, the book reveals practices that have helped company leaders stay at the center of blockchain evolution. These lessons will help you design a business strategy by creating value using blockchain and be prepared for any possible disruptions to your business model.

If you find yourself in this place where you have heard of blockchain and wondered what it is, and whether or not you should invest your time and energy into knowing more about it, then I invite you to join me on this journey. I hope that you will learn something new—maybe not what you thought you would, but something new nonetheless.

As you read this book, you will discover the promise of blockchain as a new operating system of business, providing an infrastructure layer and helping us safely exchange value. Through this book, I hope to share my passion and excitement for the socio-technological phenomenon called *blockchain*. Ultimately, I want this book to help you stay at the edge of innovation as blockchain reshapes your competitive landscape.

I hope the book makes you excited about all that blockchain has to offer and that you finally decide to take the plunge and go for a swim instead of just dipping your toes in to test the waters.

It is a book that speaks to leaders who want to leverage blockchain technology to drive business value. *Unblocking Blockchain* will help company leaders understand what blockchain can do for their business and prepare them to have meaningful dialogue with their technology counterparts. The book will also help technology leaders understand blockchain's possibilities while striving to future-proof their companies' technology foundations.

I invite you to join me on this journey of *Unblocking Blockchain*—a journey in the discovery of what's possible now and what is yet to come.

# PREAMBLE

## BLIND MEN AND THE ELEPHANT – A POEM BY JOHN GODFREY SAXE (1816–1887)

It was six men of Indostan, To learning much inclined,
Who went to see the Elephant (though all of them were blind),
That each by observation, might satisfy his mind.

The *First* approach'd the Elephant, and happening to fall,
Against his broad and sturdy side, at once began to bawl:
"God bless me! but the Elephant is very like a wall!"

The *Second*, feeling of the tusk, cried, "Ho! what have we here,
So very round and smooth and sharp? to me 'tis mighty clear,
This wonder of an Elephant, is very like a spear!"

The *Third* approach'd the animal, and happening to take,
The squirming trunk within his hands, thus boldly up and spake:
"I see," quoth he "the Elephant, is very like a snake!"

The *Fourth* reached out an eager hand, and felt about the knee:
"What most this wondrous beast is like, is mighty plain," quoth he,
"'Tis clear enough the Elephant, is very like a tree!"

The *Fifth*, who chanced to touch the ear, said, "E'en the blindest man,
Can tell what this resembles most; deny the fact who can,
This marvel of an Elephant, is very like a fan!"

The *Sixth* no sooner had begun, about the beast to grope,
Then, seizing on the swinging tail, that fell within his scope,
"I see," quoth he, "the Elephant, is very like a rope!"

And so these men of Indostan, disputed loud and long,
Each in his own opinion, exceeding stiff and strong,
Though each was partly in the right, and all were in the wrong!

# CHAPTER 1

# WHAT IS BLOCKCHAIN?

———

"I keep hearing about blockchain, and you keep reading so much about it. Help me understand. What is it?" my wife asked me one fine day.

"Blockchain? It's an immutable distributed ledger in which data is cryptographically stored on different nodes using a consensus protocol. Each transaction is stored in a block, and the blocks are chained together," I replied.

Crickets.

This was the first time I encountered the challenge of trying to explain—what *is* blockchain? This chapter was, unequivocally, the hardest one to write because of this reason. With other emerging technologies, it is relatively more straightforward for people.

With 5G, a user gets higher speeds, which you can experience for yourself. With the "internet of things" (IoT), we have visions of "the minority report" with people walking into stores and getting served up snazzy advertisements based on all the scanning technology around them.[12] With AI, we have OpenAI writing human-like articles.[13] It's all instantly relatable. However, unlike these aforementioned technologies, blockchain works behind the scenes and is much more of an abstract concept. In large part, people would not even know that blockchain has anything to do with some of the things they will take for granted in the coming years.

Therefore, it is difficult to explain what blockchain is without helping others relate it to something they do in their daily lives. A translation is needed—a second-level explanation. I can define blockchain, and your first response would be, "So, what?" And rightly so. The answer to the question "What is blockchain?" is neither simple nor easy.

After attempting to explain blockchain to my wife, I have encountered this situation multiple times. I have realized that it is better to start with a business-focused description of blockchain technology instead of a tech-centered answer.

Let us get started.

**BUSINESS DEFINITION**

**BUSINESS ELEVATOR PITCH:**

*Blockchain is a record-keeping system shared across multiple computers. These records are practically undeletable, stored securely, and collectively maintained.*

---

12  Spielberg, "Minority Report"
13  GPT-3, "A Robot Wrote This"

Let me break it down for you.

Blockchain, as a record-keeping system, stores data in the form of a ledger. It is an ever-growing list where new transactions are constantly added. You sell stock to another person: That's a transaction. Your warehouse receives the goods from the shipping company: That's a transaction. Blockchain can store all such transactions between entities.

Whoever has an interest in the data can get access to this ever-growing list of transactions. The sharing gives all of us one common version of the truth. Having a shared reality means that there is no need to maintain *my* version of truth versus *your* version of the truth. There is an underlying promise that what I see is what you see.

Multiple computers, over a peer-to-peer network, have access to this shared data. Copies of the data are sitting on different computers that are part of the blockchain network.

Once recorded on the ledger, it is practically impossible to change any of the transactions. It is theoretically possible in very few cases, but given the state of technological advancement today, there is not enough computing power to make changes to the data without being detected. Thus, the data is resistant to manipulation by bad actors.

This data is also stored securely using cryptographic encryption technologies. This method of storing information is similar to a common approach to storing passwords today. Suppose you lose your password to an online account. In that case, the administrators generally ask you to reset your password instead of just telling you what your password is. That's because they don't know your password.

When you try to log in and submit your password, the plaintext password gets scrambled, and this scrambled version is compared to the scrambled text that was generated when you first created the password. If the two strings match, you get access. Nobody can reverse engineer and find the actual password even if they know it's scrambled form.

In the same way, cryptographic encryption secures the transaction data stored on the blockchain. The use of cryptographic encryption also makes it possible to limit access to data only to parties that have permission to do so.

This data is also common-property in that it is maintained collectively by multiple participants interested in the data. They all care about the data and want to transact with each other, even though they may not necessarily trust each other. The data is stored on the ledger only after the majority agree that it is indeed the correct data to be stored.

Here is a visualization that might help further clarify the process. Think of blockchain as an ever-growing list of transactions in a shared spreadsheet. There was a time when people needed to collaborate on a spreadsheet; you would create one, complete your work, save it, and forward it to another team member so they could make their updates. In today's world of shared spreadsheets, you could all be working on the same spreadsheet at the same time. Blockchain works similarly. The difference is that, on a blockchain, multiple computers store the data. If all participants agree that it is the correct data,

data gets stored. It is also encrypted, and deletion is practically impossible.

Now let's look at the technical definition to give added color to our understanding of blockchain.

## TECHNICAL DEFINITION
### TECHNICAL ELEVATOR PITCH:

*Blockchain is a distributed database technology that stores data across multiple nodes over a P2P network. This database is append-only, cryptographically secured, and committed to using consensus mechanisms.*

At its core, blockchain is a distributed ledger technology. The ledger is a chronological record of transactions. The distributed nature of the ledger comes because multiple computers store it over a peer-to-peer network. A node is one of the computers on the network that can save the data. All nodes have the exact copy of the data, giving us a shared reality with the same version of the truth.

Mainstream database technologies allow for create, read, update, and delete functions to be applied to stored data. Blockchain, however, is an append-only data technology. You are only allowed to create or read a record. No deletion or updates are permitted. This characteristic gives blockchain its immutable and tamper-evident characteristics. Suppose you need to make changes to a previous entry. In that case, you need to create new entries nullifying the prior transaction before adding new information.

Before being added to the ledger, various consensus mechanisms are used to confirm a transaction's validity.

As the transactions are confirmed and added to the ledger, they are grouped in a block. As the new blocks keep getting added, they link to the previous block using cryptographic encryption. This linking of blocks of transactions creates a continuous chain—hence the name blockchain.

The following picture brings it all together:

## WHAT IS BLOCKCHAIN

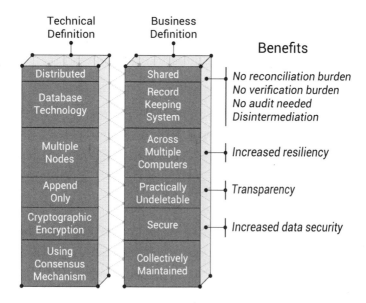

## BLOCKCHAIN BENEFITS FRAMEWORK

Blockchain has a unique value proposition to help us in real-world situations based on benefits derived from its various qualities. Let's take a look at this benefits framework.

### SHARED TRUTH:

Since the blockchain data is shared, everyone has access to the same data. There is no need to maintain two different copies representing that data. Suppose two parties want to transact with each other based on this data. In that case, it eliminates the burden of verifying, reconciling, or auditing the information. Any associated costs for those activities also go away. Consequently, this also removes the added costs of maintaining intermediary services that guarantee data authenticity. Everyone viewing the same data reality makes this possible.

### MULTIPLE COMPUTERS ON A PEER-TO-PEER NETWORK:

Having various distributed copies of the data makes the system resilient. Because there is no single point of failure, it protects against denial-of-service (DoS) attacks. Suppose one of the peers is inaccessible for any reason. In that case, you can still access the data sitting on other computers, adding to the overall resiliency.

### IMMUTABILITY:

Since, practically, no one can delete the data, we have transparency into a common stream of data reality. This increases trust in the data as it can be traced and audited for any changes. Traceability enables us to trust the data without the help of a verified third party or a central authority.

## CRYPTOGRAPHIC ENCRYPTION:

The use of cryptography in blockchain leads to increased data security. The use of digital signatures allows two entities, who do not trust each other, to participate in a secure exchange.

## CONSENSUS:

Consensus is the approval mechanism for all peers on the blockchain to reach a joint agreement on the transactions added to the blockchain. It ensures that a transaction is genuine and acceptable. The use of consensus allows for not needing a central authority to verify and validate the transactions and cuts out the middlemen and the associated costs.

Overall, it's about trust. I know peers have validated this data. I know nobody has tampered with it. I can also see it as it evolves. I see the data is secure. All of these aspects build trust in data on the blockchain.

## SMART CONTRACTS

In addition to recording transactions, meeting certain data conditions can also automatically execute code that implements business rules. For example, when your warehouse records a transaction for receipt of goods, a vendor's payment can automatically be released. This code is called smart contract and makes it possible to automate the execution of the business workflow.

Typically, contracts help when two people want to transact but do not necessarily trust each other. In the current paradigm, they trust an independent third party to enforce the contract's execution. These third parties are typically large institutions like government bodies, banks, lawyers, and accountants. Instead, smart contracts build the logic for the automatic execution of those contracts onto the blockchain. We get a consistent and predictable output with deterministic input.

## BLOCKCHAIN VS. DLT

We should keep in mind that distributed ledger technology (DLT) is the umbrella term, and blockchain is one type of DLT. Perhaps because it is catchier, the word "blockchain" has seen more industry traction. Throughout our conversation in this book, I'll use blockchain as the generic common noun to refer to all kinds of DLT. In the end, all DLTs possess similar characteristics and aim to achieve similar outcomes. Their methods may be different, but their results are identical. A few examples of these are IOTA Tangle, Ripple, and Hedera Hashgraph.

## BLOCKCHAIN VS. BITCOIN

We should also keep in mind that blockchain is not Bitcoin, and Bitcoin is not blockchain. I consistently notice that people often mistake blockchain for Bitcoin. When I gave the first two chapters of this book to my friend, Glenn—to ask for his feedback—he said, "Oh, I did not realize Bitcoin could do all that?" after reading the excerpts. This is even despite the fact that I did not mention the word Bitcoin once in any of those chapters.

Blockchain is the underlying technology that enables Bitcoin. Blockchain did get introduced to the world as Bitcoin. Since then, Bitcoin has also been the most visible of blockchain use cases as a form of cryptocurrency. With the introduction of smart contracts, blockchain technology's utility has moved beyond the confines of cryptocurrencies and into the realm of value addition in other processes.

**WHY SHOULD YOU CARE?**

If you look at blockchain like any other data storage technology, why should you care? Isn't it just a database? In the end, blockchain is not introducing any new technology. It is just a unique combination of existing technology concepts like ledgers, linked lists, peer-to-peer networks, encryption, and databases. What is the big deal?

Businesses don't work in isolation. They continually transact with other companies, governments, institutions, etc., forming business networks. Human enterprise is thus a series of transactions. Any object you see around you has reached you after changing hands multiple times across various parties. We live our lives surrounded by a web of transactions transferring value between parties.

A record of those transactions sits on ledgers everywhere. We may not call them ledgers, but that's what they are—a continuous stream of updates to records. As you sit in your room with the lights turned on, your utility company continually records the amount of electricity used. They also calculate the amount to charge you for it. For settlement, you may receive a bill at the end of the month. But a continuous record is maintained about your electricity consumption and the money you owe. Your purchase records sit on some ledger, along with what you paid in exchange. We continuously keep an account of happenings around us.

Keeping records of transactions is key to our daily lives—both for individuals and companies. These records give us a view of the past and also help us plan for the future. Transactions can be completed quickly, but settlement can take much longer, and maintaining records of these transactions can be time-consuming and error-prone. It also adds to the cost of doing business.

For example, you press the "sell" button, and you sell the stock in your online brokerage account. If you want immediate access to funds, that will not happen because the settlement process takes a few days. This settlement will involve various parties who have their versions of the ledger for the same transaction. Each of those entities cannot see each other's ledger and spend time and effort reconciling the records. These transactions are also inherently conflictual. They provide value to both participants, which is why the participants agree to the transaction. But the transaction happens at an equilibrium. Tilting that balance in their favor would be of interest to all parties. That leads to the issue of whether you can trust the other party's record or not.

Societies need trust for these transactions to continue. They try to maintain that trust through various methods. At a social level, we have a notion of ethics and morals that encourage trustworthy behavior to maintain one's reputation. At a more formal, institutional level, societies try to discourage untrustworthy behavior by implementing rules and laws that govern the boundaries and conditions under which transactions can occur. We don't trust that each of the parties will act in accordance with moral norms and the law; therefore, we implement all kinds of checks and balances.

These measures take the form of auditors, third-party trusted organizations, legal structures, etc.

All of this taken together allows for the creation of *trust*. Let's take the example of financial transactions. I can buy groceries in a store without handing over any money just by swiping a card. I can make purchases like this because both me and the merchant trust a third party—the financial system. I am willing to put my money in the banks, knowing very well that I may wake up tomorrow, log into my account, and find a zero balance. I trust the bank would not wrong me as they want to protect their reputation and continue to be in business. Even if a bank were to go rogue, government bodies have created laws to protect me.

Blockchain shifts the need to place trust in people and institutions by directing that trust toward technology instead. With that, it provides the potential to eliminate the costs associated with the infrastructure built solely to provide trust all around us. On the blockchain, transactions are transparent to all. There is no need for intermediaries to certify, which helps reduce costs.

Today, when two companies do business together, they will typically keep separate records of their work. There will be discrepancies in those records from time to time, which cause disagreements that are frustrating and time-consuming to resolve. Blockchain gives an elegant approach to the shared set of records. Both (or many) companies agree that data is correct before recording it on the shared ledger.

Once you have that trusted and shared set of records, you can now explore automated business processes on top of it. This trusted data enables a smoother inter-organizational workflow. Blockchain allows for the creation of this underlying infrastructure, which promotes collaboration among competitors.

## THE PARADOX OF COOPERATION AND COMPETITION

Over the years, as management theory has evolved, companies have shifted their strategy to include collaboration to increase their profits. Increasing their profits through competition used to be the primary strategy for companies. In trying to get a competitive advantage, that strategy has expanded to include collaboration with various partners. This cooperation with competitors has manifested itself in the form of strategic alliances.

Varying degrees of competitive and cooperative behavior among rivals can exist at the same time. Competitive behavior amongst rivals can vary from open warfare to subtle friction. Cooperative behavior amongst organizations can range from full-on integration to sporadic collaboration. This collaborative advantage can get companies more access to skills and resources than they would have on their own.

Organizations commonly exhibit the existence of these "simultaneous opposites" with contradictory elements. "The key characteristic in paradox is the simultaneous presence of contradictory, even mutually exclusive elements."[14] This paradox of cooperation and competition in strategic alliances

---

14    Clarke-Hill, "The Paradox of Co-operation."

is called "coopetition." The primary precondition needed for coopetition to happen is an overlap of interest between competing companies. Then, they can be motivated to work together in their quest to create more value than what could have been created by them working by themselves. Blockchain will supercharge coopetition. It will enhance the realm of possibilities for cooperation between companies.

Look at blockchain as more than just new technology; it introduces a new way of looking at the world. Instead of being a pure technology play, blockchain is a techno-sociological innovation. It helps change the behavior of groups of people in a manner that we did not see earlier. It is more of a techno-sociological construct that will help achieve a win-win for all parties. It shifts the mindset to try and grow the pie together instead of slicing it up as corporations compete in the marketplace. That is a paradigm shift in doing business that creates more value for the customer by opening up the silos called companies.

**So, what is blockchain?** Is it a database? A ledger? a trust layer? Immutable? Secure? Trustless? Tamper-proof? Dis-intermediating? Blockchain can be all of these or any of these. That is up to you to choose. Like the blind men of Indostan, blockchain's reality is different depending on whom you ask.

This chapter should have given you a good overview of what blockchain is. Now we are ready to explore. How do you get started on a successful blockchain adoption journey?

# CHAPTER 2

# DO YOU KNOW WHY YOU ARE USING BLOCKCHAIN?

———

## THE DICHOTOMY

Gartner's new business value forecast methodology quantifies the value of a technology's innovation. It looks at factors of customer experience, new revenue, and cost reduction. According to this methodology, in the context of blockchain, "The business value-add of blockchain will grow to slightly more than $176 billion by 2025, and then it will exceed $3.1 trillion by 2030."[15] We are talking big numbers here. With such expectations from the technology, everyone wants to get involved. They want to make sure they are not getting left behind. Although, the critical question is, are you getting involved in blockchain for the right reasons?

---

15   Gartner, "Forecast: Blockchain Business Value."

Stephanie Hurder is a founding economist at Prysm Group, an economic advisory firm focused on implementing emerging technologies, and an academic contributor to the World Economic Forum. She has been an active participant in enterprise blockchain initiatives. Working with various projects, she can see some familiar trends showing up. She explains, "You'll have a consortium announced that they have a proof of concept or that they're going to do a pilot for a specific use case. And then a year later, you come back, and you say, 'Oh, I wonder what happened to that pilot, sort of never heard from again,' and we just see this pattern over and over again."[16] The projects just didn't bring in the results.

This observation can also be backed by data. According to a PricewaterhouseCoopers survey, of the respondents who report a blockchain project in the pilot stage, 54 percent say the effort sometimes or often didn't justify the result.[17]

"My investors are asking about our blockchain strategy, and I need some tutoring on the topic," my friend Sandeep said. Of course, he got the help he needed, but it left me wondering. His reason to look into blockchain technology was not a business problem that he was trying to solve, for which blockchain was identified as the solution. Instead, he needed to look into the technology for external reasons.

---

16  Hurder, "Why Enterprise Blockchains Fail."
17  PwC, "Make the Blockchain Business Case."

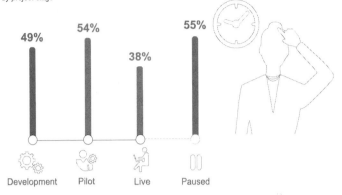

*Percentage of respondents who said blockchain efforts sometimes or often didn't justify results, by project stage*

49%    54%         55%
              38%

○        ○         ○         ○

Development   Pilot    Live    Paused

Note: Bases: 44, 193, 62, 90.
Q: For your organisation's blockchain projects, have you faced any of these challenges?
Source: PwC Global Blockchain survey, 2018

On one side, there is such potential, but on the other hand, the potential seems to be faltering. Blockchain can add significant value to companies, but they need to be clear on what the value drivers are and who is getting the value. Many projects are unclear on their reasons for using blockchain technology instead of existing technologies in the context of a particular use case. If projects just follow the hype and do not link their efforts to value, they increase their chances of not being heard from again.

As per a 2019 Gartner prediction, "Ninety percent of current enterprise blockchain platform implementations will require replacement by 2021."[18] A key reason for that is not linking use cases with the business benefits of blockchain.

## ON STAYING COMPETITIVE

One lens through which companies can look at new technology is this: What can this technology do to hurt my business? Looking through this lens is all about competitive advantage. If competitors use this technology to disrupt the competitive landscape, we will be at a disadvantage. The question then really is: How do we get ahead of the curve?

"A 2019 study by the Enterprise Strategy Group showed that most leading organizations already see the essential nature of emerging technologies. Eighty-two percent of organizations agree or strongly agree that without emerging technology, they will not be able to transform. And if they don't transform, a competitor will disrupt their business."[19]

Staying competitive is what prompted Siam Commercial Bank (SCB) to look at blockchain.

As Orapong Thien-Ngern explains, "We realized that one of the ways for the bank to continue growing or recover the low return on equity is to branch out from the traditional business. We are still mainly a financial institution, but we start looking at the financial world in a different way. Can we adopt new technologies? Can we start creating new products and services that are off the traditional way? And that's why we're so interested in this distributed ledger and

18   Gartner, "Gartner Predicts 90%"
19   Dell Technologies, "Creating Value in a Digital World"

blockchain."[20] Orapong is the CEO of Digital Ventures, which is a subsidiary of SCB.

SCB, the oldest bank in Thailand, was established in 1904, and has been one of the market's top performers.[21] It is also one of the largest banks in Thailand in terms of assets and profits. To stay competitive, SCB is continually looking at innovation in services offered. And emerging technologies are one way of looking at innovation.

Traditional banking market dynamics are such that every player is trying to protect their market share. "For example, two years ago, we created what we believe to be the leading mobile application for banking, for us to gain market share. We announced zero fees, all free transactions on mobile banking. Within half an hour, every bank matched the offer," says Orapong. [22]

It is challenging to gain additional revenues or profits in such a competitive environment, even though you may allocate heavy investments. The situation forces banks to branch out of traditional business. They look to see into ways to adopt new technologies to get a competitive advantage. Can they start creating products and services in the current processes that are different from the traditional way of doing things?

Using blockchain, SCB looked to tackle procurement management—specifically the procure-to-pay (P2P) process—and

---

20  Thien-Ngern et al., "Blockchain for Procure-to-Pay"
21  Nikkei Asia, "The Siam Commercial Bank"
22  Thien-Ngern et al., "Blockchain for Procure-to-Pay"

seek new possibilities. P2P kicks in when a company works with its suppliers to purchase raw materials or services needed to conduct business. In the case of procuring goods, a buyer typically issues a purchase order (PO).

After approval, the PO goes to the supplier, who then ships the product with a shipping document. The goods come to the buyer's warehouse. After inspection, the warehouse issues a goods receipt (GR) acknowledging the receipt of goods. The goods receipt goes back to the supplier, who then issues an invoice back to the buyer's accounts payable department. The accounts payable department then takes all of these documents and verifies them. Typically a three-way match is performed between the purchase order, the vendor invoice, and the goods receipt.

Different departments in a company manage various functions like sourcing, procurement, and account payable functions. The organization of these departments optimizes the tools and processes for their functioning. This siloed functioning creates processes that are unintegrated, manual, and error-prone. Additionally, a large company can have thousands of suppliers who are using their systems. These systems do not talk to each other. Their data is not integrated, leading to manual and document-heavy processes.

With existing technology, this integration between buyers and suppliers is challenging because of the large number of entities involved. Getting all the data integrated across organizations gets expensive very quickly with point-to-point integration.

As Orapong explains on the use of APIs, "Technically you could. But economically, it might not be feasible. One buyer could easily have ten thousand suppliers. Even if you have APIs, how many integration points would you be able to manage? How much testing do you need to make sure that everything is correct? Once data starts being exchanged, how can you make sure that everything is secure, traceable, and auditable?"[23]

With a blockchain-based solution, there is no need for multiple documents in the P2P process. It all becomes one ledger. If there is a problem, you don't have to worry whether that record can be audited and has integrity. It comes built-in as part of the technology stack.

"That's why we believe that blockchain will change the world. It will enable different business models. If you can conduct trades as easily as you send a text message or send an email today, imagine how many changes will occur in the business world if you can conduct the trade as easy as that."[24] SCB is using blockchain because they could not use the existing technology stack in an economically feasible manner.

SCB started the project in 2017, and March 2018 saw the launch of the first version of a proof of concept (POC). The POC proved that the solution worked. They started scaling it up from there and launched production with real trades in August 2018. From there, it took them a year to scale up to one hundred suppliers. Initially, the progress was slower

---

23  Ibid
24  Ibid.

because, as happens with many IT projects, real-world implementation in production served up its own set of complications. All kinds of edge cases and exceptions showed up, e.g., someone was shipping partial quantities. Some goods were getting rejected due to quality. Sometimes parts were getting substituted, and so forth. It took them a year to identify and fix the exceptions. Now, they can scale at about one hundred suppliers per week. They have more large corporations showing interest in joining the network. When you see that kind of response, you know that the participants see some real value.

What is that value for participants in the case of the SCB project?

"It's productivity," says Orapong. He goes on to add, "If you look at the world today, you have multiple players. You have one big buyer, multiple suppliers, the buyer's payment bank, and the suppliers' financing banks."[25] With so many players involved, with no integrations, the process becomes cumbersome. After the supplier submits an invoice, it might take two to three weeks to complete the approval. This amount of time is needed to complete a three-way match, i.e., matching the invoice with the purchase order, goods receipt, and shipping document. After an invoice submission, there is a need for continuous follow-ups to clarify its receipt, handling, and processing by the buyer's accounts payable department. "From the buyer's point of view, the accounts payable department needs to spend a lot of time processing these documents and answering questions along the way. This platform solves

---

25 Ibid.

all of this. We are able to approve an invoice within the same day it is submitted."[26]

Banks also see many benefits. As Orapong confirms, "In the past, if a supplier needs to finance the cash flow, they have to wait three weeks for the invoice to be approved, which means that for those three weeks, the bank cannot provide lending. Right now, we shorten this time to one day, which means a bank has three more weeks to provide invoice financing to the supplier."[27]

Because of the transparency in the solution, banks can see the trade from the very beginning, from the point of issuance of the PO to the end with the invoice submission. Having this increased visibility significantly reduces the collection risk for them, enabling them to price the financing at a lower rate because they don't have to compensate for the risk. Also, they can do away with invoice financing processing fees because they can see the trade themselves. "With that, rather than providing financing at 18 percent, now you are providing it at less than 5 percent—because of no cost and no risk."[28] To drive the point home, early adopters like Siam Cement Group have reduced procure-to-pay process time by 50 percent and costs by 70 percent.[29]

**ON CREATING BUSINESS VALUE**
Another frame of reference for companies looking at emerging technology is increasing their profits. Profit increase

---

26   Ibid.
27   Ibid.
28   Ibid.
29   R3, "Blockchain for Procure-To-Pay."

comes from either increasing revenue or reducing costs: "What is it that we can do with this technology to benefit our business? And generally, technology does one of three things, in my mind. It lowers cost. Or it increases the speed of doing something. Or the convenience of doing something," explains Tony Little. Tony is senior director of integration strategy at Optum (part of UnitedHealth Group) and a key contributor to the early blockchain strategy at Optum. For correctly using your project's use case, he goes on to explain, "What problems exist, amongst a common, competitive set of companies in health care? In which, no company, if they solved it themselves, would have a significant advantage over the other? And no one company can completely solve it themselves. Basically, you're looking at problems that you need to crowdsource, and everybody wins." In short, you are looking for common pain or common gain among multiple players.

In 2016, Optum decided to evaluate blockchain technology. The team's first order of business was to understand blockchain basics and do an evaluation to clearly understand the beast—what it is and what it is not. With that understanding, the next question to be answered was: How might it impact their business? A company-wide call for use cases went out to collect a set for evaluation. This methodical approach helped the team make some objective conclusions on the real risks and the real benefits. A two-day working session brought together business and technical leaders.

The outcome of the mind-meld resulted in the creation of an outline of the health care industry from a data perspective. Whiteboards with every type of data and broad use-case got

filled. Things like medical records, claims, charges, and cap-
italization models were considered. These use cases covered
the entire health care continuum that United Healthcare
is involved in, i.e., basically all of health care. Next was
comparing this map to blockchain technology keeping in
mind the maturity of the technology and its possibilities
and limitations. It was then time to cross off things that
blockchain couldn't help solve at the time. All crossed-off
items were mapped to why it wasn't a good fit for a blockchain use case.

Finally, the team settled on the use case of "improving
provider data accuracy." Provider data is a semi-public list
of the doctors with their demographic information, e.g., a
doctor's first and last name, their clinic's phone number,
their address, information on whether they are accepting
new patients or not, etc. This data is kept current for every
in-network provider of the insurance company (i.e., the
payer). Insurance companies reach out to the providers
a couple of times a year to validate the information and
ask, "Hey, did anything change?" For all the doctors in the
insurance companies' network, they have to reach out and
confirm the data. This information also goes stale fast. Data
has to be continually updated and creates a verification burden that happens multiple times for all of the insurance
companies.

Insurers across the health-care system collectively spend
more than 2.1 billion USD every year managing the process of keeping their records accurate on provider data.[30]

---

30   Synaptic Health Alliance, "Improving Provider Data Accuracy."

On the side of doctors (or the providers they are associated with), there is a constant burden to keep answering calls or filling out forms to update the same data multiple times a year. All the insurance companies are asking the same questions.

Technologies exist today that can try and tackle this issue. But they are challenging to use. Because these technologies don't provide a possibility of tackling the challenge in a decentralized fashion, all insurers have to collect their version of the truth. As an aggregate of all insurers, this becomes significantly burdensome. Curating their source is not only technologically burdensome, but it is also an organizational issue. Additionally, there is also a burden on the providers because they have to manage the constant stream of requests from multiple insurers asking for the same information.

Optum technologies started on its blockchain journey with the goal of finding a few national insurers who would want to participate in an experiment. The experiment's goal would be to see what benefits would be derived if they tackled some of the use cases with blockchain. We are talking more than just technical benefits. There could be economic, political, and operational benefits when everyone works together. Attending various blockchain health-care conferences allowed the Optum team to build relationships with other insurance companies like MultiCare and Humana and start a conversation about creating an alliance. With that, Synaptic Health Alliance came into existence.

With the use of blockchain, Synaptic Health Alliance members can significantly lower the cost of verification. Doing it right can bring it almost down to zero. Insurers look at the shared version of data reality and see that the other trusted insurer has attested to the data. That is essentially as good as calling them up and asking, "Hey, did this person change their name from Dr. Jones to Dr. Smith?" Instead, it's right there on the database: Insurers can simply run a query and grab this information, and they do not have to take the load of verifying the same provider data over and over again.

In the SCB and Synaptic Health Alliance cases, we can see how the participants can derive value using a solution rooted in blockchain technology. But, as HFS research found, "Only around half of the 940 blockchain projects reported are the ones that make business sense and created real value for respondents."[31] We have to keep in mind that blockchain is not the answer to everything, as the hype would lead you to believe. Indeed, there are relevant use cases among all the noise. Still, they have to be chosen carefully. Before starting the initiative, look at the strategic horizon to identify what you are trying to accomplish. Pain points that are targeted to be solved should be evaluated using key parameters before confirming that blockchain technology is a good fit. Maybe other technologies are more appropriate to help you get to the end that you are seeking. All in all, you are looking for shared pain or shared gain so that other stakeholders are willing to fund and help effectively govern a blockchain initiative.

As Tony Little explains, the critical question is: "How do you create a network that is one, self-bootstrapping; two, rewards

---

31   Gupta et al., "Ignore Blockchain at Your Peril."

those who participate with quality data to a particular use case; and three, so there are a ton of incentives for them to continue participating in that manner." Answering that question for the chosen use case is what gives an edge in the use of blockchain technology. Because of the use of crypto-economics, this works well in public blockchain networks like Bitcoin. In the case of enterprise blockchain, we have to be very careful to evaluate the blockchain network's self-sustaining nature from an economic perspective. As Tony goes on to confirm, "If I participate with quality data and I am going to be economically rewarded by the network; that means it's self-sustaining, and you can get little players to play along too. Now all of a sudden, you have network effects." We have to look at some of these subtleties and evaluate why it is cheaper and better for a company to participate in a business network in this fashion.

The economics are really where it gets interesting with blockchain.

## SHOULD YOU USE BLOCKCHAIN?

| | |
|---|---|
| Will multiple parties benefit by sharing and updating data? | **If not, blockchain may not help** |
| Will multiple parties be coordinating their processes? | **If not, blockchain will likely not help** |
| Are there current barriers to share data or coordinate? | **If not, a traditional database may be a better option** |
| Do trusted intermediaries add complexity and heavy cost to provide services? | **If not, you are better off with an intermediary that adds trust to the ecosystem** |
| Can parties agree to common data standards? | **If not, you will transfer problems to a different system** |
| Can data sources be trusted or secured to provide accurate data? | **If not, blockchain cannot help - Garbage In, Garbage Out** |

# CHAPTER 3

# IT'S ALL ABOUT THE ECONOMICS, STUPID

———

## ON THE ROLE OF CRYPTO-ECONOMICS

Torrent sites have used a decentralized peer-to-peer system to share files without much success. "In a torrent system, anyone can share their file with a decentralized network. The idea was that people would download them and keep seeding, aka sharing the file with the network for others to download. The problem was that this worked on an honor system. If you were downloading a file, then you were expected to seed as well. The problem is that humans are not really the most honorable of creatures, and without any economic incentives, it made no sense for people to keep seeding a file which took up unnecessary space in their computers."[32] In a blockchain network, though, crypto-economics can help. It brings together aspects of cryptography and economics. It provides incentives for the participants to get the work done to keep the network going in a self-sustaining manner.

———

32  Rosic, "What Is Cryptoeconomics?"

Suppose you are going through the rigor of creating a blockchain-based solution for companies. In that case, you are doing it because you think it will create economic value for all the participants. The intention is to save money and time for the participants or create new opportunities to increase revenue. In the case of Synaptic Health Alliance (discussed in Chapter 2), by putting multiple data sources contributed by various network participants into the same database, they hoped to get synergies that would allow for cost savings. As part of this economic rationale, you have to think about different stakeholders and their incentive to join and contribute to the system as good economic citizens of the consortium. Participants may have a line of sight into the value they derive from the solution, but how can you incentivize them to participate and contribute to the alliance's health?

Blockchain can provide a working model to offer participants an economic incentive to be good network citizens and pull their weight. In the case of Synaptic Health Alliance, the idea of a data marketplace was floated. That helped pave the way to figure out the model for network economics. Anyone who wants to use the data and amend their provider directory, updated by another payer, would need to buy it from the entity that submitted it. The buyer's willingness to pay will depend on the history of how accurate the data is from that insurer. The network rewards the participants for contributing accurate data. This will also provide a way to shoehorn a lot more companies in and allow them to onboard and use the network in a way that they're not freeloading on everyone else's data. Otherwise, there is no incentive to participate as a model citizen of the network. "If I could do it over again, I would push much harder to help them understand the need for an economic model," explains Tony Little.

## ON THE NEED FOR FOCUS ON NETWORK ECONOMICS

In general, there is a tendency to overlook the "economics" part of the equation because typically, people who come forward and take the initiative to drive technology projects are, well, technologists. They approach the solution from the perspective of creating a technology solution. Buy-in from business teams at the outset of the project will increase the chance of success. HFS Research reports that "Seventy-five percent of respondents look at blockchain as a strategic priority today, but the budget for more than 90 percent of blockchain initiatives is emanating from IT budgets. Only 7 percent of business unit heads are allocating budget for blockchain initiatives, which leads us to question their overall commitment."[33] This observation is also echoed by Tony in his work with Synaptic Health Alliance: "What would have been great is if we would have had economists or the business people come in and say, 'Okay, we're creating a marketplace.' And the requirements for the technology should have been driven off the marketplace idea." This would drive the conversation about the economics of the blockchain solution.

Suppose the focus of a blockchain project is more on the technical aspects and not on economic incentives. In that case, there is a risk of missing the big picture. "Much of the power of blockchain-supported decentralized networks derives from the fact that they have the potential to draw

---

33   Gupta et al., "Ignore Blockchain at Your Peril," 16.

in participants by leveraging economic incentives."[34] In all parts of a business network's value chain, the participants can derive economic value from a blockchain project. However, all improvements that a blockchain network brings to the table may not be apparent to participants up the stream in the value chain. It is essential to focus on value for all participants and bring it in focus to have appropriate visibility.

In a supply chain consortium like Vinturas, a consortium of logistic service providers (LSPs) in the finished vehicle logistics (FVL) industry, the participants expect to derive increased benefits as more companies throughout the supply chain join the network and represent all types of stakeholders.

"So, blockchain technology enables collaboration and enables value creation for all stakeholders in the ecosystem . . . in a world where we are all more and more afraid of bigger organizations, giants, middlemen taking away your data and making money themselves. Our position at Vinturas is that we all benefit if we collaborate together in a blockchain-based network."[35] We all benefit; this is how Jon Kuiper, CEO of Vinturas, explains it. That is what blockchain is all about. But for everybody to benefit, you have to be clear about how everybody will benefit and be set up for everybody to benefit.

The FVL industry encompasses all the activities of shipping a new consumer vehicle from the factory to the dealer. Since we are talking vehicles, the shipping requires more specialized activities than what we might be aware of with the standard

---

34   SettleMint, "Why Enterprise Blockchain." 23
35   Kuiper., "Supply Chain on the Blockchain."

everyday consumer packages. There is a need for specialized transportation, skilled drivers who can handle these deliveries, specialized storage, pre-delivery inspections, etc. Due to the nature of transportation and handling of vehicles, there is also a high risk of damage. In the FVL industry, due to today's supply chains being global in nature, there is added complexity. The complex and dynamic nature of the industry presents unique challenges.

In FVL, LSPs are a significant player and are outsourcing entities that manage the storage, distribution, and transportation of vehicles. For a vehicle to reach the dealer from the production facility, multiple hand-offs happen between original equipment manufacturers (OEMs), i.e., the companies producing the vehicles, and various LSPs. These LSPs and OEMs do not use any standardized data exchange among themselves. In addition to that, all the processes supporting the handovers are paper-based. This situation leads to an opaque supply chain. The result is that the OEMs do not have end-to-end visibility in their supply chain, leading to poor inventory management.

The dealer knows when the vehicle has been produced in the factory but has no idea when it will arrive at the dealership for the customer to take possession. This lack of visibility leads to poor planning of the last mile processes for hand-off to the customers. Consumers accustomed to better experiences with online retailers for their other delivery needs are left underwhelmed in comparison.

In a situation rife with such inefficiencies, the only way LSPs can lower their service pricing is by cutting down on profit margins. With profit margins under pressure and all the focus on cutting costs, the companies cannot invest in upgrading their processes and tools. Supply chain control towers are one of the industry's initiatives; here, the more prominent players try to optimize the economics by consolidating smaller players' contracts. This approach only ends up introducing more structural inefficiencies into the process. The supply chain control towers end up operating as middlemen, thus adding cost to the overall infrastructure. This introduction of intermediaries in the value chain also creates a threat of marginalization for the logistics service providers.

With his extensive experience working with supply chains, Jon appreciates the value that blockchain technology can bring to address the FVL industry's challenges. As he explains, "Like in many industries, collaboration is a new theme in the world, in general terms, and certainly in relation to blockchain technology. Blockchain technology is a fantastic technology to collaborate, and collaborating creates additional value. At the same time, it's fair to say that the companies that are now working together in Vinturas are, on the floor and operational levels, competitors. So this requires a mindset of identifying the value that we will collectively have, if we collectively digitize our world, in a safe and fair way."[36] In comparison to a cost-cutting focus, collaboration makes it possible to create more value.

Vinturas believed that the right technology could help fix the finished vehicle supply chain's inefficiencies. They

---

36   Ibid.

created a blockchain-based digital collaboration infrastructure to benefit the whole ecosystem. "We—and by 'we,' I mean a number of logistics service providers in Europe—said . . . 'Well, we need to take the initiative to create this digital infrastructure, this collaboration infrastructure, where we will all benefit and not only as logistic service providers . . . but also other stakeholders in the ecosystem,'" explains Jon.[37]

Like Vinturas, first, you should decide to use blockchain technology for the right reasons, i.e., to create value. After that, you also have to define how the value will be generated for various participants. The focus should be on value provided to all players throughout the value chain. Value can come in the form of savings it brings for the participants, or it can come from enabling new ways of generating revenue that were not possible earlier. Keep in mind that various stakeholders will derive value in different possible ways. Vinturas is setting themselves up for success by considering the incentives needed for all participants, including the ones upstream in the value chain, like the OEMs. The business architecture of the network thus needs to be emphasized from the beginning of the project.

Vinturas started with three companies in Europe, and over time, have added three more shareholders who want to collaborate. Vinturas now represents approximately 25 percent of the market of new vehicle movements in Europe. In the case of Vinturas, the focus was on the critical efficiencies provided to the FVL companies and all other players in the

---

37   Ibid.

value chain (including OEMs and claims processors). Collective use of one standardized data set can show the state of the end-to-end supply chain. With that, the ecosystem can get rid of the common enemy, i.e., all the paperwork rife in their processes. The move away from paper-based processes will go a long way in helping optimize the cost structure.

**BLOCKCHAIN NETWORK MATURITY MODEL**

# Blockchain Network Maturity Model

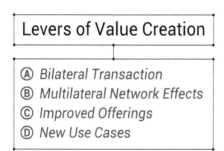

Levers of Value Creation

Ⓐ *Bilateral Transaction*
Ⓑ *Multilateral Network Effects*
Ⓒ *Improved Offerings*
Ⓓ *New Use Cases*

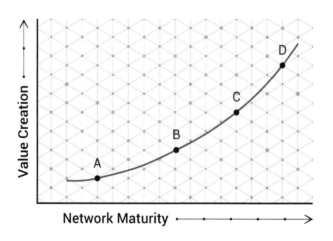

Typically, a new blockchain initiative is going to start with a small group of initial founding partners. The hope is that the consortium will eventually grow and deliver ever-increasing value to all the participants. As the business blockchain network goes through its life cycle and matures, it helps to focus on different levers of value creation. We can use a blockchain network maturity model to help look at these levers during the business network's growth. It is essential to identify which lever will deliver more value at different times in a network's lifecycle.

### BILATERAL TRANSACTIONS: VALUE CREATION BY TWO PARTNERS CONTRIBUTING TO THE DATASET

When you are starting out, you can stage the network economics first to tackle the bilateral use cases. Working first on bilateral use cases will enable the participants to get some value early on. These use cases are not necessarily dependent on adoption by a large number of participants to provide value; for example, in a use case using smart contracts to enable automatic release of payments for goods received at the warehouse. In a non-blockchain world, one of the frictions present in all kinds of settings is how challenging it can be to monitor and enforce contracts. Just because you have a contract with another party does not guarantee that the other person or entity will follow through on what they said they were going to do. One of the promises of smart contracts in blockchain is that the contract will automatically execute whenever the contract conditions are met. Having a smart contract adds value by increasing the credibility of both parties' commitment to the business relationship. It takes away the counter-party risk.

## MULTILATERAL NETWORK EFFECTS: VALUE CREATION BY MULTIPLE PARTNERS CONTRIBUTING TO THE DATASET

This layer of value creation refers to the network effects. Network effect comes into play when you bring together various participants. They have increased value because others are now participating. You can then expand the use cases that the network is tackling. You can now include use cases that will benefit from multilateral transactions as the group matures and grows. In the case of Synaptic Health Alliance, multiple insurance payers come together to share a set of data. Here, the network's value is higher if more participants are adding to the data pool. Growth in the number of participants will more likely be the case as the group matures.

## IMPROVED OFFERINGS: VALUE CREATION THROUGH BETTER SOLUTIONS USING EXISTING DATA

Improved offerings come about by taking data that others have contributed, analyzing it, and coming up with better solutions. In the case of Siam Central Bank, the banks could reduce the cost of loans because of reduced risk. As Orapong explains for SCB, in the past, because invoice approval would take three weeks, banks had to wait for long periods before being able to provide financing. Now banks have three more weeks to offer invoice financing to the supplier because the invoice approval time has gone down to one day. In developing countries, banks also have added risk because the supplier could be using the same invoice to approach multiple banks for invoice financing. Banks need to price the funding to compensate for the risk. But with this platform, SCB is the payment bank and financing bank. The bank sees this trade from the time of PO issuance to the point that goods were shipped and the invoice issued. So they know the invoice is real, and they do not have any collection risk: "With that, rather than providing financing at 18 percent, you are providing at less than 5 percent."[38] This situation enables them to provide improved offerings based on the same dataset using a blockchain-based solution.

**NEW USE CASES: VALUE CREATION ON NEW USE CASES ENABLED WITH EXISTING DATA**

Next, see where you can use the consortium that has been bootstrapped for one use case and launch another use case. When looking to build new use cases, you should first look at the data that has already been contributed. Based on that, decide the next use case to launch. It is not advisable to start on a use case that would require a whole new set of data and participants being onboarded. Try to build it off of the success of the previous one.

The blockchain network maturity model is not to say that value creation will always be linear. Depending on how ambitious the team is, you can choose to tackle value creation using any levers. However, understanding which lever you are using and matching that to the network's maturity will increase chances of success.

All in all, blockchain can deliver much economic value to groups trying to use it to solve a common challenge. But it would help if you were clear about what drives the creation of that value. Additionally, have a line of sight into who is getting the value. As we saw in Chapter 2, one of the pitfalls

---

38   Thien-Ngern et al., "From Siam Commercial Bank."

is that it's not always clear to the project participants what exactly blockchain is intended to do compared to existing technologies. In the case of a blockchain project, you have to look at value for all participants, bringing in aspects of network economics. Individual participant value is all well and good. Still, without considering the value derived by all participants, we are setting ourselves up for failure.

# CHAPTER 4

# THE ROI DILEMMA

## THE NATURE OF ROI

"I went in and said, 'Yeah, we have something new. It is very promising. But we have no idea what we are going to get out of it,' . . . I had one picture that I showed to them at the beginning. It's a picture that tricks your eyes. If you look one way, it looks like a bird. If you look the other way, it looks like a rabbit. So I told them at that point that I don't know if I am selling you a bird or a rabbit. If it's a bird, it will fly. If it's a rabbit, it'll dig a hole, and you will never see it again."[39]

As we saw in Chapter 2, Orapong has been deeply involved with the blockchain efforts of SCB. At the start of the conversations, Orapong positioned their blockchain project to Siam Central Bank's partners in this fashion. When making decisions on their investments in a blockchain project, senior company leaders find themselves at the same crossroads. Even if the team has done its due diligence and identified

---

39   Thien-Ngern et al., "From Siam Commercial Bank."

value for all the project participants, the question is: is it worth the cost?

Return on investment (ROI) directly measures the net returns on a particular investment relative to its cost. Return is the quantification of the business value that we expect the blockchain project to provide. Cost is the other aspect of the ROI calculation. However, this basic ROI calculation ignores the impact of time on the investment in the blockchain project. When comparing blockchain projects to other competing investment options in emerging technologies available to company leaders, time can sway decision-making.

**TIME AS A FACTOR: THE NEED FOR MORE TIME**
The aspect of time is vital in the case of blockchain projects when making early decisions. Various factors come into play that can contribute to more time being needed for a blockchain project to show returns. Blockchain projects come with change. People naturally resist change. It is, therefore, necessary to have a long-term perspective and lots of patience to allow time for people to adjust to the new normal. With multiple stakeholders' involvement, getting numerous organizations aligned and moving forward in a new way of working as a cooperative is difficult for blockchain projects. The need to have a consensus as the way to move forward also requires an investment in time.

A core part of the value from blockchain is due to network economics. Businesses built to harness network effects generally take years to become profitable. "If I had to give one piece of advice, it would be to really understand what is the value that blockchain and a blockchain network are bringing to your project, and be really precise about that. And then be patient. The network businesses, the social networks that we look at now took years to build, right? Their value really came from getting, you know, two-thirds of the world's population on Facebook or whatever else you want to talk about. And so the value from blockchain-based networks are going to be similar," says Stephanie Hurder, who we met in Chapter 2.[40]

We have various examples of network businesses that took years before becoming profitable around us. Facebook is one example, as is Twitter.[41] For any product or service that relies on network effects, the making of big money for the founding members will be several years into the future. Looking at an ROI number in the short term would be an incorrect metric to make decisions about pursuing a blockchain project. Can a senior leader in a technology company adopt such a long-term perspective in the face of investor scrutiny?

### INVESTMENT AS A FACTOR: THE NEED FOR MORE INVESTMENT

"Something like blockchain and distributed ledgers—they require a critical mass to achieve the benefits. And getting enough people educated, getting enough people through that POC journey, getting enough people through their investment committees and to the end of it, with extra money to spend on commercialization, has taken a lot longer because you need that network effect for it to be successful," says Andrew Speers.[42] Andrew has worked as director of products

---

40  Hurder, "Why Enterprise Blockchains Fail."
41  Thompson, "Facebook Turns a Profit"; Kollewe, "Twitter Makes First Quarterly Profit in Its History."
42  Speers, "User Experience on the Blockchain."

and innovation at Royal Bank of Scotland (RBS). RBS is an international banking and financial services company. They are involved with various blockchain initiatives in partnership with other industry players: first, Coadjute, working on streamlining the UK property market; second, Marco Polo, a finance network of banks, technology partners, and corporations working on transparency in trade finance; and third, Contour (formerly Voltron) working in the trade finance industry, starting with the Letter of Credit. With his involvement in blockchain projects at RBS, Andrew has developed a good insight into the efforts needed to move blockchain projects forward.

Working with multiple blockchain projects, RBS realized that many factors increase the costs in ROI calculations. Besides giving time for network effects to play out, you also have to make early investments in learning about the technology. With large banks like RBS, if any bank's business customers have a multi-product need, their experience is typically very fragmented. And why wouldn't it be? A user's journey does not necessarily influence product design. In banks, typically, product creation revolves around the silos of specific expertise within the bank. While getting service for a complicated need, a corporate customer will have to go through silos like originations function, the credit assessment, forex, trade finance, insurance, risk, etc. Going through all these silos ends up creating a very disconnected experience for the customer.

One cause of the disconnected user experience is how larger financial organizations acquire other smaller companies with their own systems and processes. At times, the acquiring company's response could be to keep the acquired company as separate organizations, continuing to use their own systems, which will need to be integrated. This approach further adds to the internal fragmentation contributing to poor user experience.

To respond to these and other industry challenges affecting user experience, RBS identified an opportunity in blockchain quite early. As Andrew says, "Technology—distributed ledger technology is coming to a maturity point now, where it's helping people knit some of this together. The technology is catching up. We can create client-centric user experiences by having a distributed architecture with identifiable data that we can seamlessly stitch together into bespoke propositions. So, you can have a little bit of FX attached to a little bit of credit assessment, attached to a little bit of trade finance, etc. Once your data goes into the distributed machine, smart contracts can then send the data to where it needs to go and transact on it automatically, or more automatically than it is at the moment, to improve the user experience."[43]

With blockchain, very early on, RBS had engineering teams with some brilliant people take a look at the technology. Engineers tested and played with and got used to the technology. Once it got to a point where it was clear that there were enough use cases, they created a community of practice with its center of excellence around blockchain.

When companies are at the beginning of their blockchain journey, the organization's understanding of commercializing

---

43   Ibid.

an emerging technology will be limited. Having it run through a centralized function focused on blockchain technology helps evaluate the extensive list of use cases. An investment in building a COE is an upfront cost contributing to the denominator in an ROI calculation. As Andrew confirms on the choice made by RBS, "Any organization needs to be prepared to burn a little bit of money as something new is coming up, to test it, and play with it. And we did that very early on in the picture."[44]

### EXTRA COST DUE TO PARALLEL RUNNING OF THE SYSTEM

Because blockchain is in such early stages, there is a need to prove the benefits of new technology. The ability to compare and contrast with existing technology also helps with decision-making. A shift of production systems in a phased manner can help facilitate that. As the new blockchain-based solution runs parallel with existing solutions, it adds to the costs. This duality is good in the long run as it manages risk while building confidence in the technology. Because you are effectively running two systems in parallel, it does come at a higher cost in the short run. It creates even more reasons to have a long-term outlook for ROI. Once we have a winner, between the old and the new, we can start seeing the gains that we were targeting by using blockchain.

Dustin Helland confirms this process "requires the new solution to match up against whatever the legacy solution is and prove itself worthy. In order to do that, it does initially require some additional investment and expense."[45] Dustin

---

44  Ibid.
45  Helland, "State Farm's Blockchain."

Helland has been part of the leadership team driving State Farm's blockchain strategy since 2016.

State Farm was founded back in 1922. It is one of America's major insurance companies, insuring more cars and homes than any other insurers in the country. They also provide other products to their customers, like life insurance and other financial services. For their blockchain use case, they chose to work on the netting of auto claims subrogation payments between insurers on the blockchain as one of the projects to pursue. USAA insurance has been their co-founder for the subrogation product. They shared the same vision and saw similar opportunities with a common thought process and approach.

Subrogation is not a common word in everyday parlance, and I had to dig into it a little more to understand what it is all about. Let's say your car gets rear-ended, and the other driver is at fault. You will go ahead and start insurance claims. That's when the subrogation process kicks in. In the context of an insurance claim coming in, "subrogation" is the process through which your insurance company collects money from the at-fault party or their insurance company.

The US auto insurance industry handles a large number of individual claims subrogation payments each day. Subrogation is a highly manual process with dependence on snail mail and paper checks. Using blockchain, they have built a system that can maintain accounting for each transaction electronically. It then calculates a net manifest based on all those transactions. It passes that net on to the organization's existing electronic payment system to enable electronic payment. This move to a blockchain-based solution has reduced processing time and increased efficiency, helping State Farm pass on the benefits to their policyholder.

State Farm understands that blockchain solutions will need to be run parallel with the existing solution to compare old and new solutions. Simultaneously, it does mean an increase in costs as you are effectively running two systems.

**ON THE DIFFICULTY OF QUANTIFYING BLOCKCHAIN ROI**
As we discussed earlier in the chapter, blockchain in enterprises is a network economics reliant technology. You don't succeed with blockchain on your own. Besides the need to give the network time to mature, the companies don't know how big the network will grow at the start of their journey. The hope is that every stakeholder in the industry will join in. That may eventually happen. But, in the beginning, you do not know how long it will take for that end state to pan out. The success of the network depends on many unknown variables. In light of this situation, you have to make projections based on assumptions about the network size. These assumptions bring in uncertainty around the ROI projections.

The ROI is challenging to quantify because blockchain is still relatively new. You can't rely on many available examples for guidance. You can't lean upon any real precedents. Blockchain was first introduced to the world in 2009 with Satoshi Nakamoto's white paper on Bitcoin. That was just over a decade ago. Their packaging as blockchain has been recent, even though the various concepts that make up blockchain have been around for a few years. More importantly, the use of blockchain for solving issues faced by companies is even more recent. Hyperledger and Ethereum were introduced in 2015 with the added layer of smart contracts. This addition made blockchain more viable for companies. With such a young technology, you don't have much to lean on for inspiration. There is no guidance on how to use it effectively. Quantification of demonstrated value is also missing.

On the other hand, with the newness of the technology and not having a large body of work behind it, blockchain knowledge is scarce. It is also evolving very fast with new developments in this nascent space. The ever-changing landscape of blockchain technology makes it difficult and expensive to find people with relevant blockchain knowledge. The technology will mature over time, and current limitations will eventually be solved. Meanwhile, you should consider the evolution of this technology and plan for higher costs.

Other comparable options to solve the same problems include setting up manual processes. The use of existing technology can help get these tasks done in a quick and dirty manner. The availability of these options makes it difficult for leadership to justify emerging technology's business case in a shorter-term time frame. Remember, you can get there faster with incumbent technology, but you give up on sowing the seeds to set up blockchain as an enabling technology for your company and get its advantages. Over a longer life cycle, your cost will decrease if you bring automation enabled by adopting blockchain technology into the picture.

## INCREMENTAL VALUE HELPS WITH ROI DILEMMA

Collaborating with competitors is new and uncharted territory for businesses. You may start your journey corralling everyone around one use case. But as we saw in Chapter 3, with the blockchain network maturity model, as the network grows, new use cases will evolve based on how the group matures. In reality, there would be multiple use cases that the consortium can tap into. All of them necessarily may not be visible from the start. When you are looking at ROI, if you can prove that the returns on one use case show a pretty good cost-benefit, you should consider going forward with it. Eventually, newer ones that show up over and above the starter use case will add to the returns part of the ROI, even though you can't quantify them at this time.

Looking for some early traction helps with the ROI situation. It helps to focus on how early users can get some value from their participation and investment. You should think of it more in terms of incremental returns to start with. Eventually, as the network grows, there should be an expectation of higher returns coming in.

When designing your system, you look at the use cases and determine that the real value comes when many industry stakeholders are on the network participating in multilateral transactions. It would then make sense to provide that rich feature set at the launch. However, suppose the actual value comes after many players have been on-boarded. In that case, you will have a long period during which there isn't much value coming from the network while you wait for everyone to show up. While you may have big goals after the network matures, you should balance that against early quick wins to encourage adoption by more participants in the long term. And as the momentum builds up with more players adopting the network, you can also build up functionality toward a more feature-rich solution.

As Dustin Helland put it, "When you think about different types of use cases, and you are looking at how, quickly, can an organization begin to achieve some level of value, there are some use cases that you can start to achieve some level of value with a smaller network . . . if you have a use case that's targeting business to business transaction efficiencies—while you need a larger group to be involved to really get significant value—you can get some value right out of the gates with a smaller network."[46]

On their part, State Farm approached the project by breaking it down into phases. Through each phase, they gain additional insights for ROI projections. The first phase was a prototype that was evaluated at the end of the phase. Phase two is the shadow network phase, where they implemented the system in production in parallel to the existing processes. This dual implementation proves the solution and validates the expected business process efficiencies. "So we've taken an iterative approach to both development and revisiting the actual business case ROI," explains Dustin.[47] The blockchain network maturity curve (from Chapter 3) is one way to look at a possible progression and decide on the kinds of use cases to target as you look at incremental ROI.

---

46   Ibid.
47   Ibid.

It would be best if you looked at blockchain technology's benefits holistically over the long term. Otherwise, you will miss the intrinsic benefits that blockchain brings to the table to build distributed solutions with other companies, get cost synergy, and enable new revenue opportunities. Concluding in the words of Dustin Helland: "Sometimes you are willing to invest upfront for future returns, and time is a risk factor. But maybe there's a bigger opportunity at the end of that, and you are willing to invest in it and take the risk."[48]

---

48  Ibid.

## CHAPTER 5

# ALL ABOUT CONSORTIA

___

**ABOUT CONSORTIA**

Merriam-Webster online gives this definition of a consortium: "An agreement, combination, or group (as of companies) formed to undertake an enterprise beyond the resources of any one member." One part that we are looking at here is "group of companies."[49] Many times, these groups of companies will comprise participants that are competitors in the same market. And the second aspect that we are looking at is "beyond the resources of any one member."

Because the current business world primarily doesn't operate like this today, this state of coopetition can be challenging to establish. However, it is worth pursuing because companies can look to get returns that would not be possible independently. In that pursuit, companies looking to use blockchain technology come together in some form of a consortium to build the solution together. As Deloitte's 2019

___

49   Merriam-Webster, s.v. "consortium (n.)," accessed February 15, 2021.

Global Blockchain Survey found, there are various reasons why companies might look to join a consortium.[50]

As companies start looking into and experimenting with blockchain, they get to the point of trying to figure out how to best work with other players in an organized fashion. As we saw in Chapter 2, Optum technologies started by learning about blockchain technology. They evaluated blockchain's impact on their business, decided the use case to pursue, and started looking to build relationships with other insurers interested in working together. The idea was to find a few national insurers who want to participate in the experiment and benefit by trying to solve the use case with blockchain.

This chapter explores blockchain consortia.

Participating in various blockchain health care conferences allowed the Optum team to build these relationships with other insurers like Humana, Multiplan, Aetna, etc. These were the efforts that paved the way for consortium conversations. At a high level, the consortium's founding partners signed a memorandum of understanding to start using the use case to improve provider data accuracy. Each entity had to negotiate up the leadership chain, and the Synaptic Health Alliance was born as a consortium.

**TYPES OF CONSORTIA**

That's the route Synaptic Health Alliance took. However, different forms of consortia take shape as companies try to figure out how to best cooperate with competitors. One framework to

---

50   [2]Pawczuk et al., Deloitte's 2019 Global Blockchain Survey

view the developing consortia trends in the blockchain space is to look at the leadership available to bring the ecosystem together. A consortium steward provides the lead in defining the working relationship of business network partners to help drive the blockchain solution from concept through development and industry adoption. There are two emerging patterns to structure these consortia. First is a founder-led consortium where the consortium steward is one of the companies in the industry ecosystem. The second is where an independent entity provides leadership as the consortium steward.

### FOUNDER-LED CONSORTIUM

A founder-led consortium typically involves an industry leader providing an early lead in the adoption of blockchain technology. Often the founder acts as the steward of the business network and is responsible for providing technological and organizational leadership and bringing its business partners along in adopting a blockchain use case. Sometimes a dominant industry player fills this role. At other times, a group of companies comes together to agree and solve a shared business problem. Still, one of the group's peers would end up taking the lead as the steward of the network. One of them, however, does provide leadership to the group in structuring the alliance.

Irrespective of the consortium steward's profile, all participants work together to build out the solution, prove it, and invite others in the industry to join in. In this case, the maturation of the product and the consortium would likely progress in parallel. Technical maturity, among other things, includes the progression of developing the solution, establishing standards protocols, defining integrations, etc.

Organizational maturity consists of the group's progress in defining the operating model, governance, etc., and growing the network by making it attractive for other partners to join the consortium.

## Benefits organizations expect from consortia

Cost saving and learning opportunites are top benefits that respondents expect from consortia participation.

*Survey question: What benefits does your organization or project get or expect to get from a cosortium? (Percentage of respondents who cite that factor as a benefit from joining consortia)*

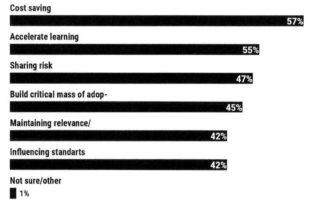

**Cost saving**
57%

**Accelerate learning**
55%

**Sharing risk**
47%

**Build critical mass of adop-**
45%

**Maintaining relevance/**
42%

**Influencing standarts**
42%

**Not sure/other**
1%

N=1,386 (global enterprise).

Note: Percentages total more than 100 percent because respondents were allowed to submit more than one answer.

Source: Deloitte's 2019 Global Blockchain Survey.

This consortia structure typically starts with a smaller number of participants, which helps better manage the politics of competitors needing to adjust to the new paradigm of working together toward a common goal. A steward of the blockchain network has to tackle technology, economics, and politics as different facets of the consortium. Having a smaller number of starting members helps not to complicate the politics. If the speed of decision-making is an important factor for the consortium's success, having a consortium steward helps move things forward at a relatively faster clip. If other consortium partners have a similar idea of the solution, it helps with quicker decision-making.

Although a smaller number of consortium members helps with faster decision-making, there is still a need to have large enough numbers to form a minimum viable ecosystem. After all, network effects influence the consortium's chances of success. You can't start a really good blockchain use case that provides value with smaller industry players. It is unlikely to have enough weight. It's a delicate balance—keeping the numbers small to keep it manageable but large enough to have the outcome be material and attract other industry participants.

On the flip side, though, this structure might cause friction for newer members of the consortium. They might fear that initial members will benefit more and rules are skewed against them. This can give newcomers a reason to hesitate and thus provide friction for adoption and get in the way of growing the consortium.

An example of this consortium is in the retail industry centered around food safety. Walmart has been heavily involved in this initiative. Walmart is one of the world's largest retailers and one of the first to pilot blockchain technology. Frank Yiannas, the vice president of food safety at Walmart, has come to appreciate the transformative possibilities of blockchain technology. As he explains, "I happen to be a big believer that blockchain is a new and emerging technology that has extreme relevance for food. But I have to tell you, when I first started at this, I was a major blockchain skeptic.

But after working with it, and more importantly, piloting it, I've become a blockchain believer for sure."[51]

The Centers for Disease Control and Prevention (CDC) and the US Department of Agriculture (USDA) data have documented the impact of contamination in food supply chains. The CDC estimates that one in six Americans get sick from contaminated foods or beverages each year, and three thousand die as a result. The USDA estimates that foodborne illnesses cost more than $15.6 billion each year.[52]

With technological advances, the food supply chain has grown a lot. Still, it comes with the challenge of keeping food safe throughout the system. Food contamination episodes have a widespread impact on companies in the ecosystem, starting from the producer to the retailers. It also negatively impacts consumer confidence. Consumers may eventually stop buying certain food products for fear of health hazards. Even if one lot has problems, retailers have to remove entire shipments from the shelves because it takes a long time to trace and identify the problem's origin. They want to err on the side of safety.

Origin tracing is difficult and time-consuming because of various reasons. No one has complete visibility into data on the movement of goods across the entire supply chain. Typically each player in the supply chain only has knowledge of their transaction up the chain with their supplier and down the chain with their customer. A complete picture needs

---

51  Yiannas, "Leading Food Safety."
52  Centers for Disease Control and Prevention, "CDC and Food Safety."

to be put together, one piece at a time. Stitching it together isn't easy either because much of the record maintenance is not standardized. There is also widespread use of paper documents, which means that tracing has to be done manually and takes much longer than it would if digital records were being used. Because the records have been maintained manually—on paper—there is also a higher chance of data mistakes due to user error. The errors need to be reconciled to get an accurate picture. Many foods see commingling from multiple sources coming in from different countries, and traceability is further complicated.

With the early adoption of blockchain, Walmart has seen some early gains. Walmart is focused on food safety, using blockchain technology to help them better manage their supply chains. They decided to tackle two use cases to run pilots—pork in China and mangoes in the US. These pilots have helped Walmart reduce the time it takes to track the origin of items and allows the retailed to have better availability of associated data through the supply chain to improve food safety and reduce waste. In their blockchain pilot on the pork supply chain in China, they could reduce the time needed to track down the meat source from twenty-six hours down to a few seconds. For the pilot on mangoes, as confirmed by Frank Yiannas, "We tried to trace mangoes, sliced mangoes back to the source. The current process took us about seven days, you know, pretty much the industry benchmark. Maybe a little bit faster than at times that happens in some of these health investigations. After blockchain, we could do it in 2.2 seconds."[53]

---

53    Yiannas, "Leading Food Safety."

Food safety is an area ripe for the use of blockchain technology. Players in the food safety ecosystem have an incentive to work together to solve the problem using blockchain technology. By its very nature, the ecosystem lends itself well to what blockchain can bring to the table. Because food safety is not a competitive issue, participants in the whole ecosystem have an incentive to cooperate. When a food safety issue happens—nobody wins. Suppose there is an E. coli outbreak with consumption of fresh spinach in the interest of consumer safety. In that case, all the spinach that is difficult to trace gets pulled from the shelves. This inability to quickly trace the source also hurts those whose supply chain did not carry the tainted products. This motivates the industry participants to work together and make the solution work. Over and above that, the overall system is too big for any single player to solve it by themselves, making sense to co-operate with the competitors.

To provide traceability throughout the complete supply chain, this kind of effort needs leadership from a key player. That company coordinates other stakeholders and shows them what blockchain technology can offer to solve their collective challenges. The consortium has grown to include Dole, Driscoll's, Kroger, Tyson Foods, and more. As we learned in Chapter 3, the consortium steward has to define the value for all participants in the ecosystem for its efforts to be successful. Otherwise, wider adoption by breeders, processing plants, cold storage facilities, distribution centers, and retail stores will be difficult to pull off.

### NEUTRAL THIRD-PARTY-LED CONSORTIUM

A startup company or an independent software vendor (ISV) develops a blockchain-based solution to solve a shared problem within the industry in a neutral third-party-led consortium. This independent company brokers the consortium's workings and manages the operational and governance structure to attract participants in the ecosystem to join the network. This neutral third party provides the lead in building the solution, starting from the product's initial conception, and working toward development, and finally, implementation and support.

In this scenario, because there is no one company leading the effort, there is less fear amongst other partners about working in the shadow of a big brother imposing on them. That makes for easier recruitment of newer members to grow the network. Because it is a neutral environment, it is also relatively more straightforward for competitors to start working together. This neutral environment helps reduce any drag on adoption.

As we see in other business situations, when you have many decision-makers at the table who have an equal say in matters of decision making, the going can be slow. Different opinions and points of view need to be reconciled to achieve consensus. That can be challenging and time-consuming. In such a situation, this model can help move things along faster.

As Dan Salmons, CEO of Coadjute, explained to me, "It seemed to us that the answer was to create a company that could present a solution rather than wait for one to be agreed on." Coadjute is on a mission to digitally connect the UK's property market by bringing together various disparate players in the industry: estate agents, conveyancers, surveyors, brokers, lending banks, etc. The end goal is to improve the customer's home buying experience.

"I had a problem here that I didn't know the solution to. I was out hunting; how on Earth would you give a comprehensive end-to-end experience to customers in a very fragmented property market?" explained Dan. The home buying process is pretty complex because a buyer needs to engage with multiple businesses. Just think of all the steps you have to take when you buy a home. First, you find a real estate agent and start looking for a home.

Meanwhile, you also need to figure out how big a home you can afford. How large of a loan will the bank give you? You work with a bank for the preapproval. And then, at some point in time, you need a home inspector to help you understand what you are walking into. You work with a mortgage broker to find the right loan for you. An appraiser will come in to help before the loan is closed. You probably don't know what exactly every entity providing a service to you does throughout this long process, but there are associated fees.

Each of the entities you interact with during the buying process is part of a vertical sub-industry, i.e., real estate agents, banks, home inspectors, mortgage brokers, assessors, etc. "Each one of these verticals—state agency has been digitized in some great platforms. . . . Conveyancing has been digitized, the legal piece with some great platforms if you want to do that. Brokering has been digitized. Mortgage lending is being digitized. Surveying is being digitized. But collectively, when you go on this process, you have to knit all that together," explains John Reynolds, founder of Coadjute.[54]

---

54   Reynolds, "Real Estate on the Blockchain."

The individual pieces work well, but the end-to-end value chain is fragmented. It's tough for a consumer to get through it all. A buyer has to stitch it all together as they go through this process across different verticals. This situation leads to a longer buying time, which can go up to four or five months, with increased cost going up to 4 percent of the property values. John goes on to explain, "If I want to buy your house, and your name is on the land register as owning the house, really all we're trying to do is change that to my name and put some money in your account. But to do that, we've got like these six companies and all these things we will navigate through."[55] Buying a home is a watershed moment in people's lives. But the home buying process often brings along stress and frustration.

For Coadjute, it all started as a research project. Looking at different UK government agencies, you can't expect them to close down their systems and move to a single government platform. Could they create a distributed ledger that would keep their databases in sync? When the UK Land Registry department floated a bid, they went for it. A POC was built to test the shared ledger concept for the complete home buying process—from someone starting to list their house until someone moves in. They created nodes for each of the different players in the value chain. When they put out an invitation for companies to test it out, they received an overwhelming response.

Fifty nodes were set up across twenty-two countries to create dummy properties and complete transactions around them.

---

55    Ibid.

The POC proved that such a solution would go a long way in reducing the repetition, cost, and friction involved in the whole home buying process.

But the move from POC to production is enormous because it is about adoption. The POC showed that the solution will work technologically, but will industry participants be willing to adopt it? So, the next question was how to move into production successfully. The team realized that the industry participants already have systems they use, and it would be difficult for them to move off those systems and onto a new platform. The research around this challenge gave birth to the idea that Coadjute will be this network of platforms. So, they went and talked to leading platform providers in different verticals to work closely with them.

With that group, they moved into a non-production MVP. They connected the Coadjute platform to test environments of these other industry-leading platforms and make them available as a mobile solution. With this platform's help, a buyer can track their home buying journey and get a mortgage and move home in one simple online journey. By bringing together leading actors at each stage of the value chain, they can now create this end-to-end experience for the consumer.

To some extent, governance is not tricky for Coadjute. They are not targeting disintermediation or disrupting the industry, nor are they threatening the existing players. They are helping facilitate the end-to-end process for the current industry players. Some players in the property market have been very keen to see the Coadjute solution built. Others are interested but a little bit more ambivalent. There is a varying degree of commitment. There is also considerable variation in the types of companies involved. You have small software companies and also very large banks. This fragmented market with many small players leads to distrust that a big player might try and take it over. With all of this variability, following the third-party model seems to be a good fit.

As Dan explained, "We are seen as a trusted, independent, sort of objective third party by all the players in the market. Coadjute means collaborate, and you'll hear us say that we don't intend to disrupt the market. We want to support it. We've gone out of our way to try and be a good friend and supporter of all the companies involved."

Consortia are turning out to be the vehicle for collaboration utilized to tackle use cases that are beyond the means of one single company. Many ecosystems are adopting this approach to come together and learn about blockchain technology and build industry-wide solutions. Consortia enable the participants to take advantage of blockchain technology and solve common problems while maintaining the needed boundaries as competitors.

Next, let's take a look at some aspects that have helped others come together and play to win.

## CHAPTER 6

# CREATING COLLABORATION INFRASTRUCTURE

———

"Collaborating with your competitor is not always easy; it requires a different mindset than the one you've had for maybe twenty, thirty, or forty years," explained Jon Kuiper.[56] Blockchain provides the infrastructure for safe collaboration where competitors can collectively derive value. Bringing together competitors to be part of a successful ecosystem requires a multipronged approach, as I discovered listening to Lisa Butters talk about GoDirect Trade.

GoDirect is an Amazon-style marketplace for used aerospace parts that brings buyers and sellers together and simplifies their experience. It is part of Honeywell, a Fortune 100 company. Within aerospace, Honeywell wears many hats. They are an original equipment manufacturer (OEM),

---

56   Kuiper, "Supply Chain on the Blockchain."

manufacturing everything from components up to engines. They are a repair facility. And they are also into trading used aerospace parts.

"In a call this morning, we were talking about used aerospace parts and why people are so hesitant to do their transactions online. And we talked a lot about how there are a lot of parallels to the used car industry. So, buying used automobiles—and I think that some of the perceptions are that in order to buy a used car, people feel so compelled to negotiate on price. It's just what they do. They feel like they're not getting the best price unless they negotiate it. And I think that really is a good parallel to used aerospace parts. People feel almost like they're not being responsible if they're not negotiating the best price on these parts," explains Lisa Butters, general manager for GoDirect Trade. [57]

Never mind used cars—I think we all go into new car purchases with the same mentality—all geared up to negotiate.

According to ICF, the used aircraft parts market was valued at $5.4 billion last year, 60 percent of which was engine-related and 36 percent, component-related. The expectation is that the market-size will grow to $7.7 billion by 2026.[58] The industry sees most transactions offline via traditional routes of picking up the phone and calling somebody you know or sending them an email. You work only with someone you know and trust. Because of this, a transaction takes a long time to complete.

57   Butters., "Blockchain Airplane Parts."
58   Shah., "Honeywell Brings Blockchain."

As a *Wall Street Journal* article reports, "Before blockchain, a transaction took, on average, two phone calls and four emails to arrange, and two days to close. The sale of larger parts such as engines could take weeks of sending quotes and exchanging documentation."[59]

The buying process is manual and works offline mainly because of two reasons:

- First, these are typically high-value transactions due to the nature of the parts that the marketplace deals with. There are small items like nuts and bolts, but then we also have multimillion-dollar engines for sale and everything in between. The average transaction size is about $10,000.
- The other reason is that there is a high safety bar in the aerospace industry. These parts need to be safe enough to reinstall back in an aircraft so you can fly passengers safely.

Other players who have tried to shorten the buying cycle have run into a few problems. To reinforce buyer trust through the process, these players are trying to get quality documentation from sellers; although, they are falling short on their will to enforce it. Not being able to give buyers consistent transparency into the quality of purchased parts makes these marketplaces prone to failing. Seller adoption of the platform also runs into headwinds. They are not accustomed to having an online storefront to conduct business. After all, they have been selling over email and phone for years.

---

59   Ibid.

As the platform went live, the GoDirect Trade team knew that online transactions were not just going to happen overnight. They started an inquiry into what it would take to encourage buyers and sellers to move onto the platform and away from old behaviors. They started calling and emailing people to get a pulse on the market. They realized that for people to participate in e-commerce, a good customer experience, and the three Ps—price, pictures, and paperwork—are just table stakes. It will take more than that to help the whole industry move away from archaic paper and offline transactions. There is a reluctance to trust due to the high dollar amounts associated with the transactions. The aerospace industry's high-quality standards throw in more friction in the trust process from a quality perspective.

As Lisa explains it, "We believe that it really all boils down to trust. There isn't enough trust in that e-commerce transaction because the average orders are high-dollar, and there has to be a lot of inherent trust from a quality perspective. And so we need to look at other technologies such as blockchain to try to chip away at that boulder of mistrust. Because it's not going to just be about a good customer experience, but about providing transparency to the consumer that's going to move this channel into the digital era."[60]

For the aerospace industry, where the adoption of blockchain technology is yet to catch on, Honeywell is focusing on collaborating with other industry players. As Lisa explains, "For Honeywell, I wouldn't say that we're going at it alone. If anything, I can't think of a company with aerospace that's

---

60   Butters, "Blockchain Airplane Parts."

a bigger cheerleader for trying to collaborate and work with others—whether it's a mom and pop or big business—to try to collaborate on blockchain trials. And the reason why is because blockchain is truly a team sport. If you go at it alone, you get really nothing out of it. You get just your own data, and you have no other benefits, right? You might as well just have a database."[61]

Different industries are in various stages of adopting blockchain technology. Industries will mature around their understanding of blockchain technology as various consortia come together. Let us look at a few steps to take that help strengthen this collaboration infrastructure and set us up for higher chances of success.

### LOWERING RELATIONSHIP-SPECIFIC INVESTMENTS

One of the challenges in contracts and agreements is the holdup. Suppose that you and I consider entering into a business contract. To keep my side of the deal, I have to make several investments that I would not have otherwise made. For example, I may have to buy some new software, implement it, and adjust my business process to make it work. I have to adopt the new software, and it will be helpful only if I do business with you. But, if I leave the partnership, it is entirely useless. These are called relationship-specific investments. The hold-up problem occurs when I have made relationship-specific investments. You may then refuse to honor your side of the agreement unless we renegotiate the contract in your favor. If things go wrong, I will have wasted my resources on a relationship-specific investment. I may

---

61   Ibid.

not want to enter into a potentially profitable business partnership with you because of this risk. Relationship-specific investments are generally an impediment to a fruitful business partnership forming up. These kinds of situations are a source of friction to get started on business partnerships—to the extent that an agreement may not even materialize if there is enough mistrust.

The good thing with the blockchain environment is that in a data-sharing consortium, we have distributed consensus. Using nodes as validators, all companies have their own up-to-date copies of the ledgers. This setup can help reduce the risk of hold-up. The goal should be to think about how we can alleviate some of the risks that are typically involved with relationship-specific investments. For instance, a big problem when you are entering a data-sharing consortium is that you are worried you won't have access to your data anymore if you want to leave the consortium. It might be stored in a proprietary format or just be inaccessible. You may need the consortium software to read it. If you ever want to leave, you are stuck with a data format that you then have to pay someone to convert into a usable form for you.

As we have come to understand, blockchain technology's value comes from the robustness of the business network in the consortium. In service of the network, a consortium steward can help by alleviating the concerns of newer consortia members. To start with, blockchain is a technology that can help manufacture digital trust that enables smart contracts. Smart contracts, with their automated execution, can provide added commitment from all parties to execute on the terms of the agreement and reduce holdup risk.[62]

Since value gets derived from the network's vibrancy, expanding the network should be an active topic for consortia governance structure. Consortia stewards should focus on trying to reduce those kinds of frictions. One way to enable other companies to get involved is to make their entry into the network easier with less friction.

In the case of State Farm, as Dustin Helland explains, "One of the ways that we've enabled other insurers to get involved easily and with low entry investment is through a beta test. So this involves us providing the other insurance company with access to a node where they can exercise the application and run through some test scenarios with us. We also provide them with a full copy of the code, if they'd like to, where they can stand up their own node on their own and work through those same test scenarios."[63]

These actions make the newer members of the consortium feel welcome and start them on the right footing.

### CHOICE OF RIGHT PARTNERS TO START WITH

There is a need to find other industry players that would be willing to participate in an experiment. Choosing the right partners to start with can be pivotal in the initial success of the effort. Bringing together the right partners is an essential start in the journey of a consortium. Early on in the life

---

62   Holden et al., "Can Blockchain Solve."
63   Helland, "State Farm's Blockchain."

cycle of blockchain technology, when there are not many players involved in the blockchain ecosystem, it can be even more challenging.

Siam Central Bank appreciated this factor as they started on their journey with blockchain. As Orapong explained, "We started this in late 2017. At that point, there were not that many players. So, we have to assess because we're about to do something that is quite new and not stable yet—who could be the best partner? And who would be able to support us?"[64]

SCB understood that what they were attempting to do was very new and shaky with instabilities as the technology itself was evolving. They started working with Siam Cement Group (SCG), which is a manufacturing conglomerate. It is one of the largest companies in Thailand ($15 billion USD). It is also recognized as one of the most efficient and innovative companies in Thailand, winning several quality awards.

"If you are going to prove that new technology works, you better start from the top. If you can make the best company the most efficient company by improving their productivity, then you know what you have works," confirms Orapong.[65]

### PARTICIPATORY DECISION-MAKING
Blockchain technology brings to the fold a distributed nature to the data. It also allows the consortia members to have shared control of the data without any specific entity

---

64  Thien-Ngern et al., "From Siam Commercial Bank."
65  Ibid.

having complete control. Translating that further into the governance model of the consortia helps further solidify the confidence of network participants. The governance should be structured such that the participants can decide together.

## Challenges of joining blockchain consortia

Consortia face a full array of challenges to attract new members, with rules and participant roles and responsibilities heralding the list.

Q. What do you feel are the greatest challenges in participation in a blickchain consortium?

■ Percentage of respondents who feel the issue is a challenge in participation in a blockchain consortium

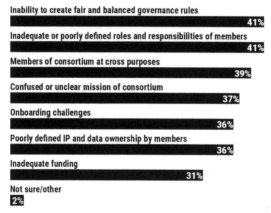

Notes: N=1,488. Percentages equal more than 100% because respondents were allowed to submit more than one answer.

Source: Deloitte's 2020 Global Blockchain Survey.

As Silvia Attanasio (whom we will meet in more detail in the next chapter) from ABI explains, "Our mission is to put the banks together and let them decide together. . . . We have a metaphor that guided the project from the very beginning, which is this group of soldiers who are very organized, who step together, who go on together, who protect each other. So we needed to work at the same time, to work always in a synchronized way. And this was really important."[66] That should be the guiding principle for the consortium. With that spirit, the consortium steward is more of a facilitator. Things like the companies' size or being a founding member should not matter as they are equal participants.

This approach can slow down things regarding decision-making. And that's a delicate balance that the consortium has to tread—the speed of decision versus building confidence in participants for continued participation. As Deloitte's 2020 blockchain survey found, many consortia that begin with good intentions often fail because of infighting and perceived inequities over different issues. [67]

### TIMING OF MONETIZATION

Very early on in the life of consortium, you are getting the network members to come together. At that time, you have to be thoughtful about who is getting value at each of the different maturity stages. The monetization decisions of the consortia should take into account the network member's willingness to pay. In the case of the Synaptic Health Alliance (Chapter 2), should you charge the doctors and insurance companies to participate in the business network? The answer to that depends on who is getting the value from the network.

The value proposition for the insurance company is apparent because insurers are legally required to maintain physician data. On their part, they are trying to figure out ways to collaborate to make their provider data accurate and do

---

66    Attanasio, "Blockchain for Italian."
67    Pawczuk et al., Deloitte's 2020 Global Blockchain Survey

that with a lower cost of maintenance. However, the doctors have the associated load of completing the paperwork for the insurance companies. Their pain of administrative burden in dealing with multiple insurers will surely go down. However, will it be enough that they will be willing to pay to join the network? That is not such a strong proposition.

As Stephanie Hurder suggests, "I think you really need to understand, what are the costs and benefits that the different types of stakeholders are getting? And what is their outside option for not participating?"[68]

To further mature the Synaptic Health solution, it would be beneficial to the whole ecosystem if the providers can self-serve and contribute to the data. The goal here would be to get more and more physicians onboard the system. And suppose the initial monetization strategy charges them to come on board to provide data for this use case. In that case, you are creating more friction for the network adoption as a whole. Instead, the network might be served better by looking to monetize with the doctors on a subsequent use case, which has a more compelling value addition for the doctors. When you develop your early monetization strategy, you focus more on the insurance companies because the value they are getting is clear and obvious.

This chapter looked at a few things that consortium members can do to make for a stronger partnership. Next, let us look at steps on the project level that others have taken to make their blockchain journey a success.

---

68  Hurder, "Why enterprise blockchains fail."

# CHAPTER 7

# SET YOURSELF UP
# FOR SUCCESS

———

Companies typically start their blockchain journey by learning with the community and running proof of concepts (POCs). As they get to know more about blockchain, they realize that it is a team sport, so they go about strengthening relationships in the industry and focus on building a business network, perhaps in the form of a consortium. Next, they get to a point where they can run a pilot and commercialize the solution. With that backdrop, let's look at a few items that have shown up in my conversations as ideas that can help make that journey smoother.

**MANAGING PERCEPTIONS**

As I learned more about blockchain, I reached a point where I was looking to define a financial engine to power my blockchain business. I wanted to join a mastermind group that could act as an advisory system and a support group to stay on track. After a few web searches, I decided to approach a company that would bring together a group of people in cohorts to start mastermind groups.

To their credit, they were very meticulous in their approach to forming a group. The first part of their process included filling out a questionnaire, followed by an interview. One question was to link a web page describing my company's services. I gave my blog as the link. As the interview started, the first thing the woman tentatively asked me was, "So you do something with Bitcoin?"

At the time, I found it funny because, on my blog, there is not one single mention of the word "Bitcoin." Instead, it is all plastered with the term blockchain. The title of the blog was *The Blockchain Stream of Consciousness.* And yet, she had registered Bitcoin in her mind.

As I am talking to more and more people, it is clear that projects centered around blockchain technology face headwinds of perception.

Blockchain and Bitcoin are tightly intertwined in general perception. And by extension, blockchain has to fight Bitcoin's tainted connections with nefarious activities like money laundering, funding of terrorist activities, the dark web, Silk Road, etc.[69]

As the early enthusiasts of blockchain start conversations with folks in their companies, it is necessary to manage this association and perception about a blockchain project. Be

---

69  Department of Justice, "US Attorney Announces Arrest."

prepared to answer the question: "Isn't blockchain the same as Bitcoin?"

"One barrier is perception. When you use the term blockchain, people hear cryptocurrency. They hear Bitcoin, and they don't hear blockchain. We just started calling it 'Digital Identity' and not so much blockchain because it distracts people," says Doug McCollough.[70]

Doug is the CIO of Dublin, Ohio, and is currently leading the charge for the city to integrate emerging technologies into its daily operations. Dublin is a small community of around fifty thousand people in the northwest corner of Ohio. It is a technocentric city that has embraced using technology to advance its economic development interests. And from there, they have embraced the idea of being a leader and innovator in smart cities.

Doug is very aware of the possibilities of digital disruption to the government. He tries to keep his city ahead of the curve by embracing emerging technologies in city operations. But nobody sees disruption coming. Most of the time, the prevalent narrative is of the status quo with incremental changes.

One example of government disruption is how people now trust map services in deciding whether or not to travel on the road. If your GPS and mapping service says a road is open, you think it is open. However, somebody might have removed a sign that city officials put up. If mapping services advise

---

70  McCollough, "Dublin Digital Identity."

people to undertake actions according to themselves—that is a disruption.

Cities are moving onward in their journey to become smart cities and rely on data-driven decisions. Software companies, not the government, pioneer all the technology that is going into making connected vehicles. And when software companies get better at directing people's traffic and keeping them safer, governments are no longer doing it. The government is no longer the primary safety partner in citizen's lives—that is a disruption.

"We tend to look at cities and say, 'Stay in your lane, plow the snow, mow the grass, fix the potholes, cut my taxes, and I'll be happy.' We don't think about all of the various services and things that a city does and has been doing. If cities do not innovate, then we are going to be disrupted just like any other business. . . . We are candidates for innovation just like anybody else. I do believe that there's going to be a new distributed data environment. Just as the web changed everything, blockchain and distributed data environment are going to change everything," explains Doug.[71] For Dublin, that has been a driver for pursuing the blockchain-based digital identity project—to prepare for possible disruption by the technology.

Besides the challenge of association with Bitcoin, using the word blockchain starts distracting people on other fronts too. They start associating the project with the flavor of the day and associating it with following the hype. The conversation strays away from looking at the merits of the project

---

71   Ibid.

deliverables. That also starts coming in the way of the funding available for these innovative projects.

## INVEST IN CREATING A COMMUNITY

It helps to create a community of enthusiasts that would help define the use cases. On his part, Doug McCollough started the Dublin blockchain group. He wanted to bring together tech companies and individuals in the Dublin area interested in blockchain, who were probably experimenting behind the scenes. With that effort, a few companies started emerging as the ones who were passionate about blockchain.

The group's activities helped start the conception of the idea about what would be a great use case for how the government could be using blockchain to create value for its citizens. And now, the Dublin blockchain group helps create a sense of community and accelerates learning among people who are curious about blockchain technology and are experimenting in the background.

Besides community building outside the company, investing in innovation teams internally looking at various use cases for blockchain will go a long way. Organize them into a community of practice or center of excellence. As we learned in Chapter 4, to respond to industry challenges, the Royal Bank of Scotland (RBS) identified an opportunity in blockchain quite early. And they were prepared to spend some budget at the beginning to play with and test blockchain, which was something new that was coming up.

Very early on, they had engineering teams look at the technology and get used to it. It then got to a point where it was clear there were enough use cases to justify investing in a community of practice with its center of excellence around blockchain.

"And that would be my number one piece of advice to any organization early on in their journey or starting to commercialize projects on the blockchain. You'll have different technological camps sitting there and saying, 'I like iPhone; I like Samsung.' You are going to have the same viewpoints to blockchain technology," says Andrew Speers.[72]

At the beginning of your blockchain journey, your company will have a limited understanding of commercializing new technology. Having it run through a centralized function focusing on blockchain technology helps evaluate the use case more robustly. This will also help identify the proper use cases to pursue as you start your blockchain journey. On their part, State Farm began to look at blockchain in 2016. As Dustin Helland (who we were introduced to in Chapter 4) explains, "We were able to pretty quickly identify that the blockchain technology underlying Bitcoin could have applications much broader than just cryptocurrency and we established a group in innovation area to prioritize and explore potential opportunities."[73]

Because you are working with competitors, you have a need for a new way of organizational thinking for blockchain projects. An approach leading with education and collaboration will help, and the community can help with the whole process. For State Farm, initially, the teams focused on working

---

72   Speers, "User Experience on the Blockchain."
73   Helland, "State Farm's Blockchain."

across multiple business lines—for example, subject matter experts in the claims department, underwriting, financial services, etc.—to educate them on the capabilities of the technology. They also worked to identify and evaluate any potential use cases that State Farm thought might be of value.

The focus then shifted into learning by aligning a few of the identified business opportunities with some development teams and created early prototypes. Eventually, they moved to a stage where the focus was on product delivery and business value realization based on the technology. The flagship project out of those efforts is Auto Claims Subrogation, built collaboratively with USAA.

In addition to community, it takes a change agent who can be one of the early people in a company that is evangelizing the emerging technology forward. It helps if they are trusted and knowledgeable within the organization. They need to be subject matter experts who understand this technology and what it makes possible. Blockchain technology reaches into the depths of an organization's plumbing. It's essential to take the time to spread the gospel of blockchain.

As Shahar Steiff from PCCW pointed out to me, it helps to have the person at the top, with the executive behind the project. Communication of a clear vision goes a long way, and that needs to be done with patience and persistence.

"For most participants, this is not just technical evolution; it is also some sort of internal revolution within the company. Telcos and cloud providers today understand they are no longer delivering a service; they're delivering an environment and an experience. They are becoming a technology company. And it is not easy to take a legacy telco and turn it into a technology company. It needs to be a complete mindset shift. It needs to be driven by management," explained Shahar.

Shahar Steiff has been leading PCCW Global's development of blockchain-based platforms to support automated-service life cycle. PCCW Global is a leading communications service provider participating in the Communications Business Automation Network (CBAN). CBAN is a network of telecom industry leaders collaborating around emerging technologies to benefit the global carrier ecosystem. And one of the initiatives underway is blockchain-assisted automated settlement.

Consumers generally identify the telecom industry as a single entity. Even though, to deliver services across countries, multiple operators need to come together behind the scenes. The data traffic has to flow through one carrier's infrastructure to another before reaching the consumers' devices. When you and I, as users, make a telephone call, we pay our telecom company for the services rendered. In turn, our telecom company pays the various information and communication technologies (ICT) providers along the telecom supply chain. This telecom supply chain eventually establishes an end-to-end connection from a phone in one country to a phone in another country. ICT providers complete the settlement for all these transactions. We, as consumers, have no visibility into what's happening behind the scenes.

To activate a business relationship that serves us, the consumers and two ICT companies will typically sign a master services agreement (MSA). The agreements are still commonly done manually. The MSA defines the terms and conditions of their relationship. Based on these agreements, to deliver a service to the customer, a price quote is configured. Service delivery gets set up after understanding the customer requirements, designing the solution, submitting the quote, and securing an order. And this delivery can take anywhere from a few seconds to a few months. Data can start flowing to service the customer only after the service delivery setup is complete.

As the customer starts using the service, all the data usage is recorded, and the telecom providers generate invoices. As the operators verify the invoice charges submitted to them, they typically find incorrect charges. The discrepancy could be because of various reasons, like miscalculation of time service or use of the wrong rate. After identifying these disputes, they go into the dispute resolution process to settle the amounts. The actual time varies a lot, but it takes about three months to get the service up and running. From the time they provide the service to the time they get paid after the invoices' settlement, it takes about eight weeks. These extended times are primarily caused by the manual processes involved; they reduce the company's profitability and create a negative customer experience.

With the blockchain-assisted automated settlement, disputes due to record mismatch were eliminated. The usage is measured and compared through blockchain in real-time, drastically reducing the chances of discrepancies. All in all, they can reduce the time for the price quotation process from days to seconds. Service delivery timelines are reduced from months to minutes. Traffic measurement and reconciliation have been reduced from days to seconds. And the settlement itself has been reduced from weeks to seconds. Overall, they have achieved cost reduction, acceleration of processes, and the ability to build new revenue streams from services that they were not able to deliver earlier.

As I marveled at their results and asked Shahar about the lessons he gleaned going through the experience, he explained, "The companies that joined forces in that project were very much driven by CxO-level executives to make it happen. They were driving the product teams and development teams. Industry adopts three horizons. Horizon one is our existing services. Horizon two is what we are building today, i.e., tomorrow's services. And horizon three is what will happen three to four years from today. Horizon three is something that really needs management with the right mindset. With a mindset to push toward something that will only realize and give revenues in a few years. Maybe by the time that the respective executives will not even be working at the company."

## TRY AND CHOOSE LOW-RISK PROCESSES AS THE FIRST USE CASE

"We chose a very small process. Spunta is an internal process. It doesn't involve external customers. And it's not particularly known. So it was a good, a sort of, natural sandbox," explains Silvia Attanasio.[74] Silvia is the head of innovation at ABI (Italian Banking Association) to support innovation among the banks in the Italian Banking Association. ABI lab is a

---

74   Attanasio, "Blockchain for Italian."

consortium owned by 150 banks. They work with the banks and for the banks.

It helps lower the risk with anything new by choosing low-impact processes to start with so that it doesn't ruffle any feathers even if there is an issue. In December 2017, ABI labs began working on a project to address the interbank reconciliations process (also known as Spunta) using blockchain technology. To understand if blockchain technology could help, the team visited fourteen different back offices in various cities in Italy. They analyzed traditional processes based on how decisions are made and the organizational structure of these offices. They also focused on the interaction of one bank to another and the resulting flow of activities.

Spunta is this incredibly complex Italian interbank reconciliation process chosen as the subject of the blockchain project. This process has been in place for decades, based on interbank agreements beginning 1978. In Italy, these are bilateral accounts that are co-owned by two banks. Ownership of this account switches from one to the other bank every three years. When the account is *Nostro* and the bank has ownership of the account, they can see all the account details like balance, transfers, etc. But when the ownership switches to *Vostro* and the other bank has ownership, Bank A cannot see any details regarding the account.

Suppose Bank A needs any information in a vostro account. In that case, they need to connect with the other bank using traditional communication mechanisms and ask for the information. Back offices of the banks run the process to clear mismatches in the double-entry bookkeeping and make sure that the banks at both ends of a transaction agree on all aspects of the transaction. It gets complex because it is a single account that tries to reconcile the viewpoints of counterparties on the same ledger. And, what happens if there is a mismatch? Resolving these mismatches requires a lot of time and effort.

For ABI, the Spunta process seemed like a perfect use case for blockchain. People in the Spunta process were asking for improvement. There was a willingness to spend time modernizing Spunta and its associated agreements. It was essential to get the right people from the right organizations to participate. The conditions were right for that to happen. On the other side, the innovation team wanted to explore this emerging technology's potential using a low-risk process. It was essential to choose a relatively small internal process that does not impact the customers. It was important to select a process on which the team had the authority to make decisions. There was no reason to include other regulatory bodies or the government in making any changes.

There would be various considerations in choosing a particular use case to implement with blockchain. Factors to look at would include the potential business value opportunity presented to you with the proper use of blockchain technology. You would also need interest from other partners in the industry because, after all, you are working with WE technology. One thing to look at is the hurdles you need to jump through to drive the solution to completion. That impacts the pace at which you can move the project forward. If we use a low-risk process, we can have better control over the pace of the project.

As Dustin Helland explains, "So, net subrogation as we built it includes data that organizations are primarily already sharing, and it also doesn't include highly sensitive customer information. While we're not necessarily avoiding those challenges, we just wanted to be intentional about which ones we chose to take on."[75]

## EARLY FOCUS ON EDUCATION

Blockchain projects need a new way of organizational thinking because you will now be focusing on collaborating with your competitors. An approach leading with education and collaboration helps. Investing in building the community also helps with the whole process. For ABI, The business side did not know of blockchain technology. At the same time, the technical side of the house did not know of the Spunta process.

The first order of business, then, was to get them together. The intent was to help the business understand different competencies of the technology and the technologists to understand the ways of the business process. To further cement this cross-pollination and help gain confidence in the technology and avoid any reluctance amongst the participants, they decided to conduct a POC.

As Silvia explains, "One of the main goals of the project was to fully understand the technology, the potential and the way this technology could change traditional banking. So, we incorporate in the project also some learning phases. We've got learning sessions with the experts . . . to an audience of

---

75    Helland, "State Farm's Blockchain."

fifty or sixty people from back offices, from innovation and from IT of fourteen different banks."[76] That investment in learning helped with increased participation from the consortium members.

A blockchain project needs very different thinking, for one, because you end up working directly with competitors. But, internally also, many other groups need to get involved. Beyond the technical and business teams, to manage all the consortium-related aspects, teams such as legal, security, risk, compliance, public affairs, etc., will also need to get involved. As Dustin Helland explained for State Farm, "The way that we got the support and buy-in has been through education, collaboration, working side by side, and consistent transparency."[77]

## CAREFUL THOUGHT TO DECIDE ON THE USE OF PUBLIC VS. PRIVATE BLOCKCHAIN

One critical decision in our blockchain journey will be about the choice of public versus private blockchain—more importantly, the choice to proceed with either an open public or closed private network. Or maybe—a hybrid? Focus on deciding whether you will use a private or public blockchain network is necessary because tools matter. For enterprises, privacy and security are essential aspects to keep in mind.

*Here are a few terms to help us better frame the conversation. It is good to understand these as they are not always accurately used in discussions.*

---

76   Attanasio, "Blockchain for Italian."
77   Helland, "State Farm's Blockchain."

Public vs. Private: This is defined based on who can write data to the blockchain. If anyone can write to the blockchain, then it is a public blockchain. Bitcoin and Ethereum are good examples of a public blockchain. On the other hand, it is a private blockchain if the write access is controlled.

Open vs. Closed: This is defined based on who can read data from the blockchain. Open blockchains allow the general public to consume data. Closed blockchains control access through permissions.

Permissioned vs. Permissionless: Role-based access defines this aspect. Permissioned blockchains have the native ability to track and manage the identity of entities accessing the blockchain.

As per a PricewaterhouseCoopers survey on how businesses are managing blockchains, companies are adopting both approaches; while 40 percent are using permissioned blockchains, 34 percent are working with permissionless chains, and 26 percent are taking a hybrid approach.[78]

Looking to use case considerations, companies will decide what path to take.

Coadjute first started working on their project by participating in the UK Land Registry's procurement process. They realized that "for a government use case, a public platform enabled by cryptocurrency practically wasn't feasible. The data would need to be in the UK."[79]

---

78  PricewaterhouseCoopers, "Design Deliberately"
79  Reynolds, "Real Estate on the Blockchain."

For SCB, one major decision they needed to explore was this: Are you going to use a private blockchain network or a public blockchain network? The deciding factor was the visibility of transacting parties. As Orapong explained, "With the procure-to-pay application, you normally deal with a closed loop—a limited number of suppliers and a limited number of buyers. You cannot even identify who's the one who executed the trade. But the fact that you see information in the trade is a risk. If you see the price, even if you don't know who buys that product, but you see a different price, and you see a buy, that creates trade issues. That's why first we assess: Are we going public blockchain? Are we going private blockchain? And we decided private blockchain."[80]

For Optum, managing the politics of technology and support for tokenization were driving factors in deciding to go with a public blockchain network. "There are three legs to the stool. It's politics, economics, and technology. If you decide to make your own network, you have to tackle all three simultaneously. If you decide to piggyback on public Ethereum, and you can have a use case that runs on that, then you've essentially removed a lot of the politics around the actual execution of the network. And there are already network effects. So there's a huge advantage to moving every private permissioned blockchain to a public permissioned blockchain, as quickly as possible." That's how Tony Little explained it to me.

It makes sense to follow the general investment of dollars and time as criteria in choosing the technology. Investment

---

80  Thien-Ngern et al., "from Siam Commercial Bank."

of dollars by different players in a protocol and investment of time by developers in building the protocol means a robust ecosystem. That will help you connect your stack to proven technology. If the protocol supports tokenization, it helps you view data as an asset that can be the basis of microtransactions powering your consortium. Otherwise, you'll end up using a third party and adding transaction cost to the consortium's economy. "I think there's a whole lot of work that's being done out there today that just ends up falling flat because they don't think about this multidimensionality," explains Tony.

State Farm also looked at multiple blockchain protocols. As Dustin Helland explains, "Early on we did take a look at some of the capabilities of the public blockchains, but then like most large enterprises, quickly latched on to the need for privacy and protection."[81]

State Farm is using Quorum, which allows for an Ethereum-based private permissioned enterprise blockchain. It is an open-source technology that was initially released and governed by JP Morgan. Quorum enables permissioned network and private transactions within the Ethereum network, so they are not using the public Ethereum network in their solution. There were a few key factors that they took into account when they were deciding on a specific blockchain network.

First, they needed a permissioned blockchain as transaction privacy was essential for them. Second, they looked at the

---

81    Helland, "State Farm's Blockchain."

maturity of different platforms at the time of evaluation. One thing that made them comfortable about Ethereum was that it had gone through public network adoption for quite some time. Third, they also took input from their developers to understand the developer's point of view. What were the developers more comfortable working on? Developers look at different things like available documentation and contributions made between various individuals, companies, etc.

One notable thing to look at is how the three leading platforms' available architecture influenced their decision. For both R3 Corda and Hyperledger, the network architecture allowed for a master node, potentially having more power and authority. Whereas in Quorum, every node has the same privileges. As State Farm started on the project, choosing the architecture provided by Quorum was essential. The choice would help avoid any perception that one network participant is trying to gain some sort of an advantage over the others.

### LOOK AT WAYS TO FUND THE PROJECT CREATIVELY

For emerging technologies with no clear ROI, funding can always be an issue. You may have to get creative in getting the projects off the ground. Doug McCollough, with the city of Dublin, was well aware of scarce funding in public space. There is not much funding available for innovative projects. The public sector project environment is also very risk-averse (which could also be true for very large companies).

Instead of using startup principles and modern IT practices like agile development and iterative processes, the approach in public sector funding is to have fully baked ideas that fit into a budget. That approach helps secure budget allocations. After that, the focus is on the project's success rather than experimenting with innovative technologies. As Doug explains, "We don't have a lot of funding. There's no funding for these kinds of innovations. So you kind of have to partner and do public-private partnerships and explore a really low-budget kind of experiment. And that's why we've done a proof of concept in a very limited way."[82]

In the case of Coadjute, it was quite a joint effort where all the participants contributed. At the same time, Coadjute used its resources to build the core platform. As John Reynolds explained, "It genuinely was kind of a collaborative effort. If any one organization had tried to do it, it would have been a really expensive project. But when you spread the cost of the project across forty businesses or so, it was affordable."[83] It ended up being quite the decentralized funding model. Very much in line with the blockchain's decentralized ethos.

### PREPARE FOR CHALLENGES WITH DATA STANDARDS
Data standards will play a significant role in how the project will move forward toward success. If there are existing industry standards, it's better to adopt those instead of reinventing the wheel. For Jon Kuiper and Vinturas in the FVL space, the industry has a history of multiple costly EDI connections spread around, which leads to a lack of standards in transactional processes.

---

82   McCollough, "Dublin Digital Identity."
83   Reynolds, "Real Estate on the Blockchain."

They focused on the proof of delivery document (CMR), which is the document used to hand over the vehicle, e.g., from a transport company to the dealer, and is ordinarily paper-based and handwritten. They relied on the electronic CMR protocol approved by most European countries and created by regulatory bodies. Providing this document on the blockchain becomes essential from a fraud perspective.

As Jon Kuiper explains, "We are providing our infrastructure for these electronic CMR documents. And of course, it's blockchain, it is immutable, it's a legal document, and we can provide it to the industry stakeholders because the standard has been defined from a governmental and regulatory perspective and will be implemented in the coming years in all countries of Europe. . . . We think it's very powerful, because an electronic CMR, coming back to the fraud discussion again, for people who are shipping, it's very important that it is legal and yet not a paper-based, but electronic document."[84]

As I was talking to Jesús Pizarro about standards, he commented, "The reason I like working with IBM Food Trust is that IBM is using international standards." Jesús is the VP of financial innovation at Heifer International. He is leading strategy at Heifer Lab's blockchain offerings for agricultural development and financial inclusion. Heifer International is an international NGO with a mission to end world hunger and poverty while taking care of the earth.

Heifer is using blockchain to accelerate its mission, which is ending hunger and poverty while they take care of the

---

84   Kuiper., "Supply Chain on the Blockchain."

earth. As they started working with blockchain, they stipulated their vision to create a blockchain network in the agricultural sector where a farmer can access working capital, technical assistance, and fair markets. Their approach is one of partnership with government, universities, and other organizations.

Heifer partners with others to use blockchain to fast-track their mission. They are involved with three different projects in the supply chain: poultry, cocoa, and coffee. In poultry, they are working on the Ethereum blockchain. For coffee and cocoa, they are partnering with IBM Food Trust and the International Development Bank (IDB) on various other projects.

Heifer wants to use blockchain to improve market transparency. In agriculture, the small farmer is invisible, and the consumer is blind. The consumer doesn't know where their food came from, nor do they know how it was prepared. And we, as consumers, of course, do not know anything about the small farmer. It is the same situation with the small farmer as far as their visibility into their product's consumption is concerned. For Heifer, blockchain gives the possibility of transparency, which, in the end, will improve the markets.

As Heifer worked through the various blockchain projects, amongst other things, one of the important lessons they learned has been about the standardization process. As Jesús explained to me, "One of the problems is that we also need to do the standardization of standards. Even if you use GS1, you will find that GS1 is also very flexible. There are different ways to do the implementation of the standard. For blockchain projects to be successful, we need to be using the same standards. I would say this is the top lesson learned."

Of course, much more goes into making a blockchain journey successful. A few things are unique to blockchain due to its nature and because it is in the very early stages of its development. This chapter helped us take a look at some of those peculiarities.

# CHAPTER 8

# THE NEW MACHINE ECONOMY

———

"More than 90 percent of blockchain projects are weaving in other emerging technologies, especially the IoT and machine learning,"[85] the HFS research report tells us. We are beginning to see some attempts to harness the potential of other emerging technologies like IoT (internet of things) and AI (artificial intelligence) together with blockchain. A combinatorial approach to these technologies ends up generating a whole that's greater than the sum of its parts.

Internet of things (IoT) refers to the multitude of physical devices—"things"— that connect to the internet. All these smart devices—smart lightbulbs, connected thermostats, fitness trackers, sensors, etc.— are meant to collect data about their environment and communicate with the network without the need for any human intervention. IoT devices are rapidly proliferating our environment. Gartner, Inc.,

———

85   Gupta et al., "Ignore Blockchain at Your Peril."

forecasts that the enterprise and automotive internet of things market will grow to 5.8 billion endpoints in 2020, a 21 percent increase from 2019. By the end of 2019, 4.8 billion endpoints are expected to be in use, up 21.5 percent from 2018.[86]

Since these IoT devices' job is to collect data and feed it to the network for other devices and systems, an immense amount of data is going to be collected. One of the primary concerns with IoT devices is their susceptibility to security vulnerabilities. This lack of security is concerning with the widespread use of IoT devices in smart homes and smart cars. Blockchain as a data-sharing mechanism for IoT devices can provide another level of security with available encryption and the tamper-evident nature of the technology. With its use in conjunction with IoT devices, blockchain can facilitate data distribution in a secure and trustworthy manner.

Another challenge with this expansion in IoT devices is the load that it puts on the infrastructure. The sheer growth in the number of IoT devices anticipated to be in operation will generate large quantities of machine data that will be uploaded and need to be processed. That will heavily stress the current cloud infrastructure. Instead, it would help to build infrastructure at the edge to handle all these devices sharing data among themselves without needing to go back to the cloud. This edge infrastructure would help reduce latency and power the machine economy.

Applications of AI are also getting ubiquitous. As you look to purchase something on your favorite website, you'll find

---

86   Gartner, "Will Be in Use in 2020."

them acutely predicting what you are interested in buying. It then nudges you to look at a few more suggestions. That's AI behind the scenes. When your voice assistant offers to recognize you by your voice, that is AI in action. When the social networking site automatically suggests names to be tagged in a photo, AI is at work.

IoT collects all the data, and AI consumes it to get insights and make intelligent decisions about how to act upon that data. Today, much of AI is like a black box. With a blockchain backbone, AI will be getting clean data that has not been tampered with. Inherent attributes of blockchain can help AI produce a report card showing how data was used. An audit trail can be created from the time data is ingested to train the AI models. It can also include the provenance of data on how AI came with the predictions. This increased visibility will help users get assurances that AI is operating within design parameters and increase trust in the AI models.

"Data is just like crude. It's valuable, but if unrefined, it cannot really be used. It has to be changed into gas, plastic, chemicals, etc. to create a valuable entity that drives profitable activity; so must data be broken down, analyzed for it to have value."[87] Taking that line of thought one step further—if data is the new oil, then that data on a blockchain is cleaner and will require less processing. That makes the overall system more efficient.

Integrated solutions with a convergence approach using blockchain technology in conjunction with other emerging technologies like the internet of things (IoT) and artificial

---

87    Palmer, "Data Is the New Oil."

intelligence (AI) has the potential to open new doors for value creation. Some attempts are being made toward the convergence of these emerging technologies and the emergence of machine economy. Let's take a look at one of them.

## BOSCH GLOBAL AND THE ECONOMY OF THINGS

Blockchain can provide the trust layer to help IoT devices move away from collecting and communicating the data to devices that can participate in transactions as independent entities in the economy and as economic citizens. "An economy with an Internet of Things"—that's the push that Bosch industries are banking their efforts on.[88] The economy of things is an evolution of the internet of things that enables devices to participate in an economic transaction by their own choice.

Raghavendra Kulkarni has been working at Bosch on incubating businesses using emerging technologies like blockchain to develop new revenue streams. As he puts it, "Internet of things is all about the connecting of the physical and the digital world."[89]

The situation of connected devices has commoditized the role of hardware in the ecosystem. Devices have been relegated to the collection and transfer of data. And that's it. With the economy of things, the devices can provide added value as economic participants in the network. Devices become an integral part of the value chain instead of the collector and communicator of information, and blockchain is the very technology enabling that development.

---

88   Bosch Global, "Economy of Things."
89   Kulkarni, "Bosch's Economy of Things."

That participation starts with providing these devices with autonomy. Bosch, as a company, has done a lot with the use of sensors. They derive services from sensors and put the sensor information into the software. For now, IoT devices with these sensors help automate the physical world around us. But suppose we have to give these devices autonomy, i.e., enable them to make decisions on their own. In that case, components of blockchain have the role of a catalyst in achieving that. Blockchain will help us move from smart connected devices to economic devices.

This will help enable the economy of things, i.e., an autonomous device with a business model around them. And that gives "things" a choice in deciding whether it makes sense for them to participate in an economic transaction or not. The device can make decisions based on its resources and its availability by broadcasting whether it is open for business or not.

As Raghavendra put it, "Economy of things is not just about the technology of connected [devices] or the technology of blockchain. But once you make them participate in the transaction, participate in the business models, participate in settling of the business models is where the economic things would come into picture."[90]

**THE CASE OF DATA MARKETPLACES**
All this data produced by IoT devices creates numerous possibilities beyond simply enabling the machine economy. We should keep in mind a few things for the data produced by all the IoT devices. The sheer quantity of data produced is a

---

90   Kulkarni, "Bosch's Economy of Things."

mix of structured and unstructured data. Due to this, a lot of that data ends up being noise. Data is also temporal in nature and has a short shelf life. Its usefulness slowly degrades if it is not promptly analyzed.

We need to have a clear data strategy to make good use of all that data. That means knowing what data you need and how much of it you need. The collected data needs to be stored privately with the proper access controls in place. With appropriate access controls, the rightful owners of the data can monetize it. Today, people are given charge of their data to some extent. Still, it is also being copied and used by the companies with which they interact. There is no genuine appreciation of that data's value and how other actors are using it.

The creation of cleaner and more organized data using blockchain will allow for the emergence of new data marketplaces. Blockchain can enable individual entities to be custodians of their data because it is an immutable record that no one has to regulate. Envision people having a digital vault that contains their digital identity along with their behavior patterns: activity patterns collected by fitness trackers, media consumption patterns collected by content providers, driving behavior collected by cars, medical records collected with interaction with the health care system, etc.

We can be custodians of the data in a secure manner. We can then access this hyper-granular data and provide access as we choose. Now, if Rahul wants to go to a bar, the only needed data is this: Is Rahul over twenty-one? Yes or No. There is no need to produce the driver's license revealing the date of birth, address, and organ donor status. All that information is not relevant to the transaction and does not need to be divulged. Not only people but objects, like IoT devices, can also have their vaults. With these vaults, data becomes an inherent part of every actor in the economy.

Bosch has implemented a data marketplace for the provenance of milk with TrueFood+. One aspect of the solution tackles milk production and the farmer ecosystem. The concept is dubbed "Crypto-cow." With Crypto-cow, a farmer can record and advertise different data points for a cow's entire life cycle in a blockchain-based data marketplace, e.g., amount of milk produced, milk production forecasting, etc.

All the farmer ecosystem participants who sell to the farmer, like veterinary doctors, insurance companies, cooperative societies, equipment manufacturers, seed manufacturers, etc., are the consumers of this data. Based on the information shared in the data marketplace, these participants can offer services to the farmer. For instance, the veterinarian can look at milk forecasting and advise on possible medical interventions or changes in feed needed for the herd to influence the forecast. The financial ecosystem can look at various data points like the herd's health, milk forecast, etc. Based on this data, they can offer alternative financial products. The farmer provides the data and, in turn, receives proactive input from advisors.

Besides being a data marketplace, TrueFood+ also helps the farmer showcase their sustainability practices by providing an immutable record of that data. This industry has a high focus on sustainable practices, e.g., water consumption, kinds of feed used, well-being of the herd, etc. The use of blockchain as a component of the overall solution helps the farmer provide legitimate records of livestock maintenance practices.

The second dimension addressed in the provenance of milk revolves around milk distribution: the point from which it is collected to being available in the retail store. Here, condition monitoring of the milk is the main focus. Bosch has sensors starting from the milk barn and throughout the distribution channel, measuring various milk characteristics. Bosch has taken the data collected by the sensors and put it on a blockchain ledger. Storage of all the data generated by these sensors on the blockchain provides provenance of various parameters like temperature, humidity, etc. This data can be collected for the milk from the barn until it gets dropped off for processing. TrueFood+ can also help monitor a batch of milk using dynamic QR codes through different storage points until it is available at retail points.[91]

A seamless combination of blockchain, AI, and the internet of things will enable the next generation of solutions and open new doors for value creation. As we look to accelerate the adoption of these technologies at scale, blockchain can help provide trust in the data used with these emerging technologies—from data to information to intelligence, generated by IoT, powered by blockchain and analyzed by AI.

---

91   Robert Bosch Engineering and Business Solutions, "Transformation through Sensors."

# CHAPTER 9

# BLOCKCHAIN IN SUPPLY CHAIN

———

As per the research done by MarketsandMarkets, the block-chain supply chain market will be worth $3.2 billion by 2026 and grow at a compound annual growth rate (CAGR) of 53.2 percent during the forecast period.[92] With its use in several global supply chain initiatives, blockchain technology is showing promise to solve some issues with managing global supply chains. However, the success with the use of the technology has been varied. Let's look at a few supply chain scenarios and what experience has shown to use blockchain solutions in these situations.

### INCREASED CONSUMER PRESSURE FOR TRANSPARENCY IN PRODUCTS

"Consumers are increasingly demanding transparency in products. They want to know that if a product says organic, it's really organic. Or they want to know that if a product says

---

92  MarketsandMarketsTM, "Blockchain Supply Chain."

that it's a sustainable product, then the farm that it comes from is truly a sustainable farm. Or they want to know that the clothing they buy wasn't made by child labor. Consumers are demanding more transparency. This is a key factor for consumers in modern economies. Blockchain comes here because this is where blockchain has a unique value proposition for supply chain," David Ritter tells me in the context of Blockchain Rice, which we will discuss in greater depth.

A 2017 transparency study done by Response Media also supports David's observation. Their report confirms, "Consumers are willing to spend more on a transparent product versus nontransparent product, with Millennial Moms and Gen X Dads willing to pay the highest price for these products."[93] Their data also shows that 80 percent or more of consumers are willing to pay more in all product categories. Fresh foods top the list, with 92 percent of respondents willing to pay more for better visibility in the supply chain from farm to table. They want to know all about the source of ingredients, manufacturing, and shipping and handling of the product, along with the sustainability, charitable, and labor policies of brands.

David is the CEO of Penta Solutions. Penta's mission is to become a "universal blockchain connector." The goal here is to make blockchain available to a broader audience—mass adoption. They intend to connect not only different blockchain technologies but blockchains to existing networks like online systems, and also blockchain technology to the off-chain, brick-and-mortar world.

---

93  Pages, "2017 Transparency Study."

In 2017, Penta did their first at-scale deployment of a supply chain solution. It is a traceability platform for rice in China. They worked with a state-owned enterprise and a public company to track about thirteen million acres of rice farmland in China's northeast. The traceability was done up to consumers' point of purchase. The consumer purchases were made through JD.com, the second-largest online retailer in China.

It was marketed as part of the product offering for rice and called Blockchain Rice. When somebody would buy a bag of rice on JD.com, they could scan it and see the provenance through the whole supply chain. One of Penta's key takeaways from this project is that people are willing to pay about three times as much for Blockchain Rice as they would otherwise pay for the same bag of rice.

In the Chinese consumer context, there's a massive problem with the adulteration of rice products. People are concerned about the safety of buying rice at supermarkets. As David told me, "There's been news reports and studies have come out saying that if you buy a bag of rice at a Chinese supermarket, it might have up to 30 percent contamination."

In some cases, it might be natural additives like stones. Still, in other cases, there's also chemical contamination like glass particulates. We don't know where this comes into the supply chain. Rice is a staple of nutrition there in the diet. So, if one of your staple products has that level of contamination, it's a severe issue. Interacting with the data, consumers can pay more to see there is nothing mixed into their rice.

## WASTE IN FOOD SUPPLY CHAINS: THE ECONOMIC IMPACT

Besides consumer confidence, like in Blockchain Rice, contamination also has other impacts. Food waste due to contamination has a substantial economic impact on the apple supply chain.

As far as supply chain scenarios go, besides the consumer-facing side of things, there are also business reasons for companies to adopt blockchain. One is that there's a tremendous amount of waste that happens in the supply chain. Food waste is a huge issue. Recalls are another issue. In the US context, in particular, there are many recalls, e.g., those related to E. coli outbreaks in produce or meat.

Penta did a project with the largest apple packing house out of Michigan that delivers apples to many retailers. They were the first apple packing houses in the United States to have a recall of apples. The purpose of the initiative was to test different sensor devices in the supply chain. In the apple produce ecosystem, all sales are on consignment. Nobody upstream in the supply chain gets any revenue in a recall event for that specific supply chain. If those apples don't sell at the retail store, then the packing house doesn't get paid, and the farmers don't get paid. There is an outsized economic impact when these recalls occur.

As we learned with Walmart's example (in Chapter 5), it takes a long time to isolate the root cause of the issue in different parts of the supply chain. "I brought a package of sliced mangoes into my staff meeting. I put it on the desk, and I said to my team, 'The traceback study starts right now. Hit the clock and tell me from where did these mangoes come from, what farm, and what country.' And you know how long it took them to do that? It took them almost seven days! Seven days to do that because they had to actually contact the supplier, get paper records. . . . They then had to contact the importer," says Frank Yiannas.[94] This delay has extremely adverse effects on the producers in the supply chain.

Large retailers, of course, suffer financial harm and reputational harm, but they also have insurance that protects them. It's a motivator and a demand driver for companies and supply chains to adopt this kind of technology. Suppose we're able to pinpoint where the contamination occurs in the supply chain. In that case, you might be able to isolate other stakeholders from suffering as much financial harm. Based on that, it could realign insurance products.

## WASTE IN FOOD SUPPLY CHAINS: THE SOCIAL IMPACT

We talked about the liability side of food waste in the business context. But there is also the social impact that blockchain can create. The Food and Agriculture Organization (FAO) of the United Nations claims, "World hunger is on the rise; yet, an estimated one-third of all food produced globally is lost or goes to waste." In order to provide more clarity on food loss and food waste, FAO provides a Food Loss Index (FLI), which calculates loss estimates through the supply chain up to the retailers. "Initial estimates of the FLI tell us that around 14 percent of the world's food is lost from post-harvest up to but excluding the retail level."[95]

---

94  McDermott et al., "Breaking down Blockchain."
95  Food and Agriculture Organization of the United Nations, "Food Loss and Food Waste."

At the same time, FAO also finds that "a total of 842 million are estimated to be suffering from chronic hunger, regularly not getting enough food to conduct an active life."[96] Those numbers are unfortunately only going to go up because of mass migration and various other problems. We have this dual problem where we have a third of all produce going to waste. Meanwhile, you have many people on the planet, approaching a billion, who are either undernourished or malnourished.

As supply chains become increasingly data-driven, you should use data to address inefficiency, waste, and contamination in terms of isolating where contamination occurs. If a bag of rice is contaminated with glass particulates, or an apple is contaminated with listeria, we don't have to say to the retailer, "Okay, you need to destroy every apple on every shelf on every store." You can, instead, pinpoint the farm or the packing house or the point in the supply chain when contamination occurred. That reduces the liability and the financial harm to everybody.

As Frank Yiannas goes on to tell us, "And once we finished the proof of concept, we go to the blockchain solution and just log on. And by inputting a lot number or . . . [scanning] a QR code, how long do you think it took us to trace back? 2.2 seconds! We've gone from seven days to 2.2 seconds in the ability to track food back to the farm. And not only that, not only do we track it back to the farm, but now because we're capturing that information on the blockchain, we have additional information and insights at each point in the chain."[97]

---

96   Food and Agriculture Organization of the United Nations, "Hunger-Facts."

97   McDermott et al., "Breaking down Blockchain."

## UNIQUE VALUE PROPOSITION OF BLOCKCHAIN FOR SUPPLY CHAIN

Blockchain has a unique value proposition in helping fight food waste due to contamination in the apple supply chain. When Penta did the apple supply chain project out of Michigan, they tracked apples all over the country to different brand-name supermarkets. They discovered a few things.

One, there is existing technology in place where people use logistics and fulfillment software to help automate the ordering process. This automation helps determine which trucking company comes to pick up which order to deliver to which supermarket.

In the case of apples, sometimes they are regular logistics companies that work with the apple packing house, and sometimes they are independent contractors. The packing house company's system includes both. They go through an ordering process that determines who picks up the apples, at what time, and delivers to what place. Different supermarkets may have systems that require compliance. For example, they may require that shipments include a temperature trail. Temperature trail is a small sensor device that works as a data logger. It's not wireless and it just collects the data, so somebody has to pick it up, gather the data, scrape the data off the device, and put it into their system. Retail chains generally require this for apples.

But what Penta learned from interviews with the truckers and the people at the packing house in Michigan is that the retailer personnel may never get the data from the temperature trail. The truck comes up to the docking bay at the retailer's loading site, and that's it. The trucker has nothing to do with the apples at that point. The retailer's people come to collect the apples, and they throw away the temp trail, or they just leave it in the truck.

There is a system in place, but people aren't using it. Without that information, you can't pinpoint where contamination might have occurred. Suppose there was a temperature event, where, for example, the air conditioning unit broke in a truck. In that case, there is a high risk of possible bacterial growth or contamination. All that data gets lost in the supply chain. If the retail company then has a problem, they can't go back to their existing system and find the data.

So ultimately, the problem is trust. You have a complex value chain with multiple stakeholders, and this is why blockchain has a unique value proposition. In the apple supply chain, the retailer owns the data that comes off the temperature trail. But as the apple packing house taught Penta, each member of the supply chain can only see one step forward and one step back. That's the extent of their visibility. The problems that we are dealing with, like contamination or environmental conditions against regulations for a specific product, can occur at any point in the supply chain.

We need a robust system for data collection that collects data from all the stakeholders. That is what existing technology does not do. Each stakeholder owns their systems. And thus, the information is siloed. They don't necessarily share it with each other. Maybe they share it with the large retailers because it is a requirement set for them. But the trucking companies don't necessarily share the data with packing houses because they have possibly differing interests when it comes to sorting out a liability issue with their insurance.

As David goes on to explain, "What blockchain does is, it creates a multi-stakeholder data infrastructure that can collect data from different stakeholders in the ecosystem without compromising their proprietary information. This allows the system to have efficiency gains, visibility gains, transparency gains, etc. All those things are important when it comes to dealing with a product that has a contamination event or a consumer-facing problem in a complex value chain. So that's why we see blockchain having a unique value proposition."

### ORIGIN AUTHENTICATION

Different supply chains require different solutions because they have other pain points. So it's tough to have a one-size-fits-all type of solution in the supply chain. In the case of coffee, blockchain's value proposition is different from fresh produce. Fresh produce is concerned with waste and contamination. Coffee as a processed product is roasted coffee beans. That is what we see in stores. The value proposition to coffee brand names is for single-origin coffee, which people pay more money for. It's origin authentication, supplier authentication, and sustainable farming.

The answer to having end-to-end traceability is wireless IoT devices. That's the answer if you want trusted data at the beginning endpoint of production. The conversation around the beginning endpoint could go on and on. Does it start at the soil to make sure that the soil is organic and hasn't been contaminated? Does it start at the harvest when the product is fully grown and you're pulling the bananas off the tree? Generally speaking, there's always going to be a concern when humans provide data. Bad actors might give false data, or human error might cause inaccurate data. For that, devices are the answer.

Penta spent a lot of time testing devices in commercial environments. They concluded that the IoT devices and sensors for supply chains are not ready for primetime. Penta did a coffee project and used two different preferred device manufacturers. They put their devices in the coffee chains to track the coffee. They got different data from the same coffee chain.

That just suggests that there's a lack of standardization on these devices. They are not quite ready yet for use at scale. We are also not living in a 5G world yet. Suppose you want wireless IoT that transmits data through cell towers to your blockchain, which ultimately is how you want to get trusted data. In that case, you need the infrastructure to be in place. And it's not there yet. Even if you are using NFC chips or RFID, you have to collect that RFID device and collect that NFC device and scan it with your phone. There's always going to be a human element in there that people can question. If you want real trust and end-to-end visibility, you need to have wireless sensors in there, but we're not ready for the sensors yet.

Therefore, the next question is, for each specific supply chain, what are the key pain points you're trying to address? If it's coffee, the key questions might be origin authentication and sustainable farming. There are other ways to do it without wireless IoT. Penta has a commercial deployment with the Ministry of Agriculture in Uganda. Here, you can register a farm on a blockchain and do what is called a trusted supplier authentication. Suppose you wanted to trace coffee back to its source and verify a single origin. In that case, you could do that just with a trusted supplier authentication.

However, it gets complicated because Ugandan-grown coffee gets intermingled with coffee from other parts of East Africa. This commingling happens while being aggregated in Kenya and gets sold as Kenyan coffee, but it is also a problem for the Ugandan ministry. They want to drive more value to their production in Uganda since exports are a significant part of their industry. So there are ways to approach this without IoT devices. Trusted supplier authentication is one of them.

One of the challenges that we continually come back to is that people in the blockchain world think they have the next disruptive technology, which can change the paradigm. But, there's an educational hurdle for businesses that don't understand blockchain's value proposition in their specific business contexts. As an industry, we have to identify those unique value propositions—not just value propositions, but unique value propositions.

We try to find industries and problem-solution fits for which blockchain has a unique value proposition. It has a value proposition that existing technologies can't offer. Complex value systems are where people share data between different companies with different interests in the value chain. In that situation, blockchain is the only data solution that allows for comprehensive data infrastructure. This infrastructure enables collecting the data assets used to verify the authenticity, legality, and regulatory compliance. Because of this unique value proposition, blockchain technology will have a substantial role in strengthening the global supply chains.

On to the next chapter to wrap it all up.

"When I was a kid, I would get these headaches. And I went to the doctor, and they said that I needed glasses. I didn't understand that. It didn't make sense to me because I could see fine. And then I get the glasses, and I put them on, and I'm in the car on the way home—and, suddenly, I yell! Because the big green blobs that I had been staring at my whole life, they weren't big green blobs. They were leaves. On trees. I could see the leaves. And I didn't even know I was missing the leaves. I didn't even know that leaves existed, and then . . . Leaves!"

GREY'S ANATOMY, S5E6, "LIFE DURING WARTIME."

# CHAPTER 10

# UNBLOCKING BLOCKCHAIN

———

## THE DILEMMA OF EMERGING TECHNOLOGIES

*"After two decades online, I'm perplexed. It's not that I haven't had a gas of a good time on the Internet. I've met great people and even caught a hacker or two. But today, I'm uneasy about this most trendy and oversold community. Visionaries see a future of telecommuting workers, interactive libraries, and multimedia classrooms. They speak of electronic town meetings and virtual communities. Commerce and business will shift from offices and malls to networks and modems. And the freedom of digital networks will make the government more democratic.*

*"Baloney. Do our computer pundits lack all common sense? The truth is no online database will replace your daily newspaper,*

*no CD-ROM can take the place of a competent teacher and no computer network will change the way government works.*"[98]

CLIFFORD STOLL, ASTRONOMER AND AUTHOR

A technologically savvy Clifford Stoll wrote these comments in 1995. Fast forward twenty-five years, and we can have a chuckle as we read through the words. But Mr. Stoll's flub highlights the duality of emerging technology and its accompanying challenges.

"We overestimate the impact of technology in the short term, and underestimate it in the long term."[99] As I mulled over those lines, it made me ponder that irrespective of who gets credit for the thought, it is easy to fall into this trap with new technologies.

Emerging technologies come with opportunity and risk. Therefore, they need to be managed appropriately. On the one hand, there is an immense potential to generate new value by participating in the innovation. And on the other hand, the newness comes with its own set of risks. There is always an accompanying drumbeat that can hype up the emerging technology as the next big thing. The decision to, or not to, evaluate, invest, and implement these technologies quickly can have far-reaching impacts for companies.

For this reason, companies need to be tech-forward and figure out the right amount of time and energy to invest in

---

98   Stoll, "Why the Web."
99   Farnam Street, "Why It Matters."

**152 · UNBLOCKING BLOCKCHAIN**

emerging technology—just enough so that they know what is going on without missing the boat if it turns into something big.

The question then becomes, how do we go about evaluating blockchain as an emerging technology? Do we want to take advantage of new developments without exposing our companies to undue risk with new technologies?

## ENTERPRISE BLOCKCHAIN ADOPTION FRAMEWORK

As I followed the breadcrumbs and looked closely at several early adopters' blockchain journeys, a framework has evolved. Digital leaders can use this as a template to guide their blockchain strategy.

This picture gives a depiction of the framework.

ENTERPRISE BLOCKCHAIN ADOPTION FRAMEWORK

## LEARN

As an emerging technology shows promise, it is crucial to learn about it before jumping in with investments. To start your journey with blockchain, you first take some time to dip your toes in the water. Learning about the technology should inform future investments by a company.

That learning is accelerated if you focus on bringing together various minds who are interested in the technologies. Internally this is best done by building a center of excellence (CoE). A CoE helps centralize the company's blockchain skills and experience and build a repository for best practices. A CoE can also take the lead in executing the proof of concept and pilots. It can also provide training as part of the adoption process further down the line.

As Lisa Butters realized with Honeywell, a central team can also help illuminate new use cases. They can help the business side understand how blockchain technology could help. As she explains, "I don't really recall, a hundred percent, how I got linked to our advanced tech team at Honeywell. But we had a small group of people who were dabbling, I would say, in blockchain technology. But they didn't really have a good use case. I was able to meet with that team, introduce them to the marketplace, some of the barriers that we were faced with, how the industry operates today, etc. And that's really how it all started."[100]

Externally, engaging with the community in the ecosystem is the way to go. It helps you build relationships within the

---

100 Butters, "Blockchain Airplane Parts."

ecosystem. These relationships help down the line as efforts go into nurturing the business network for consortium conversations. It is best to embed into the community to learn more and help others. Engage with others interested in the technology by attending blockchain-specific events and connecting with people who are pursuing an understanding of the technology. Besides trying to understand what others are building or what problems they are solving, contribute to the community by providing your input.

Doug McCollough did it well with the city of Dublin, Ohio. He explains: "We actually created a group, before we thought about developing a solution here, called the Dublin blockchain group. That was my attempt to plant a flag a few years ago, where we said, 'We want all of the tech companies in the area to come out and sit down.' Hackers, you know, people in the back rooms of their companies who are really experimenting and sort of keeping this skunkworks in secret, 'Come out, and amongst friends, we're just going to discuss them.' We've had a few meetings of that, and a few companies emerged as really just being passionate about this."[101]

As you learn about the technology, it helps complete a proof of concept (POC) to get your hands dirty. The POC will help see the benefits that blockchain technology might bring and the limitations that come along with it. A POC also helps get a view into what use cases might be ripe to be tackled first. Building POCs also provide input as you present critical findings to the leadership team and discuss the business case.

---

101  McCollough, "Dublin Digital Identity."

This learning phase is the starting point to build upon further action.

## COLLABORATION INFRASTRUCTURE

In the learning process, you realize that blockchain is a team sport. It is best to play well with others. Those others might be your competitors, making it harder and different from other emerging technologies that companies would be evaluating. So evaluating market maturity becomes essential.

Is the industry ready to use the technology? Are there other players in the industry that are showing an interest in possibly collaborating? Blockchain technology cannot help achieve much if others are not ready to participate. What is the state of consortium development in your industry? Is some competitor taking the lead? Or is an independent software vendor coming up with a solution in which it makes sense to engage with them? Would data standards pose a barrier given the industry landscape?

All in all, you have to figure out and contribute to creating the collaboration infrastructure for the minimum viable ecosystem, which is the basis of successful blockchain adoption.

As you learn about the technology, you should continually evaluate the technology opportunity in front of you. One factor to keep an eye on is the maturity of the technology itself. What are its current limitations? What is gaining traction with others? How much momentum is behind solving the gaps? Which platform providers are gaining momentum and getting more market share? How is the regulatory landscape?

**COMMERCIALIZE**

As the ecosystem matures and the collaboration infrastructure comes together, you are ready to move forward. Start with a pilot to build the solution before focusing on adoption and commercialization to reap the benefits.

A pilot helps build confidence in the technology across the organization. Running a pilot proves to yourself the technical feasibility of the solution. It also builds confidence across the organization, especially with the leadership, to pursue the technology further.

As you get to the point when it makes sense to invest, it's time to act. If you want to have a higher level of influence on the solution's direction, go for a founder-led consortium. Suppose there are multiple equal players in the market. In that case, it might be better to partner with a consortium to come up with a solution. And if the industry progression is such that there is already an ISV coming up with a solution, look to see if it makes sense to join up in their solution.

**BLOCKCHAIN AS GPT?**

General purpose technology (GPT) is a technology that is a core driver of economic growth. These are few key technologies that drive economic growth and further technical progress over extended periods. GPTs permeate multiple sectors of the economy, and the downstream sectors use GPTs as input. Innovation in GPT fuels growth in the downstream sectors. Because of this, as GPTs mature, their adoption also becomes more entrenched throughout the economy. In their paper looking at technical progress and economic growth, Bresnahan and Trajtenberg looked at a few examples of GPTs like the steam engine, electric motor, computers, internet, etc. [102]

GPTs are compelling technologies with global impact. The effects of GPTs can bring change to existing economic and social structures. Over time, the efficiency of GPTs increases, and this continues to improve the downstream sector where the GPT is embedded. As GPT becomes more efficient, downstream sectors' costs go down, helping reduce prices and better products. Notably, more and more sectors find it helpful to use the GPT as input.

I could see a parallel to GPTs and how Tony Little described the way he looks at blockchain: "It's like just plugging into the electrical grid. I use the analogy of blockchain as a utility. It's not a light bulb, but it's the electrical grid you plug your light bulb into. A good blockchain use case should feel like an electrical grid. You are creating something that everyone can tie into."

Downstream sectors utilize some generic functions that GPTs perform. The generic function performed by blockchain is to enable transactions in an environment where no trust exists.

At a superficial level, blockchain looks like nothing more than a shared worksheet to which multiple parties can read and write transactions. They do it in a continuously flowing ledger format. However, blockchain is more than a shared worksheet because it puts this socio-economic wrapper around the technology.

---

102 Bresnahan et al., "General Purpose Technologies."

As Dan Fritz from Novartis highlighted, "Blockchain is a socio-technical construct. . . . This basically means it's something designed for joint optimization. This is another way to say it should be a win-win. It should benefit all of the participants that are engaged in it. . . . And that requires basically a different mindset, a different way of thinking where we're going to grow the pie, instead of just slicing it up."[103]

What transforms that shared worksheet into a blockchain is that many people can agree to the recorded transactions, even though they don't know or trust each other. For that matter, they may even have a conflict of interest and still be able to transact. On top of that, there is no one overseeing or refereeing this interaction. Blockchain makes it possible for a peer-to-peer market to exist without the need for a central authority. And these peers can also be enterprises, or IoT devices.

Blockchain can help us get to a point that we will just take digital trust for granted because it will be the least common denominator to the way we work. Just imagine all the things that ubiquitous digital trust will unlock. As Orapong wondered, "If you can conduct trades as easily as you send a text message, or send an email today—imagine how many changes will occur in the business world if you can conduct the trade as easily as that."[104]

Blockchain will be an infrastructure layer of business functions. We will not be talking about blockchain but just take

103  Fritz et al., "Healthcare Blockchain from."
104  Thien-Ngern et al., "from Siam Commercial Bank."

it for granted. We are already starting to see it permeate through various industries in the economy. It will become the underlying plumbing of enterprise workings.

Like GPT, it can spread through the economy and help everyone do more. Blockchain can help you come together with your competitors and partners in a way that a rising tide raises all boats, including yours.

## PATH FORWARD FOR BLOCKCHAIN

Before blockchain can get to be a GPT, its journey from here needs to stand the test of time.

Of all the emerging technologies, blockchain is one technology that brings value primarily when deployed across organizations. There are many headwinds for adopting the technology, like lack of education about blockchain, fast-evolving technology landscape because of the newness of the technology, immaturity of standards, and lack of much-needed love from the regulators in the US. But, coopetition being a necessary condition for success is perhaps its most significant hurdle. As a collective, the business world needs to get to a point where this idea takes root and becomes ingrained in the business ethos. Businesses need to appreciate the value coming from a shared and connected economy to realize blockchain's full potential.

Adding to that, as Alison McCauley put it, "One thing that's really important to keep in mind is there's this hangover from a really crazy hype cycle that we are going through, and so people come into it with a lot of preconceptions and a lot of emotions. A lot of emotions. And that's really difficult to navigate." [105]

For all emerging technologies, you need to be patient with the ROI. You can't expect that things will just start happening right away. First of all, few people know what to do and how to use it best to derive quick value. There is also a lack of best practices that are not available to lean on. In the case of blockchain, we must take additional factors into account. Because blockchain projects are a team sport, you have to bring everyone along to be successful. That takes time. All have to walk together. If all have to move forward together, you have to allow for time needed for coming to agreements. If there are shared goals, it will also need to be shared decisions. That takes time.

You also have to spend more time on non-technical things. As William Mougayar so aptly put it, "When you sum it up, the blockchain is about 80 percent business process changes and 20 percent technology implementation."[106]

Because technical teams champion many blockchain projects, they end up taking a technology-first approach. The primary focus ends up being the implementation of technical details instead of the economics of the endeavor.

As HFS research reports, "While most respondents are focusing on technical solutions, less than 45 percent of respondents are investing in blockchain talent, consortia, research,

---

105  McCauley, "Why Executives Struggle."
106  Mougayar, "A Decision Tree."

and intellectual property. A blockchain narrative purely centered on technology is a recipe for failure—people (stakeholder buy-in, change management, skills development) and processes (business case, governance, scaling, and service support) are equally essential to drive success."[107]

Because of these reasons, change management takes on an extra dimension because people have to learn fundamentally new ways of doing things. Newly learned behavior will take some time to manifest. I may intellectually understand something because the change management efforts have taken me through the training. I also appreciate the paradigm shift that is involved here. Before we see a behavior change, there is a process of internalization that I have to go through.

Until then, I may know it, but I might still exhibit old behavior patterns.

Just as Lisa Butters found out in her work with GoDirect Trade, "I think transparency is really hard. For sellers that are used to antiquated ways of selling, and they're scanning documents, maybe saving it to their computer and emailing it back and forth, they're not used to having an e-commerce presence. They don't know how to manage an online storefront. That's what you saw with Amazon in the 1995 to early 2000 era. You had a lot of brick-and-mortar stores that really were just not used to e-commerce activities. They felt like they didn't have to participate in it until 2010 started rolling in, and they just got left behind."[108]

---

107  Gupta et al., "Ignore Blockchain at Your Peril."
108  Butters., "Blockchain Airplane Parts."

In their current situation, people have relied on diligently cultivating relationships for success in their jobs. You cannot expect them to change and start trusting blockchain technology. You have to allow them to adjust and be patient as they go through that process. You can use organizational strategies to accelerate the process. However, you still have to allow for the organizational patience to manifest.

Ironically, blockchain—the "Trust" technology—has to earn our trust before it can achieve mainstream acceptance.

With all of that said, as we have seen in our inquiry through this book, there certainly is enough momentum in various industries with blockchain adoption. Blockchain has moved on from POC to commercialization. As Andrew Speers put it, "I think that the days of blockchain POCs are gone. We did two to three years of that. We know it works. We know what it does. Now we don't have any luxury of building things for the sake of intellectual pursuit. It's gone from emerging tech to 'Tech.' And we are just getting on with commercialization, and testing, and using with customers."[109]

### ENABLING OUR DIGITAL FUTURE

My friend Venky keeps asking me, "What is the killer app built using blockchain?" And I honestly believe there is no answer to that question right now. We are in very early stages of the technology, with many technical limitations yet to be solved. The real transformative solutions are, however, yet to come. As the technology evolves and blockchain starts

---

109 Speers, "User Experience on the Blockchain."

playing nicely with other emerging technologies like IoT, AI, 5G, robotics, etc., the real killer apps will also come.

For the end-users, blockchain has the potential to permeate our lives and make them better. It can go the way of the internet. Omnipresent in our lives. Working behind the scenes. We don't need to understand how it works, but we still use it all the time without thinking about it. Taking it for granted. If I buy something online, I don't need to know what happened behind the scenes to make the purchase happen. I just need to know that my security is not compromised, and I can easily do what I want to do.

For companies, it will open up hitherto uncharted territories. It will be the backbone of a connected digital economy and help other emerging technologies extend their potential. Blockchain will do for business ecosystems what ERP did for the single enterprise. As Brigid McDermott from IBM put it, "Blockchain has the potential to transform transactions, the way that the internet transformed communications."[110]

Blockchain is not there yet, but signs suggest that it will get there soon. When we get there, it will transform our social and economic paradigms.

Blockchain will be the glasses that we didn't know we needed. We just might see the leaves of trust for the first time.

---

110  McDermott et al., "Breaking down Blockchain."

www.locatesw.com

Locate Software sponsors this book. Best-partner-ever for your digital transformation needs. Thank you for being a Superfan and showing your confidence in me, as you always do.

# ACKNOWLEDGMENTS

———

We would not be anywhere without our support system. My support system certainly lifted me to help this book complete its journey from an intention to reality.

My "who" luck came through with a chance crossing of our paths, and *Eric Koester* changed my life's trajectory. Thank you for showing me that I, too, can write a book.

My gratitude to all the people who so generously gave me their time and shared their knowledge to make this book better: Tony Little, Dan Salmons, Shahar Steiff, David Ritter, Jesús Rodríguez, Paige Krieger, Chris Spanton, Stephen Albonico, and others who helped me with countless conversations.

Special thanks to Walid Al Saqqaf for all that you do to evangelize blockchain and continue to be a source of information and learning.

To all my backers, who came together as a community from all walks of my life and showed the confidence in me just on the promise of faith when this book was just taking wings— Thank You to Aarushi Mahajan, Abdullah Ali, Aditya Bhatnagar, Alexander Edelman, Alvaro Jimenez, Amit & Shaveta Bhatia, Amit Kumar, Amit Singh, Amol Kale, Anil Bahal, Anshuman Bhardwaj, Bhavana & Kriti Mahajan, Anthony Landreth, Anuj Gulati, Anupam B, Anurag Nagpal, Archana Mahajan, Anil & Aruna Mahajan, Arun Malik, Arvind Kunwar, Arvind Yadav, Ashish Agarwal, Ashish Rakheja, Ashish Sharma, Ashok Kumar, Ashok Mishra, Ashutosh Kumar, Ashwini Krishnan, Atanu Ghosh, Atul Gupta, Avanthi Koneru, Balaji Abbabatulla, Benjamin Schultz, Birendra Kumar, Brandon Kissinger, Brock Freeman, Chandra Prakash, Chandrika Pasricha, Charlotte Malmberg, Chetan Kudur, Christopher Spanton, Conor Bronsdon, Corey Bugni, Daibashish Gangopadhyay, David Rolls, David Vanhorn, Deepak Mogha, Dipen Chauhan, Divya Soni, Elisabeth Revell, Emily Chelius, Eric Koester, Erin Lowe, Gary J. Anderson, Gina Short, Glen Kurisingal, Glenn Holman, Graydon Britton, Guillermo Miller, Gunjan Murarka, Hari Sekhar, Hemant Albert Soreng, Jeff Jager, Jharna Madan, Jim R Ludu, Johan Nguyen, John Kuder, Jonathan G. Blanco, Kailash Purohit, Kartik Shankar, Laxmi Shirisha Vuddaraju, Lorraine Stoker, Luka Dover, Luke Bayler, Madhura Purohit, Manisha Lath Gupta, Manish Samadarshi, Manoj Naik, Manoj Sreedharan, Medha Soni, Mohit Kapahi, Muffadal Boty, Muneesh Batra, Natesh Bellal Venkat, Naveed Ahmed, Naveed Mohammed, Navendu Pandey, Nitin Daniel, Paige Krieger, Parul Prakash, Paul Rapino, Peter Chen, Pradeep Sekar, Pradeep Venkataramu, Prashant Jamwal, Praveen Sharma, Praveer Gaur, Priyadarshan Wanjari, Radhakrishna

Pillai, Rahul Dwivedi, Rahul Padhye, Rajat Sharma , Ram
Cherala, Ravi Jagannathan, Ravi Pooli, Ravi Venkatesam,
Ray Blakeney, Reema Agarwal, Riga Mann, Rishi Bhatnagar,
Rosie Odsey, Rupam Baijal, Sachin Maheshwari, Sandeep
Raju, Saurabh Gupta, Shailesh Jaiswal, Shalaka & Dar-
shan Gangolli, Shalini Chhabra, Shantanu Sharma, Shashi
Kumar, Sheen Thomas, Shivram Subramanian, Shubhra
Garg, Sid Priyadarshi, Sidharth Mohan, Som Sarangmath,
Srihari Rayavarapu, Srinivas Kasturi, Srinivas Sistla, Stephen
Albonico, Tejas Dixit, Tejinder Mann, Tina Singh, Tony Little,
Trilok Singh, Umesh Gupta, Venkat Baddipudi, Venkata Ped-
ereddla, Venkata Remella, Venkatesh Varadachari, Vijay K
Srivastava, Vikas Valsang, Vincent Wijdeveld, Vineet Ahuja,
Vivek Gupta & Will Oh—thank you for having confidence
in me.

Everyone at New Degree Press, who oh-so-gently guided me.
Unassumingly. They walked with me and helped at every
stumble on the path. I would have been so lost without
their structure.

And everyone else who is not mentioned here but helped me
continue this journey in their own unique ways.

# APPENDIX

---

## INTRODUCTION

"Growing Threat from Counterfeit Medicines." *Bulletin of the World Health Organization* 88, no. 4 (March 4, 2011). https://www.who.int/bulletin/volumes/88/4/10-020410/en/.

"The Blockchain Report 2020." *CB Insights*, 2020. https://www.cbinsights.com/reports/CB-Insights_Blockchain-Report-2020.pdf.

"The Blockchain Report 2020." *CB Insights*, 2020. https://www.cbinsights.com/reports/CB-Insights_Blockchain-Report-2020.pdf.

Aitken, Murray, Michael Kleinrock, Alana Simorellis, and Deanna Nass. "The Global Use of Medicine in 2019 and Outlook to 2023." *The IQVIA Institute*, January 2019. https://www.iqvia.com/-/media/iqvia/pdfs/institute-reports/the-global-use-of-medicine-in-2019-and-outlook-to-2023.pdf.

Behner, Peter, Marie-Lyn Hecht, and Fabian Wahl. *"Fighting Counterfeit Pharmaceuticals."* Strategy&. PwC, 2017. https://www.strategyand.pwc.com/gx/en/insights/2017/fighting-counterfeit-pharmaceuticals/fighting-counterfeit-pharmaceuticals.pdf.

Behner, Peter, Marie-Lyn Hecht, and Fabian Wahl. "Fighting Counterfeit Pharmaceuticals." *Strategy&*. PwC, 2017. https://www.strategyand.pwc.com/gx/en/insights/2017/fighting-counterfeit-pharmaceuticals/fighting-counterfeit-pharmaceuticals.pdf.

Casman, Jesse. "Top 5 Blockchain Predictions for 2019." JAXenter, December 12, 2018. https://jaxenter.com/top-5-blockchain-predictions-2019-152880. html.

Dimitrov, Biser. "How Walmart and Others Are Riding a Blockchain Wave to Supply Chain Paradise." Forbes, December 5, 2019. https://www. forbes.com/sites/biserdimitrov/2019/12/05/how-walmart-and-others-are-riding-a-blockchain-wave-to-supply-chain-paradise/.

Erazo, Felipe. "Blockchain-Powered 5G Phone Manufactured by Samsung Launches." Cointelegraph, May 14, 2020. https://cointelegraph.com/news/ blockchain-powered-5g-phone-manufactured-by-samsung-launches.

Gartner. "Hype Cycle Research Methodology." Gartner, 2018. https://www. gartner.com/en/research/methodologies/gartner-hype-cycle.

Hines, Michael. "Why Mastercard's Blockchain Focuses on Practical Applications." Built In, December 3, 2019. https://builtin.com/blockchain/ practical-applications-blockchain-technology.

Kapilkov, Michael. "Starbucks to Let Customers Trace Their Coffee's Provenance from Bean to Brew." Cointelegraph, August 25, 2020. https:// cointelegraph.com/news/starbucks-to-let-customers-trace-their-coffee-s-provenance-from-bean-to-brew.

PYMNTS. "Lending Firm Figure Technologies Raises $103M." Pymnts.com, December 5, 2019. https://www.pymnts.com/news/investment-tracker/2019/ figure-technologies-raises-103-million-continue-blockchain-based-lending/.

Rehman, Najib, and Raja Sharif. "Blockchain & AI in Pharmaceutical & Healthcare – Insights from FarmaTrust." Interview by Walid Al Saqqaf. Insureblocks, July 14, 2019. https://insureblocks.com/ep-66-blockchain-ai-in-pharmaceutical-healthcare-insights-from-farmatrust/.

Sun, Lena H. "Getting a Coronavirus Vaccine in Record Time Is Hard. Distributing It to Tens of Millions May Be Equally Daunting." The Washington Post, April 3, 2020. https://www.washingtonpost.com/health/2020/08/03/ coronavirus-vaccine-distribution-confusion/.

## WHAT IS BLOCKCHAIN?

Clarke-Hill, Colin, Huaning Li, and Barry Davies. "The Paradox of Cooperation and Competition in Strategic Alliances: Towards a Multi-paradigm Approach." *Management Research News* 26, no. 1 (February 2003): 1–20. https://doi.org/10.1108/01409170310783376.

GPT-3. "A Robot Wrote This Entire Article. Are You Scared yet, Human?" *The Guardian*, September 8, 2020. https://www.theguardian.com/commentisfree/2020/sep/08/robot-wrote-this-article-gpt-3.

Spielberg, Steven, dir. *Minority Report*. 20th Century Fox, 2002. DVD.

## DO YOU KNOW WHY YOU ARE USING BLOCKCHAIN

"Blockchain for Procure-To-Pay (B2p)—Faster, Cheaper Procurement for Corporates." *R3*, 2019. https://www.r3.com/wp-content/uploads/2019/11/R3.SCB_.B2P_CS_2019.pdf.

"Creating Value in a Digital World: The Role of Emerging Technology." *Dell Technologies*. Accessed January 23, 2021. https://www.delltechnologies.com/en-us/collaterals/unauth/analyst-reports/solutions/role-of-emerging-technology.pdf.

"Forecast: Blockchain Business Value, Worldwide, 2017-2030." Gartner. March 2, 2017. https://www.gartner.com/en/documents/3627117.

"Improving Provider Data Accuracy." *Synaptic Health Alliance*. Accessed January 23, 2021. https://f.hubspotusercontent40.net/hubfs/4801399/Synaptic_Health_Alliance_Blockchain_White_Paper.pdf.

Gartner. "Gartner Predicts 90% of Current Enterprise Blockchain Platform Implementations Will Require Replacement by 2021." June 3, 2019. https://www.gartner.com/en/newsroom/press-releases/2019-07-03-gartner-predicts-90—of-current-enterprise-blockchain.

Gupta, Saurabh, Jamie Snowdon, and Tanmoy Mondal. "Ignore Blockchain at Your Peril, but Don't Drive Blindly." *Wipro*. HFSResearch, 2020. https://www.wipro.com/content/dam/nexus/en/analyst-speak/pdfs/state-of-enterprise-blockchain-market-2020-new.pdf.

Hurder, Stephanie. "Why enterprise blockchains fail? No economic incentives." Interview by Walid Al Saqqaf. *Insureblocks*, July 3, 2020. https://insureblocks.com/ep-107-why-enterprise-blockchains-fail-no-economic-incentives/.

Nikkei Asia. "The Siam Commercial Bank Public Co. Ltd." Nikkei Inc. Accessed January 23, 2021. https://asia.nikkei.com/Companies/The-Siam-Commercial-Bank-Public-Co.-Ltd2.

PwC. "Make the Blockchain Business Case: Evolution, Not Revolution." Accessed January 23, 2021. https://www.pwc.com/gx/en/industries/technology/blockchain/blockchain-in-business/make-the-business-case.html.

Thien-Ngern, Orapong, and Sharon Yuen. "Blockchain for procure-to-pay – insights from Siam Commercial Bank." Interview by Walid Al Saqqaf. *Insureblocks*, January 19, 2020. https://insureblocks.com/ep-92-blockchain-for-procure-to-pay-insights-from-siam-commercial-bank/.

## IT'S ALL ABOUT THE ECONOMICS, STUPID

"Why Enterprise Blockchain Implementations Fail." *SettleMint*, 2020. https://mcusercontent.com/84109aac080de8b6d883c32d9/files/ee95f098-ebe7-4633-b2c6-a2c93c5fa836/SettleMint_why_enterprise_blockchain_implementations_fail.pdf.

Gupta, Saurabh, Jamie Snowdon, and Tanmoy Mondal. "Ignore Blockchain at Your Peril, but Don't Drive Blindly." *Wipro*. HFSResearch, 2020. https://www.wipro.com/content/dam/nexus/en/analyst-speak/pdfs/state-of-enterprise-blockchain-market-2020-new.pdf.

Kuiper, Jon. Vinturas – Finished Vehicle Supply Chain on the Blockchain. Interview by Walid Al Saqqaf. *Insureblocks*, February 16, 2020. https://insureblocks.com/ep-96-vinturas-finished-vehicle-supply-chain-on-the-blockchain/.

Rosic, Ameer. "What Is Cryptoeconomics? The Ultimate Beginners Guide." Blockgeeks, August 21, 2017. https://blockgeeks.com/guides/what-is-cryptoeconomics/.

Thien-Ngern, Orapong, and Sharon Yuen. Blockchain for procure-to-pay – insights from Siam Commercial Bank. Interview by Walid Al Saqqaf. *Insureblocks*, January 19, 2020. https://insureblocks.com/ep-92-blockchain-for-procure-to-pay-insights-from-siam-commercial-bank/.

## THE ROI DILEMMA

Helland, Dustin. State Farm's Blockchain – Auto Claims Subrogation. Interview by Walid Al Saqqaf. *Insureblocks*, August 4, 2019. https://insureblocks.com/ep-69-state-farms-blockchain-auto-claims-subrogation/.

Hurder, Stephanie. Why enterprise blockchains fail? No economic incentives. Interview by Walid Al Saqqaf. *Insureblocksh*, July 3, 2020. https://

insureblocks.com/ep-107-why-enterprise-blockchains-fail-no-econom-ic-incentives/.

Kollewe, Julia. "Twitter Makes First Quarterly Profit in Its History." The Guardian, February 8, 2018. https://www.theguardian.com/technolo-gy/2018/feb/08/twitter-makes-first-quarterly-profit-history.

Speers, Andrew. User Experience on the Blockchain – Insights from RBS. Interview by Walid Al Saqqaf. *Insureblocks*, January 12, 2020. https://insureblocks.com/ep-91-user-experience-on-the-blockchain-insights-from-rbs/.

Thien-Ngern, Orapong, and Sharon Yuen. "Blockchain for procure-to-pay – insights from Siam Commercial Bank." Interview by Walid Al Saqqaf. *Insureblocks*, January 19, 2020. https://insureblocks.com/ep-92-blockchain-for-procure-to-pay-insights-from-siam-commercial-bank/.

Thompson, Derek. "Facebook Turns a Profit, Users Hits 300 Million." The Atlantic, September 17, 2009. https://www.theatlantic.com/business/archive/2009/09/facebook-turns-a-profit-users-hits-300-million/26721/.

## ALL ABOUT CONSORTIA

"CDC and Food Safety." Centers for Disease Control and Prevention, June 25, 2020. https://www.cdc.gov/foodsafety/cdc-and-food-safety.html.

Merriam-Webster. s.v. "consortium (n.)." Accessed February 15, 2021. https://www.merriam-webster.com/dictionary/consortium.

Pawczuk, Linda, Rob Massey, and Jonathan Holdowsky. "Deloitte's 2019 Global Blockchain Survey." Deloitte, May 6, 2019. https://www2.deloitte.com/content/dam/Deloitte/se/Documents/risk/DI_2019-global-block-chain-survey.pdf.

Reynolds, John. Real Estate on the Blockchain – Insights from Coadjute. Interview by Walid Al Saqqaf. Insureblocks, November 30, 2019. https://insureblocks.com/ep-86-real-estate-on-the-blockchain-insights-from-coadjute/.

Yiannas, Frank. Frank Yiannas: Leading Food Safety at the World's Largest Retailer. Interview by Barbara VanRenterghem. Food Safety Maga-zine, August 28, 2018. https://www.food-safety.com/articles/5924-ep-32-frank-yiannas-food-safety-walmart-worlds-largest-retailer.

## CREATING COLLABORATION INFRASTRUCTURE

Attanasio, Silvia. Spunta – Blockchain for Italian Interbank Reconciliation. Interview by Walid Al Saqqaf. *Insureblocks*, March 22, 2020. https://insureblocks.com/ep-101-spunta-blockchain-for-italian-interbank-reconciliation/.

Butters, Lisa. GoDirect Trade, Honeywell's Blockchain Airplane Parts. Interview by Walid Al Saqqaf. *Insureblocks*, April 19, 2020. https://insureblocks.com/ep-105-godirect-trade-honeywells-blockchain-airplane-parts/.

Helland, Dustin. State Farm's Blockchain – Auto Claims Subrogation. Interview by Walid Al Saqqaf. *Insureblocks*, August 4, 2019. https://insureblocks.com/ep-69-state-farms-blockchain-auto-claims-subrogation/.

Holden, Richard, and Anup Malani. "Can Blockchain Solve the Holdup Problem in Contracts?" *SSRN Electronic Journal*, December 28, 2017. https://doi.org/10.2139/ssrn.3093879.

Hurder, Stephanie. Why enterprise blockchains fail? No economic incentives. Interview by Walid Al Saqqaf. *Insureblocks*, July 3, 2020. https://insureblocks.com/ep-107-why-enterprise-blockchains-fail-no-economic-incentives/.

Kuiper, Jon. Vinturas – Finished Vehicle Supply Chain on the Blockchain. Interview by Walid Al Saqqaf. *Insureblocks*, February 16, 2020. https://insureblocks.com/ep-96-vinturas-finished-vehicle-supply-chain-on-the-blockchain/.

Pawczuk, Linda, Rob Massey, Jonathan Holdowsky, and Brian Hansen. "Deloitte's 2020 Global Blockchain Survey." *Deloitte*, 2020. https://www2.deloitte.com/content/dam/insights/us/articles/6608_2020-global-blockchain-survey/DI_CIR%202020%20global%20blockchain%20survey.pdf.

Shah, Agam. "Honeywell Brings Blockchain to Used Aircraft Parts Market." *Wall Street Journal*, May 28, 2019, sec. C Suite. https://www.wsj.com/articles/honeywell-brings-blockchain-to-used-aircraft-parts-market-11559072819.

Thien-Ngern, Orapong, and Sharon Yuen. Blockchain for procure-to-pay – Insights from Siam Commercial Bank. Interview by Walid Al Saqqaf. *Insureblocks*, January 19, 2020. https://insureblocks.com/ep-92-blockchain-for-procure-to-pay-insights-from-siam-commercial-bank/.

## SET YOURSELF UP FOR SUCCESS

"U.S. Attorney Announces Arrest and Money Laundering Charges against Dark Web Narcotics Trafficker." United States Department of Justice, July 18, 2019. https://www.justice.gov/usao-sdny/pr/us-attorney-announces-arrest-and-money-laundering-charges-against-dark-web-narcotics.

Attanasio, Silvia. Spunta – Blockchain for Italian Interbank Reconciliation. Interview by Walid Al Saqqaf. *Insureblocks*, March 22, 2020. https://insureblocks.com/ep-101-spunta-blockchain-for-italian-interbank-reconciliation/.

Helland, Dustin. State Farm's Blockchain – Auto Claims Subrogation. Interview by Walid Al Saqqaf. *Insureblocks*, August 4, 2019. https://insureblocks.com/ep-69-state-farms-blockchain-auto-claims-subrogation/.

Kuiper, Jon. Vinturas – Finished Vehicle Supply Chain on the Blockchain. Interview by Walid Al Saqqaf. *Insureblocks*, February 16, 2020. https://insureblocks.com/ep-96-vinturas-finished-vehicle-supply-chain-on-the-blockchain/.

McCollough, Doug. Dublin Digital Identity Project. Interview by Walid Al Saqqaf. *Insureblocks*, February 2, 2020. https://insureblocks.com/ep-94-dublin-digital-identity-project/.

PricewaterhouseCoopers. "Design Deliberately: Determine Rules of Engagement." PwC Global. Accessed February 26, 2021. https://www.pwc.com/gx/en/industries/technology/blockchain/blockchain-in-business/rules-of-engagement.html.

Reynolds, John. Real Estate on the Blockchain – Insights from Coadjute. Interview by Walid Al Saqqaf. Insureblocks, November 30, 2019. https://insureblocks.com/ep-86-real-estate-on-the-blockchain-insights-from-coadjute/.

Speers, Andrew. User Experience on the Blockchain – Insights from RBS. Interview by Walid Al Saqqaf. *Insureblocks*, January 12, 2020. https://insureblocks.com/ep-91-user-experience-on-the-blockchain-insights-from-rbs/.

Thien-Ngern, Orapong, and Sharon Yuen. "Blockchain for procure-to-pay – insights from Siam Commercial Bank." Interview by Walid Al Saqqaf. *Insureblocks*, January 19, 2020. https://insureblocks.com/ep-92-blockchain-for-procure-to-pay-insights-from-siam-commercial-bank/.

## THE NEW MACHINE ECONOMY

"Economy of Things – a Technology and Business Evolution." Bosch Global. Accessed March 5, 2021. https://www.bosch.com/research/know-how/success-stories/economy-of-things-a-technology-and-business-evolution/.

"Gartner Says 5.8 Billion Enterprise and Automotive Iot Endpoints Will Be in Use in 2020." Gartner, August 29, 2019. https://www.gartner.com/en/newsroom/press-releases/2019-08-29-gartner-says-5-8-billion-enterprise-and-automotive-io.

"Transformation through Sensors, Software and Services." Robert Bosch Engineering and Business Solutions, 2019. https://media-cdn.easci.com/static/iotinactionevents/assets/event_recap_pdfs/warsaw/IIA-Warsaw-Bosch-Case-Study.pdf.

Gupta, Saurabh, Jamie Snowdon, and Tanmoy Mondal. "Ignore Blockchain at Your Peril, but Don't Drive Blindly." *Wipro*. HFSResearch, 2020. https://www.wipro.com/content/dam/nexus/en/analyst-speak/pdfs/state-of-enterprise-blockchain-market-2020-new.pdf.

Kulkarni, Raghavendra. Bosch's Economy of Things. Interview by Walid Al Saqqaf. *Insureblocks*, November 17, 2019. https://insureblocks.com/ep-84-boschs-economy-of-things/.

Palmer, Michael. "Data Is the New Oil." ANA Marketing Maestros, November 3, 2006. https://ana.blogs.com/maestros/2006/11/data_is_the_new.html.

## BLOCKCHAIN IN SUPPLY CHAIN

"Blockchain Supply Chain Market Worth $3,272 Million by 2026." MarketsandMarketsTM. Accessed March 1, 2021. https://www.marketsandmarkets.com/PressReleases/blockchain-supply-chain.asp.

"Food Loss and Food Waste." Food and Agriculture Organization of the United Nations. Accessed March 1, 2021. http://www.fao.org/food-loss-and-food-waste/flw-data).

"Hunger-Facts." Food and Agriculture Organization of the United Nations, 2011. http://www.fao.org/zhc/hunger-facts/en/.

McDermott, Brigid, and Frank Yiannas. "Breaking down Blockchain with Brigid Mcdermott: VP of Blockchain Business Development & Ecosystem at Ibm and Frank Yiannas: VP of Food Safety at Walmart." Interview by

Charles Crowson. *Outside the Box: Time > Money*, June 19, 2017. https://corporate.walmart.com/outside-the-box-podcast-season-1.

Pages, Hector. "2017 Transparency Study." *Response Media*. Response Media, April 2017. https://www.responsemedia.com/wp-content/uploads/2017/07/RM_Transparency_Survey_Final.pdf.

## UNBLOCKING BLOCKCHAIN

"Gates' Law: How Progress Compounds and Why It Matters." Farnam Street. Accessed March 2, 2021. https://fs.blog/2019/05/gates-law/.

Bresnahan, Timothy F., and Manuel Trajtenberg. "General Purpose Technologies 'Engines of Growth?'" National Bureau of Economic Research, August 1, 1992. https://www.nber.org/papers/w4148.

Butters, Lisa. GoDirect Trade, Honeywell's Blockchain Airplane Parts. Interview by Walid Al Saqqaf. *Insureblocks*, April 19, 2020. https://insureblocks.com/ep-105-godirect-trade-honeywells-blockchain-airplane-parts/.

Frawley, James, dir. Grey's Anatomy. Season 5, Episode 6, "Life During Wartime." Aired October 30, 2008, on ABC.

Fritz, Dan, and Marco Cuomo. Healthcare Blockchain from a Novartis perspectives & lessons learnt. Interview by Walid Al Saqqaf. *Insureblocks*, October 13, 2019. https://insureblocks.com/ep-79-healthcare-blockchain-from-a-novartis-perspectives-lessons-learnt/.

Gupta, Saurabh, Jamie Snowdon, and Tanmoy Mondal. "Ignore Blockchain at Your Peril, but Don't Drive Blindly." *Wipro*. HFSResearch, 2020. https://www.wipro.com/content/dam/nexus/en/analyst-speak/pdfs/state-of-enterprise-blockchain-market-2020-new.pdf.

McCauley, Alison. Why Executives Struggle with Blockchain - an Alison Mccauley Masterclass. Interview by Anthony Day. *Blockchain Won't Save the World*, June 6, 2020. https://www.blockchainwontsavethe.world/podcasts/6l2iiwr8zty9hfa2llqm5usul4qt20-d73gh-lb5c9-rblac-zhhen-87724-rlhj3-c8d6d-d3st6-dfkw9-e9hkg-2zcpe-xb785-x8n8e.

McCollough, Doug. Dublin Digital Identity Project. Interview by Walid Al Saqqaf. *Insureblocks*, February 2, 2020. https://insureblocks.com/ep-94-dublin-digital-identity-project/.

McDermott, Brigid, and Frank Yiannas. "Breaking down Blockchain with Brigid Mcdermott: VP of Blockchain Business Development & Ecosystem at Ibm and Frank Yiannas: VP of Food Safety at Walmart." Interview by Charles Crowson. *Outside the Box: Time > Money,* June 19, 2017. https:// corporate.walmart.com/outside-the-box-podcast-season-1.

Mougayar, William. "A Decision Tree for Blockchain Applications: Problems, Opportunities or Capabilities?" *Startup Management* (blog), October 30, 2015. http://startupmanagement.org/2015/11/30/a-decision-tree-for-blockchain-applications-problems-opportunities-or-capabilities/.

Speers, Andrew. User Experience on the Blockchain – Insights from RBS. Interview by Walid Al Saqqaf. *Insureblocks,* January 12, 2020. https://insureblocks.com/ep-91-user-experience-on-the-blockchain-insights-from-rbs/.

Stoll, Clifford. "Why the Web Won't Be Nirvana." Newsweek, February 26, 1995. https://www.newsweek.com/clifford-stoll-why-web-wont-be-nirvana-185306.

Thien-Ngern, Orapong, and Sharon Yuen. "Blockchain for procure-to-pay – insights from Siam Commercial Bank." Interview by Walid Al Saqqaf. *Insureblocks,* January 19, 2020. https://insureblocks.com/ep-92-blockchain-for-procure-to-pay-insights-from-siam-commercial-bank/.

Printed in Great Britain
by Amazon

84728337R00104